GLOBAL INTRIGUES

The Era of the Spanish-American War and
the Rise of the United States to World Power

GLOBAL INTRIGUES

The Era of the Spanish-American War and
the Rise of the United States to World Power

JUAN R. TORRUELLA

LA EDITORIAL
Universidad de Puerto Rico

Library of Congress Cataloging-in-Publication Data

Torruella, Juan R.
 Global Intrigues: The Era of the Spanish-American War and the Rise of the United States to World Power / by Juan R. Torruella.
   p. cm.
 Includes bibliographical references and index.
 ISBN 0-8477-1126-9

 1.Spanish-American War, 1898. 2.Spanish-American War, 1898—Influence. 3.United States—Territorial expansion. 4.United States—Foreign relations—1865-1898. 5.United States—Foreign relations—1897-1901. 6.United States—Foreign relations—20th century. 7.World politics—19th century. 8.World politics—1900-1945. I.Title.
 E715.T67 2006
 973.8'92—dc22

                    2006032919

ISBN: 978-0-8477-1126-0

The photographs between pages 102 and 103 were reproduced from:
   Library of Congress Prints and Photographs Division.

Neely's Photographs:
   Fighting in the Philippines. New York, Chicago, London: F. Tennyson Neely Publishers, 1899.

Photographic History of the Spanish American War . New York:
   The Pearson Publishing Company, 1898.

Text editor / Marshall Morris

Cover, maps and text design / Yolanda Pastrana Fuentes

LA EDITORIAL
UNIVERSIDAD DE PUERTO RICO
P.O. Box 23322
San Juan, Puerto Rico 00931-3322
www.laeditorialupr.com

To my friends Miguel Frontera and Fred Richardson,
with whom I spent memorable times and had
great debates in the jungles of Colombia.

J.R.T.
February 15, 2007

TABLE OF CONTENTS

PREFACE

Although I have researched and written this book, and it is exclusively my own work, just as in the case of most endeavors of the kind, many people contributed to its culmination.

The book is an expanded version of my thesis at Oxford University, so I wish to express my appreciation, first of all, to my advisor during my residence there, Dr. Frances Lannon, for her patience and academic support. Lacking those, it would have been more difficult to bring my scholarly work and this book to their present conclusion. In Puerto Rico, the critical commentary and expert advice of Dr. Luis González Vales, a distinguished scholar and the official Historian of Puerto Rico, were invaluable to me. I also wish to thank Dr. Brian McAllister Linn, of Texas A&M, for putting me on the track of the Filipino/Japanese communications during the insurgency of 1900, documents which were gathering dust in the archives of the Library of Congress. Gastón de los Reyes and Robert Van Kirk were both kind enough to read through early versions of the manuscript and made many useful suggestions. Gary Hoyt, an old friend and a man of many talents, not only read the manuscript and made several perceptive observations but provided several of the excellent maps included here, for which I am most grateful. I have reason to appreciate, too, the opinions and advice of my colleague and friend, Norman Stahl, which I have always found helpful.

On a practical note, there is no way to repay the help I received from my librarian, Ana Milagros Rodríguez, in getting difficult-to-find materials, and from my secretary, Nydia Feliciano, in putting my manuscripts into presentable shape. And without the technical assistance of Jeffrey O'Neill, the text of this book would still be in electronic never-never land. The help, advice and patience of Marta Aponte and Dr. Marshall Morris of La Editorial, Universidad de Puerto Rico, also deserve my recognition and gratitude.

Last, but most certainly not least, my eternal love and thanks to my psychiatrist in residence, Judy T., for her support, advice and forbearance, which have made much in my life possible.

J. R. T.
San Juan, Puerto Rico
August 21, 2006

LIST OF ABBREVIATIONS

CPFO *Correspondence respecting the War between Spain and the United States (1898-1899),* Confidential Print, 7267, Foreign Office, March, 1900.

DEEU *Disposiciones de España y de los Estados Unidos referentes a la guerra y declaraciones de neutralidad,* Ministerio del Estado de España, Madrid, 1898.

GDD *German Diplomatic Documents, 1871-1914,* E.T.S. Dugdale (ed. & trans.), Vol. II, Barnes & Noble, New York (1969).

PROFO Public Records Office, Foreign Office.

SDC *Spanish Diplomatic Correspondence and Documents: Presented to the Cortes by the Minister of State (1896-1900), Translations,* U.S. Government Printing Office, Washington, D.C. (1905).

PIP *Translations of Documents Showing Relations Between Insurgents in the Philippine Islands and Japan (1898-1900),* Library of Congress, 94 Entry 196-196A, Washington, D.C. (1902).

LIST OF MAPS

LIST OF TABLES

LIST OF PHOTOGRAPHS

(Photo insert between pages 102 and 103)

THE AMERICANS

Alfred Thayer Mahan

Henry Cabot Lodge

President William McKinley

THE SPANIARDS

Alfonso XIII, King of Spain

Queen María Cristina

Práxedes Mateo Sagasta

General Arsenio Martínez Campos

General Valeriano Weyler

General Ramón Blanco

THE CUBANS

José Martí

General Calixto García

General Máximo Gómez

Officers of General Gómez's Army at Remedios, Cuba

THE FILIPINOS

José Rizal

Emilio Aguinaldo in uniform

Emilio Aguinaldo and his chief aides

IMPORTANT OTHERS

Kaiser Wilhelm II

Queen Victoria

Lord Salisbury

Joseph Chamberlain

The Emperor of Japan

Archbishop John Ireland

CASUS BELLI
> *U.S.S. Maine* entering Havana Harbor
> *Maine* wreck, Havana Harbor

THE WARRIORS
> John D. Long, Secretary of the Navy
> Lieutenant Colonel Theodore Roosevelt
> Admiral George Dewey
> Admiral Pascual Cervera
> Admiral Montijo
> The Spanish Commandant of Manila
> American commanders against the Filipino insurgents
> The Filipino insurrection, 1899
> General Nelson Miles

THE OBSERVERS
> English, Russian, German, Austrian, Japanese and Swedish military
> attachés with the American Army at Santiago de Cuba

ACTION STATIONS
> Bombardment of San Juan, Puerto Rico
> Entrance to harbor at Santiago de Cuba
> Armored cruisier
> American troops on ramparts at Manila
> Dewey's Flagship *Olympia*
> Battleship *Pelayo*
> *Cristóbal Colón* armored cruiser wrecked

THE PEACEMAKERS
> William Rufus Day
> Signing of the peace protocol of the Spanish-American War
> Spanish peace commissioners
> Signing of Treaty of Paris
> Jules Martin Cambon
> President McKinley presenting Admiral Dewey

INTRODUCTION

Although this book deals with the Spanish-American War of 1898[1] and events surrounding it, and therefore necessarily details many of the military aspects of that conflict, it is not primarily a military history of that event. The purely martial incidents of this "Splendid Little War"[2] have been adequately covered elsewhere.[3] Thus, its various clashes will be discussed only as necessary to provide context to the main theme of this account: the attitudes and actions of the so-called non-belligerents, and how these intrigues affected the war and resulted in significant changes in the global balance of power, thus contributing to the rise of the United States to its present dominant position.

The term "non-belligerent," rather than the more common term "neutral," is used advisedly: as will be clearly demonstrated, it is easier to determine who does not engage in actual warfare than to sift through the conflicting and often unclear evidence of partiality that usually surrounds the formal declarations of neutrality by nations. Such proclamations, even when solemnly made, hardly ever reflect what actually takes place behind the scenes in the world of international affairs. In this, the Spanish-American War was certainly no exception.

Historical events can be best understood when placed within the context in which they develop. This focused probe of the Spanish-American War begins with a description of the general geopolitical framework within which this conflict took place, namely the 19th Century and especially the latter half. Circumstances throughout the world, some interrelated, some unrelated, had a decided influence on the war and its participants and helped to shape the stance taken by the non-belligerents and direct the course of their actions. The 19th Century was, in fact, one of vast change for the existing and emerging empires. Therefore, we will begin by discussing the history and circumstances of the principal empires of the period, both internally and in relation to their international spheres. These empires can be said to have been in ascendancy or at their peak (the British, German, French, Russian, Japanese and US empires) or in decline or decay (the Ottoman, Chinese, Austro-Hungarian[4] and Spanish empires).[5]

This analysis is followed by a recounting of the actions, views and sympathies of the various countries not directly involved during the period immediately before the commencement of hostilities and to a lesser extent afterwards. Their sentiments and conduct were reflected in the statements of the several national spokesmen, in the reports in their local press, and in specific actions they took, including the diplomatic initiatives which were attempts to prevent the outbreak of fighting. To cover the global spectrum fully, the views of smaller or less influential countries, as well as those of the more powerful nations, are recounted, even though the minor ones clearly had a lesser impact on this wide-ranging if brief international controversy.

The intrigues in which the major non-belligerent powers engaged, before, during, and immediately after the Spanish-American War – these are our main concern here – are set out in Chapter III, which deals with the specific actions of Great Britain, Germany, France and Japan, all of whom formally declared their neutrality yet hardly paused as they proceeded to breach this status blithely, though they did so with varying degrees of intrusiveness. The simple fact is that their national interests drove their actions, and not much more need be said in that regard.

The influence exercised by these non-belligerents permeated the peace negotiations and the Treaty of Paris, which is the subject of Chapter IV. Their ascendancy had a lasting impact upon the new world order that emerged from the final dismemberment of the remnants of the Spanish Empire, a matter which is analyzed in Chapter V.

Despite its importance in propelling the United States into the very center of the world scene, the Spanish-American War is an event that has been largely relegated to a back burner of United States national history. Why this is so is not entirely clear because the conflict, and the circumstances within which it developed and flourished, have current relevance.

Given more attention and review, the Spanish-American War may provide considerable insight into the present state and conduct of the international affairs of the United States. In fact, its study may very well shed light on what the future holds in store.

A limited discussion of this topic appears in the Epilogue. Though it is not meant to be an exhaustive analysis of this complicated, and seemingly unfathomable subject, that last chapter should be kept well in mind, or even read first.

NOTES

1. This name has not been accepted unanimously, and the different names used reflect a degree of ideological content. At the time, Americans referred to this event as the Spanish War. Thereafter, historians in both the United States and Spain called it the Spanish-American War ("La Guerra Hispano-Americana"). Philip S. Foner, in his two-volume account, called it the Spanish-Cuban-American War. *The Spanish-Cuban-American War and the Birth of American Imperialism 1895-1902*, New York (1972). The most inclusive title is the Spanish-American-Cuban-Filipino War. See Thomas G. Paterson. "United States Intervention in Cuba, 1898: Interpretations of the Spanish-American-Cuban-Filipino War," *History Teacher*, 29 (1996), at 341-61. Benjamin R. Beede and others have simply called it the War of 1898. See *The War of 1898 and U.S. Interventions 1898-1934. An Encyclopedia*, ed. B.R. Beede New York/London (1994). The Cubans call it the Cuban War for Independence of 1895-1898. Even the term "American," although used in the United States to refer to the United States of America and its nationals, can be understood to apply to the Americas as a whole and to the inhabitants of the Americas. Nevertheless, throughout this book American is used as it commonly is in the United States.

2. After the war concluded, the U.S. ambassador to Great Britain wrote to Theodore Roosevelt, "It has been a splendid little war; begun with the highest motives, carried on with magnificent intelligence and spirit, favored by that fortune which favors the brave." Cited in Hugh Thomas, *Cuba, the Pursuit of Freedom*, Harper & Row, New York (1971), at 404. See also F. Freidel, *The Splendid Little War*, Little Brown & Co., Boston (1958).

3. See generally, Ivan Musicant, *Empire by Default, The Spanish-American War and the Dawn of the American Century*, Henry Holt and Company, New York (1998); Albert A. Nofi, *The Spanish American War, 1898*, Combined Books, Conshocken, Pa. (1996); David Trask, *The War with Spain in 1898*, Macmillian Publishing Co., New York (1981); Pablo Azárate, *La guerra hispano-norteamericana de 1898*, Ediciós do Castro, La Coruña (1993); Donald Chidsey, *La guerra hispano-americana 1896-1898*, Grijalbo (1973); Salvador E. Casellas, "Causas y Antecedentes Diplomáticos de la Guerra Hispanoamericana: 1895-98," *Revista de Ciencias Sociales*, University of Puerto Rico, 9 (March 1965): 55-76.

4. The Austro-Hungarian Empire was geographically limited to the European continent. It is nevertheless discussed because it was still considered at the time to be one of the great European powers, and as such, had some influence on the Spanish-American War scenario.

5. The Portuguese Empire, although at one time one of the most extensive in geographic expanse and duration, existing well into the 20th Century, is only discussed in passing in Chapter II. A similar treatment is given to the Dutch, and Italian Empires, the latter which only came to life in modern times, and at that in a limited way, half way through the 19th Century. The Belgian Empire, which consisted of what eventually became Belgian Congo, is discussed even more summarily and only in the interest of comprehensiveness.

CHAPTER I

The Big Picture:
The World at the End of the 19th Century

The Industrial Revolution began in Great Britain toward the end of the 17th Century and continued in crescendo into the first half of the 19th century.[1] Thereafter, during the second half of the 19th Century, a fairly integrated global economy formed, centered on Western Europe but still led by Great Britain. A particular sequence of events promoted these developments.

The defeat of Napoleon in 1815 and the resulting general settlement at the Congress of Vienna established an overall balance of power in Europe. Thereafter, it became difficult for a conflagration to break out on the scale of those that took place before 1815. Thus, until 1914, no general war occurred in Europe,[2] a condition that allowed for the accumulation of capital in need of investment. Much of this capital went into manufacturing industries, which consumed large amounts of raw materials from abroad and in turn produced surplus goods in need of foreign markets.

This state of relative European tranquility and the accumulation of capital available for investment led to the spread of the Industrial Revolution outside of Great Britain, especially after the 1860s, and this began to alter the balance of the world's economic and political forces.

In 1800, notwithstanding the Industrial Revolution in Great Britain, agriculture was still the basis of both European and non-European societies. This would change in varying degrees throughout the world during the course of the 19th Century. At the beginning of this period, however, because of the huge Asian populations and the large number of craftsmen and home industries in China and Greater India, the production of goods by the "Third World" was twice that of Europe as a whole –or 67.7% of the

1

world's entire manufacturing output, compared to Europe's 28.1%.[3] By 1900, however, this had changed dramatically, with Europe out-producing Asia –62% to 11%[4]– despite the fact that Europe's population rose from only 187 million in 1800 to 268 million in 1850, while Asia's increased from about 400 million to approximately 700 million in the 19th century.[5] The reason for this change in the relative productive capacities of these geographic areas, which proved to be a stunning blow to Third World economic competition, was the technological advances of the Industrial Revolution in the West. These allowed the Western economies (Europe and the United States) to produce goods more cheaply than non-industrialized nations in Asia, Africa and Latin America. This led to the elimination of Third World manufacturing competition, particularly in Asia, and the conversion of their immense populations into captive consumer markets.

The Industrial Revolution also brought about a reconfiguration of the geopolitical scene in other ways, for as the technological advances of the Industrial Revolution gradually were adopted in the military and naval fields, the result was that the nations that possessed the most powerful weaponry reigned supreme. Although this sequence of events had some impact in Europe (and in the United States during its Civil War), it was in the colonial conflicts between Western and Third World nations in Africa and Asia (while Europe was enjoying peace and prosperity), that the disparities in firepower decided the outcome of these colonial wars. For example, in the Battle of Omdurman in the Sudan, in 1898, it took the British forces under Lord Kitchener, using rapid-firing guns and repeating rifles, only a few hours to eliminate over 10,000 Dervishes, this while losing only 48 of their own troops. In this fashion, Western control of the world leapt from 35% of the land surface in 1800 to 67% by 1878, and to 84% by 1914.[6]

That control was, of course, not uniformly distributed among the Western nations, as there also existed firepower disparities among them, and following the same rules of force that applied in colonial wars, these differences more or less determined which Western[7] nation acquired which colonies at any given time. Thus the end of the 19th Century has been described as a period of "colonial redistribution."[8] In particular, Lenin called the Spanish-American War "the first war for a [re]distribution of the world already distributed."[9]

During the 19th century, acquisition of colonial empires was still the preferred way to assert national predominance. Of course, not all empires were equal. Lord Salisbury appropriately stated, in 1898, that the world was divided into the living and the dying powers.[10]

Three extant empires were in advanced stages of decay: the Spanish, the Chinese and the Ottoman. The Austro-Hungarian Empire, the only purely European empire, would disappear after World War I. Three others were definitely on the rise: the German and the Japanese empires, and in a different territorial sense, the empire of the United States. The British, French, Dutch and Portuguese empires had more or less reached their peak by this time, although the latter two were never in the same category with the British and French empires. The Russian Empire was still expanding, principally in Central Asia and the Far East, and had extended across the Bering Straits into Alaska.

The British Empire

The popular saying that the sun never sets on the British Empire was literally true on the eve of the Spanish-American War (see Map 1). Although an exhaustive inventory of that empire is unnecessary here, it did cover an expanse of 12 million square miles, having grown at an average annual rate of about 100,000 square miles between 1815 and 1865 alone,[11] spreading over land on every continent and the waters of every ocean and most seas.[12] It encompassed within its jurisdiction perhaps a quarter of the world's population, and included both the formal empire, that is territory over which British sovereignty had been established, and the informal empire, meaning lands ruled or controlled through various indirect arrangements, in which different degrees of influence or control, short of full sovereignty, was exercised by Great Britain.[13] In essence, the British had at least a latent interest, and in many cases an active one, in almost any conflict or international action occurring almost anywhere on the globe, particularly if there was a potential for redistribution of territory. And that meant that almost no dispute failed to arouse some degree of British interest in the outcome. It also meant that the British Empire was faced with a world-wide list of contenders, exercising varying degrees of pressure at all times across the empire's great expanse. Historian Paul Kennedy aptly synthesizes the problems of this mega-empire when he states:

> In the critical year of 1895, for example, the [British] Cabinet found itself worrying about the possible breakup of China following the Sino-Japanese War, about the collapse of the Ottoman Empire as a result of the Armenian crisis, about the looming clash with Germany over southern Africa at almost exactly the same time as the quarrel with the United States over the Venezuela-British Guiana borders, about French military expeditions in Equatorial Africa, and about a Russian drive towards the Hindu Kush.[14]

This contentious existence was evident, too, in the specific geographic areas involved in the Spanish-American War –Cuba and Puerto Rico in the Caribbean, and the Philippine Islands in the Pacific Ocean, off mainland China. The rise of US power in the Caribbean might affect British interests in that area, and as the country with the greatest share of China's foreign trade, a conflict in the Philippines could have a substantial impact on the emergence of new forces or a redistribution of territories in the vicinity of China. This was felt to be particularly true with regard to its crown colony, Hong Kong,[15] which was only about 500 miles from the Philippine Islands across the South China Sea.

The British Empire was supported by the Royal Navy, which at that time was equal in power to the two next largest fleets combined, those of France and Russia, with 499,000 and 383,000 tons, respectively, as compared to Great Britain's naval force which weighed in at 1,065,000 tons.[16] The British fleet protected the sea lanes of the empire, allowing its merchant fleet, also the largest in the world, to bring home raw materials for Britain's factories, and conversely to export its manufactured goods to the world's markets. Even in the late 19th Century, Great Britain was still the world's greatest trading nation, with London the financial center of the global economy.[17]

Although the British Empire had not yet finished expanding geographically,[18] in the period between 1815 and 1865, it had already reached the zenith of its hegemony in industry and commerce.[19] By the end of the century, however, Great Britain was beginning to feel the effects of a change in the world's economic balance in favor of continent-states such as the United States and Russia, as well as of Germany.[20]

This shift was caused by increased industrial and agricultural competition from these countries, and by the emergence of new technologies developed particularly in Germany and the United States.[21]

A comparison of the relative share of world manufacturing output of selected nations from 1800 to 1900 shows how this balance inclined dramatically away from Great Britain and toward the United States and Germany, especially during the last twenty years of the 19th Century.

TABLE 1
Percentage of World Manufacturing Output

	1800	1830	1860	1880	1900
United Kingdom	4.3	9.5	19.9	22.9	18.5
France	4.2	5.2	7.9	7.8	6.8
German States/Germany	3.5	3.5	4.9	8.5	13.2
Austro-Hungary	3.2	3.2	4.2	4.4	4.7
Italian States/Italy	2.5	2.3	2.5	2.5	2.3
Russia	5.6	5.6	7.0	7.6	8.8
Japan	3.5	2.8	2.6	2.4	2.4
China	33.3	29.8	19.7	12.5	6.2
United States	0.8	2.4	7.2	14.7	23.6

Source: Table 6, in Kennedy, *The Rise and Fall of the Great Powers*, supra, at 149.

It should be noted that although the most dramatic increases between 1880 and 1900 were those of United States and Germany, all the other countries shown increased their share of world manufacturing output except Great Britain, China and Japan.

As will be discussed presently, these fundamental economic changes would be reflected in the strategic decisions taken by these nations during the eventful period that surrounded the Spanish-American War. This was particularly true in the case of Great Britain, which saw in that conflict the potential for the disruption of its crucial interests in China, where it was already feeling pressure from the incursions of Germany, France, Russia and Japan.

The French Empire

In the period surrounding the Spanish-American War, notwithstanding other diversions responding principally to its own vast colonial empire and its desire to expand it still further, France was obsessed by a spirit of revanche against Germany which grew out of its humiliating defeat in the Franco-Prussian War (1870-71), as a consequence of which Paris was occupied and France was made to pay substantial reparations to Germany.[22]

In the meantime, in the late 1880s, France attempted to challenge Great Britain in Egypt and West Africa, with negative outcomes for France, except in Senegal. It was unable to counter British occupation of Egypt in 1882, and in 1898, at Fashoda, French forces suffered a mortifying defeat at the hands of Lord Kitchener. This resulted in the loss of the Nile Valley and the Sudan to Great Britain. Nevertheless, despite these and other setbacks, mostly caused by conflicts with British colonial interests, between 1871 and 1900, France acquired an additional 3.5 million square miles to add to its already vast colonial expanses. And that made the French Empire second in size only to the British Empire.[23]

On the eve of the Spanish-American War, the French held territories in three areas that might be affected by that impending conflict: in the Mediterranean, on which it bordered, as did Spain, and on whose southern shore it possessed Algeria (1860) and Tunisia (1881); in the Caribbean, where it had the island colonies of Guadalupe and Martinique, approximately 300 miles from Spanish territory in Puerto Rico, and French Guiana further away on the northeastern shoulder of South America; and in Southeast Asia, where it was expanding its Indochinese foothold (Cambodia and Cochin China in 1867, Tongking and Annam in 1885) on the southern fringes of China, approximately 800 miles across the South China Sea from the Philippine Islands (see Map 2).

Meanwhile, France's internal politics bordered on the chaotic. This affected its naval policy, with frequent changes in building programs, leaving its navy with a heterogeneous collection of ships that were no match for either the British or German fleets.[24] The army was likewise affected by a host of military-civilian clashes that weakened the fabric of French society and called the loyalty and efficiency of the army into question.[25]

Too much politics unquestionably had short- and long-term deleterious effects upon France's armed forces.

France's strong economy and considerable wealth, on the other hand, made it possible to sustain its foreign policy, particularly against Germany. By satisfying Italy's need for capital, France was eventually able to separate Italy from the Triple Alliance and thus weaken Germany's strategic position in Europe. France further isolated Germany diplomatically by financing Russia's efforts at modernization and by raising the money for Franco-Russian loans to China. It also made substantial investments in Turkey and the Balkans, and thus effectively blocked German advances there.

Nevertheless, the fact remained that by the eve of the Spanish-American War, France had slipped to fifth place among the great powers, well behind Great Britain, the United States, Russia, and Germany. Still a power to be reckoned with, and as its actions in relation to the Spanish-American War show, it was very active diplomatically and refused to be discounted, even if it was not directly engaged.

The German Empire

In the first half of the 19th Century, what was to be Germany was distracted by the internal problems of the various, fractious German states, and it was thus impeded from playing a principal role in European and world affairs. However, by the 1860s the largest and most aggressive of these states, Prussia, was able to unite the various parts into a single Germany.

The key to Prussia's success was its superb educational system, and the resulting scientific, technical and industrial establishments which it produced. By the later half of the 19th Century, this excellence was reflected in the best equipped and trained army in Europe, led by a highly qualified and professional general staff and officer corps. Furthermore, this war machine was capable of rapid mobilization and transport over a modern and efficient network of railways.

The Germany that was unified by Prussia in 1870 had a population of over 40 million inhabitants, which by 1890 had reached 49 million, and by 1900, 56 million; in Europe, it was second in population only to Russia.[26]

On the eve of the Spanish-American War, the Industrial Revolution had fully developed in a united Germany. Furthermore, the fruit of this revolution was wide-spread. By mechanizing and applying new scientific methods and technology to its agricultural processes, Germany increased its crop production to the point of having the highest yield per hectare of any of the great powers. Nevertheless, even with substantial tariff protection, the production costs of German agriculture were still higher than those of the United States and Russia.

However, it was in manufacturing and industrial production that Germany excelled. Germany's industrial expansion was nothing short of spectacular (see Table 1). In 1860, prior to unification, the combined production of the German States accounted for only 4.0% of world manufacturing output. By 1880, however, Germany had raised this figure to 8.5%, already above France's 7.8% and Russia's 7.6%, and by 1900, Germany's share of world manufacturing output had risen to 13.2%, exceeded only by Great Britain and the United States. The United States was another emerging economic powerhouse, whose share of world manufacturing had risen from 14.7% in 1880 to 23.6% in 1900, thus taking the lead from Great Britain, which dropped from 22.9% to 18.5% during that same period. This was an unmistakable sign of the future: Germany and the United States were on the rise, and Great Britain was in relative economic decline. These realities would bring about important strategic and geopolitical consequences that would have to be taken into account as the forthcoming Spanish-American War, and its predictable global impact, loomed.

During this period, Germany became a disturbing factor for Great Britain for other reasons than these economic considerations. With its thorough trouncing of the French in the short but decisive Franco-Prussian War of 1871,[27] Germany gave notice that it was a force to be reckoned with (see Table 2).

Already by the 1880's, Germany had replaced Russia as the principal threat to British interests,[28] particularly in Africa (where France was also causing difficulty) and in the Far East.[29]

On the Continent, Germany's strategy was to isolate or at least neutralize France. This game plan called for the creation of the Triple Alliance, entered into in 1882 with Austro-Hungary and Italy.[30] Thereafter, further agreements were reached regarding the Balkan possessions of the Ottoman Empire and Italian aspirations in North Africa.

TABLE 2
Military and Naval Personnel (1880-1890)

	1880	1890	1900
Great Britain	367,000	420,000	624,000
France	543,000	542,000	715,000
Germany	426,000	504,000	624,000
Austro-Hungary	246,000	346,000	385,000
Russia	791,000	677,000	1,162,000
Italy	216,000	284,000	255,000
United States	34,000	39,000	96,000
Japan	71,000	84,000	234,000

Source: Table 19, Kennedy, supra, at 203.

The resignation of Bismarck in 1890 was a crucial moment in German history. After Germany's victory in the Franco-Prussia War, Bismarck had tried to convince the great powers that Germany had no further territorial ambitions in Europe. But after his departure, Kaiser Wilhelm II and his advisers took a more aggressive stance in foreign affairs. During the following four years, Germany embarked on its so-called "New Course," a national strategy that called for acquiring new territories almost anywhere they could be found.[31] Failure to renew the Reinsurance Treaty with Russia, and the protective agricultural tariffs imposed against Russian farm goods drove the Russians into the French camp, resulting in a Russian alliance with France. Thus Germany was confronted by potential enemies: on the East by Russia and on the West by France.

Kaiser Wilhelm II's anti-Russian prejudice and Anglophile sympathies (Queen Victoria was his grandmother) were hardly the basis for a coherent foreign policy. When Prince Chlodwig zu Hohenlohe assumed the chancellorship in 1894, an attempt was made to normalize relations with Russia, and Germany entered into a commercial treaty with Russia. Nevertheless the Franco-Russian treaty remained in place, a situation that rankled Kaiser Wilhelm, as in practical terms, Italy was an unreliable ally. Only Austria-Hungary could be counted upon to remain loyal in the event of problems with France or Russia.

A momentous change took place in German policy in the closing years of the 19th century[32] with its pursuit of Weltpolitik, looking beyond the confines of Europe toward wider participation on the world scene, particularly in Africa and the Far East.[33] This new German policy would not only bring her into conflict with the established empires, but most important, would set her at loggerheads with Great Britain over issues of "navalism,[34] a problem whose solution Germany deemed indispensable to its exercise of global power.[35]

Germany's naval strategy was inspired by the postulates of Alfred Thayer Mahan, the American naval theorist.[36] Mahan's theories were later put into practice with the enactment of Germany's Naval Law of 1898. It was Germany's naval expansion that most alarmed the British (see Table 3), committed as they were to defending their far-flung empire and dependent upon it for their industrial and economic prosperity.

TABLE 3
Warship Tonnage (1880-1910)

	1880	1890	1900	1910
Great Britain	650,000	679,000	1,065,000	2,174,000
Germany	88,000	190,000	285,000	964,000
Austro-Hungary	60,000	66,000	87,000	210,000
France	271,000	319,000	499,000	900,000
Italy	100,000	242,000	245,000	327,000
Russia	200,000	180,000	383,000	401,000
United States	169,000	240,000	333,000	824,000
Japan	15,000	41,000	187,000	496,000

Source: Kennedy, supra, Table 20, at 203.

Although it was not until after 1900 that Germany embarked on becoming the naval powerhouse it was by 1910, by then the second largest fleet in the world, this was clearly the product of an impressive shipbuilding program in place since the 1880s and which became massive after the 1890s. Between 1880 and 1890, Germany's naval fleet doubled in size, and thereafter, it continued to grow. By the end of the first decade of the 1900s, it had leapt to three times its 1900 tonnage. Although all this was taking place in the context of a world-wide naval arms race, only Great Britain surpassed Germany overall, a measure of the importance placed on sea power by Great Britain and a confirmation of its justified concern over the actions of others, particularly Germany.

The Austro-Hungarian Empire

By the time of the Spanish-American War, the Hapsburg Empire was more of an anachronism than a great power. Emperor Franz Joseph ruled over territories inhabited by 8 million Germans, 16 million Slavs (Czechs, Slovaks, Poles, Ruthenians, Croats, and Serbs), 5 million Hungarians, 5 million Italians and 2 million Rumanians.[37] In his army, orders had to be issued in 15 languages. In an attempt to forestall an early dissolution of his empire, the emperor agreed in 1867 to allow Hungary to become a separate state (*Ausgleich*), with its own constitution and a nearly independent status. The Austro-Hungarian Empire continued to serve a purpose in that it helped to freeze the settlement reached at the Congress of Vienna in 1815 and thus keep relative peace among the great powers in Europe. Even so, there was little question by the end of the 19th century that it was in decline as a great power, a tendency that would culminate with its fragmentation after World War I in 1918.

The seeds of its demise were in its diverse and fractured ethnic composition. Ideas and movements of national self-determination, inspired by the French Revolution, had made their way over time into the Austro-Hungarian Empire despite Metternich's attempts to suppress them. The outcome of World War I eventually led to the severing of the tenuous bonds that had kept that racial, religious and cultural mix together for longer than it was reasonable to expect. Metternich's actions not only were unsuccessful and counterproductive, but they in fact served to consolidate these nationalistic movements, as the brutal methods employed by his minions alienated the support of various international sectors, including Great Britain, which had been a traditional ally of Austria-Hungary. The constant struggle to suppress these movements gradually exhausted a

Habsburg Empire already weakened by the Napoleonic Wars. Unable to raise taxes to improve its infrastructure because of internal political problems that arose from its composition and its weak commercial and industrial base, the Empire faltered. Lack of adequate funding for its army was a major contributing factor in the defeat of Austria-Hungary by Prussia in its brief but decisive intramural encounter to determine who would control Germany in 1859.

In a population of 49.2 million in 1890, the third largest in Europe after Russia (116.8 million) and Germany (49.2 million), there were significant regional differences in per capita income and productivity, which led to enormous disparities in wealth.[38] Unfortunately for the long term unity of the Empire, this uneven economic situation was most prevalent in the most populous parts, the Slavic regions, which were also a hotbed of nationalistic fervor. Although the empire as a whole employed 55% of its population in agriculture, over 70% of the people in the economically depressed areas depended on farming. In contrast, the Austrian and Czech provinces became highly industrialized. Nevertheless, Austro-Hungary's per capita level of industrialization remained one of the lowest in Europe, having a mere 4.7% of the world's manufacturing production in 1900, a minimum increase over its 1880 level of 4.4% (see Table 1).

Of the major European powers, the Austro-Hungarian Empire was the least involved in the intrigues surrounding the Spanish-American War. In large part, this was due to the fact that Austria-Hungary, unique among the great European powers, lacked an overseas colonial empire.[39] That is not to say that it had no interest in what was happening in the Spanish-American conflict. It did, if for no other reason than because the Queen of Spain, Maria Cristina of Austria, was a Habsburg princess. There were, of course, older historical ties to Spain dating from the time both countries were part of the Hapsburg dynasty in the 16th Century. But the fact is that the Austro-Hungarian Empire had no direct stake in the Spanish-American War.

The Russian Empire

De Tocqueville's prediction that Russia would be one of the two great powers of the future[40] was more or less prophetic, depending on the historical period one chooses to look at. After the Napoleonic Wars, Russia went through a period of relative decline notwithstanding its huge army and even larger land mass. Although there were certain positive indicators that supported De Tocqueville's view –such as Russia's increase in industrial productivity (see Table 1), a population that swelled from 51 million in 1816 to 76 million in 1860, large growth in the number of its factories and industrial enterprises from 2,400 in 1804 to over 15,000, and a doubling of its iron manufacturing during that period– Russia was, if general economic and technological advances were considered, losing ground relatively rapidly to the other great powers.[41] Great Britain, for example, increased its iron production thirty fold during that same period.[42]

It took the Crimean War (1854-1855) to bring Russia's underlying crisis to a head and fully expose the backwardness of the Russian Empire, for Russia was not only lagging economically and technologically. This conflict showed that its massive military machine, although numerically impressive, was unwieldy and largely ineffective. Although individually Russian soldiers fought well, the army was ill-equipped and poorly led.[43] Furthermore, the size of the army itself presented almost insurmountable logistical problems considering the territorial expanse to be defended (approximately 8.6 million square miles), in a country which in 1850 had only 500 miles of railroad tracks. In the course of that war the Czarist armies had to fight Allied forces in the Baltic, the Turks in the Caucus, and Anglo-French armies in Crimea, as well as defend its territories in the Far East. The Crimean War presented the Russians with a multiplicity of supply nightmares in addition to numerous other problems caused by the inefficiency, corruption and backwardness that were endemic to the empire.

The Russian Empire as a whole was simply not up to the task. It suffered from major underlying systemic malaises, some of which remain to this day, which would in time bring down Russia's own ancient regime.

At the end of the 19th century, Czarist Russia was not just an autocracy (*samoderzhavie*), it was a state in which the monarchs vehemently resisted the erosion of any of their sovereign powers, to the point that, until 1906, despite a substantial body of codified law, the law was subordinated regularly to the czar's will. There was, again before 1906, no national legislature, no national suffrage, and no legal political parties.[44] Russia was thus, in the late 19th Century, still a politically feudal nation.

Nevertheless, after the Crimean War, particularly by the 1880s, there was a period of extraordinarily rapid growth, a considerable part of which was in the vital area of transportation. The railways increased from 1,495 miles of track in 1861 to 18,282 in 1887. At the same time, the industrial base showed an increase in the number of factories during these years from approximately 15,000 to 38,000.[45] The population had grown from 100 million in 1880 to 116.8 million in 1890, with the industrial work force expanding from roughly 700,000 workers in 1865 to 1,432,000 by 1890.[46] This rapid industrialization brought problems of its own. A portent of things to come was the St. Petersburg textile strike of 1870, a watershed in Russian labor history.[47]

Still there was no way around the fact that Russia was essentially a peasant society, with 80% of the population earning its livelihood from agriculture.[48]

That in itself was not necessarily negative, except that Russian agriculture was very inefficient: The crop yield for wheat was less than a third of Great Britain's or Germany's, and in the case of potatoes, it was about half.[49] Nevertheless, throughout this period, Russia's export trade consisted of approximately 60% agricultural produce and 10% timber products, most of which went to pay for American farm equipment, German machine tools, and interest owed on the country's large foreign debt. Thus the state of the country's agriculture was crucial to Russia's economic health.[50] Unfortunately, increased agricultural productivity during these years (of about 2% annually), was counter-balanced by population increases of about the same rate.[51]

The debacle of the Crimean War led to the implementation of a series of top-down reforms, the most important of which was put into place on February 19, 1861 by Czar Alexander IIs when he signed a law freeing the serfs[52] –ironically at about the same time the American Civil War was being fought to achieve similar goals. Although the suppression of serfdom was past due, this system was so ingrained in Russia that its abolition, far from solving the many problems caused by that untenable social condition, put in motion a series of other destabilizing situations with far-reaching consequences. Among the most immediate was a general undercurrent of social unrest that promoted numerous disturbances (1,889 in 1861, 842 in 1862, 509 in 1863, and 156 in 1864).[53] Nevertheless, a series of other reforms came of the so-called "Crimean Syndrome," including attempts at local self-government, improvements in the judicial system and the rebuilding of the army along Western lines.

This liberalizing trend came to a halt, and was followed by a wave of reaction and repression, when Czar Alexander II was assassinated on March 1, 1881. His successor, Alexander III, who reigned until 1894, at on the eve of the Spanish-American War, issued a manifesto shortly after becoming the czar reaffirming the fundamental principles of autocracy in Russia. This included the "Russification" of the empire from border to border.[54] In keeping with this effort to unify Russia's vast territory the construction of the Trans-Siberian Railway began in 1891. When completed in 1916, it would be the longest rail line in the world.

Territorial expansion seems to be the one constant in Russian history regardless of regime or internal problems, only some of which have been mentioned here. Russia in all its political forms has demonstrated an insatiable desire to absorb its neighbors, be they nations or tribes, almost without temporal interruption, and the 19th century was no exception. It has been argued, probably with some validity, that the acquisition of buffer zones around the Russian heartland has been a response to an ingrained national reaction to the 12th and 13th century invasion and occupation of the Russian homeland by Mongol hordes.[55] In addition to this "Mongol Syndrome" there is no question that another factor leading to this perennial quest for territory has been Russia's historical aspiration to acquire ice-free ports. This has been instrumental in fueling Russia's recurrent incursions toward the Mediterranean, Central Asia and the Indian subcontinent,[56] and thus, to its numerous confrontations with the British and Ottoman Empires.

The 19th century saw the Russian Empire expand into Finland in the Baltic, parts of Poland and Romania (Moldova), the Caucus down to the Black Sea (including Georgia, Armenia, and Azerbaijan), most of Central Asia north of Iraq (including present day Turkmenistan, Kazakhstan, Uzbekistan, Tadzhikistan, and Kirghistan), Iran and Afghanistan, and extensively into territory on the northern border of Manchuria, from the Pacific Ocean to Siberia (See Map 3). Of course, Russia also had outposts commencing in the 1740s in North America, from Alaska to Oregon, and a permanent presence in Alaska until 1867, when it sold that territory to the United States.

Thus the Russian Empire was, in the late 19th century, a Far East/ Pacific power and risked being affected by a redistribution of Spain's colonies in that area, particularly if the beneficiary happened to be Japan. Notwithstanding Russia's considerable internal difficulties, which affected its international performance in the Crimean War and would do so even more obviously in 1904 in its war with Japan, its size and its enormous wealth of human and material resources made it difficult to ignore by the other great powers. Thus, Russia was a decidedly interested non-belligerent during the Spanish-American War, but one which did not actively engage in acts that violated its neutral status.

The Ottoman Empire

The Ottoman Empire –which at its zenith in the 1600s encompassed lands from Algeria to Egypt in Northern Africa, the entire coast of Arabia bordering on the Red Sea, the Middle East from present day Iraq to the Mediterranean, including from Anatolia to the Bosporus, the European land mass surrounding the Black Sea and all the way to the outskirts of Vienna (see Map 4)– was by the end of the 19th century reduced to Egypt, the Red Sea coast of Arabia, the Middle East including present day Syria, Lebanon, Palestine/Israel, Jordan, and Iraq, and a small area on the European side of the Bosporus. During the course of those territorial losses Greece gained its independence (1830), the French occupied Algeria (1830) and Tunisia (1881), and Serbia, Montenegro, Bulgaria and Romania became independent (1878), and Austria occupied Bosnia (which it eventually annexed in 1908). In the meantime, in 1869, the Suez Canal was completed within its territory, in Egypt, passage through which became a key link between Great Britain and its Asian colonies, particularly India. Predictably, Great Britain occupied Egypt in 1882, partly because of perceived threats to its free passage through the Suez Canal.

Of the three moribund empires in existence at the end of the 19th century, the Ottoman Empire[57] was the least relevant to the events unfolding around the Spanish-American War, although in fact it was in a strategic position to affect Spain's global concerns with regard to its own lifeline to the Philippine Islands. The Suez Canal and British control over the theoretical owners of that passageway, the Ottoman Empire, were the subject of one of the most notorious intrigues engaged in by a non-belligerent during the course of the Spanish-American War.

The continued existence of the Ottoman Empire was of concern to Great Britain in its global strategy, as it related to both Germany[58] and Russia. British strategy substantially entailed using the Ottoman Empire as a buffer[59] to prevent Russia from gaining access to the Mediterranean, which would have threatened Great Britain's lines of communication with India.[60]

Although there were commercial considerations of some importance with respect to the Ottoman Empire –and these involved not only Britain, but also France, Germany and Italy– petroleum was not yet a strategic imperative in the area.[61]

The Spanish Empire

The Spanish Empire, which was at its apex during the 16th and 17th centuries[62] (see Map 2), began to break up in the aftermath of Napoleon's invasion of Spain in 1807.[63] Thereafter, King Ferdinand VII attempted to reestablish control over Spain's American colonies as part of his absolutist restoration in 1814.[64] This action provoked the eruption of independence revolts throughout almost all of Spanish America and by 1825 had brought about the separation of all of these colonies. The exceptions were Cuba and Puerto Rico, in the Caribbean, and in the Pacific, the Philippines and other smaller island groups.

Thereafter, Cuba, which had been called, through Spanish self-delusion, the "Ever-Faithful Isle,"[65] was also infected by the spirit of independence. Thus, in 1868, it revolted in what became known as the First Cuban War of Independence, a ten-year conflict whose ferocity and mutual atrocities became the mark of Cuban independence conflicts.[66]

The interlude between the end of that war, and the commencement of the Second Cuban War of Independence in 1895, was a period of opportunities wasted by Spain in failing to solve the "Cuban Problem."[67] In Spain, two factors came together to impede its resolution: the internal politics of Spain and the economic interests of the dominant groups.[68]

The sole goals of the Queen Regent, María Cristina, appeared to be the preservation of her son's crown and the retention of what remained of the Spanish Empire. A version of this view was expressed by Spanish Prime Minister Práxedes Mateo Sagasta in a speech to the Spanish Senate on March 8, 1895, when he stated in forceful, if perhaps, unrealistic terms, that "the Spanish Nation is willing to sacrifice its last peseta and the last drop of blood of the last Spaniard, before it consents to having a piece of its sacred territory taken from it."[69] Of course, he was already too late.

In early April, 1895 a small band of revolutionaries led by José Martí landed at Playitas in southeastern Cuba.[70] Thus began Cuba's last war against Spain, spawned from the ashes of the first one and merging into the Spanish-American War in April 1898 upon the active intervention of the United States.

Meanwhile, on the other side of the globe, Spain's Far East-Pacific empire, consisting of the Philippine Islands, the Carolines, and the Palaus, had remained relatively tranquil until late in the 19th century. In the Philippines, there was nothing before 1872 to show any serious discontent with Spanish rule.[71] During the preceding three hundred odd years of Spanish sovereignty, these Islands were administered more like a Catholic mission than a colony, basically run by the Catholic Church through its various religious orders.[72]

But in 1872, there was a serious challenge to Spanish tutelage.[73] It was the first time that a cry of "independence" from Spain was heard in the Philippines. The uprising was squelched by native troops led by Spanish officers. Thirteen leaders were executed, including one Filipino priest, who was garroted.[74]

Among those executed was the principal rebel leader, José Rizal. Like his Cuban counterpart, José Martí, Rizal was a poet and a true leader of his people. Like Martí, he also became martyr to the cause of independence, in Rizal's case before a Spanish firing squad.[75] Suppression of the revolt merely drove the resentment that existed underground, with most issues continuing to be ignored and unresolved by the Spanish authorities.

In 1896, another serious insurrection erupted, stimulated by Spain's attempt to exercise more central control over the administration of the islands,[76] but also by internal disputes between the Catholic Church's Spanish and native clergy.[77] This time, however, the uprising was largely a product of discontent among the Filipino lower classes. The leader was Andrés Bonifacio, himself a night watchman at a warehouse in Manila.

This revolt principally involved the provinces of Cavite and Batangas south of Manila. At the time, the Spanish army in the Philippines consisted of approximately 18,000 men, of whom only 2,000 were Spaniards, almost all of these officers and non-commissioned officers. Again, the native troops remained loyal to the Spanish authorities, and thus they were able to hold Manila and Cavite until reinforcements arrived from other outlying areas. However, aid from Spain did not arrive until February, 1897. Not only was the logistical problem caused by the formidable distances difficult to overcome, but there was a shortage of troops available because of the ongoing Cuban situation and the recurring Carlist Wars in Spain proper, all of which augured what was to come. By December 1897, the revolt had been suppressed, but the underlying issues again remained unresolved. The leadership of the movement, by then in the hands of Emilio Aguinaldo,[78] merely moved to Hong Kong to bide its time for an opportune moment to recommence hostilities. Considering the terms of the peace settlement agreed to by the Spanish authorities,[79] this was a revolution waiting to happen.

This moment arrived with the outbreak of the Spanish-American War and Admiral Dewey's annihilation of the Spanish fleet at Manila on May 1, 1898. Shortly thereafter, Aguinaldo's aid was enlisted by the U.S. consul-general in Hong Kong, Rounseville Wildman. As the representative of the Hong Kong Junta, Aguinaldo arrived at Cavite Bay on May 19 aboard the *U.S.S. McCulloch*, with two companions, to organize an insurrection against Spain under the sponsorship of the United States.[80] These efforts were soon to be redirected against the United States, when it became apparent that the United States intended to keep the Philippines as a base from which to advance its China policy.[81]

The Chinese Empire

As it turned out, one of the most important considerations in the geopolitics of the Spanish-American War was China –and the apparently imminent disintegration of its empire.

The Chinese Empire, one of the longest in duration in pre-modern times, as well as one of the largest in territorial extent[82], had by 1800 fallen on bad times.[83] It was ruled autocratically by the Ch'ing dynasty of emperors, who were Manchus (Q'ing).[84] They governed China through an entrenched and deeply conservative bureaucracy, the Mandarins, who insulated the emperors from the millions that made China, even then, the most populous nation in the world.[85]

This population was hardly homogeneous, however. It included the principal Han majority, which itself was diverse enough that 528 Chinese dialects were spoken, many in reality different languages, as well as large numbers of non-Han peoples such as the Zhuang,[86] the Uygur,[87] the Hui, the Yi, the Tibetians, the Miao,[88] the Mongols, the Buyi, and the Koreans, among the major ethnic groups, as well as numerous other smaller ones, all of whom had their own languages, traditions and cultures. This was not a formula for stability or unity, and consequently China was wrecked by internal dissent and rebellions that the central government had to put down. The Daoguang reign (1821-1850) of Emperor Xuanzong was one of the most tumultuous in Chinese history, during which the greatest rebellion in China's entire history began, with the possible exception of the most recent one lead by Mao Tse Tung.

In addition to the many secular problems endemic to so large and diverse a country, China was affected by periodic natural calamities, namely the disastrous floods and course changes of the Hung He (Yellow) and Yangtze Rivers. These disasters not only devastated the most populous areas of China but regularly caused havoc to China's principal agricultural crop, rice, upon which a large part of the population depended for survival, thus disrupting its economy and the stability of its government. Millions died in the resulting famines and civil disturbances.

As China entered what was the 19th century by the Western calendar, it soon became the object of interest to the industrial nations of the West as well as of its aggressive neighbor, Japan. As the world map was increasingly covered by the pin flags of the imperialist nations, it became clear that, at the very least, China, with its immense population, was a huge market waiting to be exploited commercially, and possibly also a target, because of its relative weakness, for territorial expansion.[89]

Great Britain was one of the first Western nations to break into the China market.[90] From 1773, the East India Company, which had a monopoly on the growing of opium in India, was trading the drug with the Chinese in exchange for tea, even though opium was illegal in China.

The rise of the opium trade coincided, and undoubtedly was correlated with, the decline of the Chinese Empire. In 1839, the Chinese government, disturbed by the harmful effects that opium was having on its population, decided to put an end to its importation. The British reacted to the curtailment of its commercial interests, and the result was the First Opium War (1841-42), in which the British handily defeated the technologically inferior Chinese.[91] Under the Treaty of Nanking, which ended that conflict, Great Britain was granted a long-term lease of Hong Kong, and Canton, Amoy, Foochow, Shanghai and Ningpo were opened to British commerce. A naval station and coaling facility was set up in Shanghai, and British naval ships were allowed to patrol Chinese rivers and coastal waters.

The First Opium War not only had far-reaching consequences in China, but most importantly, it tipped the balance of world economic power in favor of Great Britain. Great Britain became the principal commercial and military power of the region, further strengthening its already dominant global position. But by exposing China's technical backwardness and vulnerability, the war alerted other countries to the possibility of easy pickings in this commercially fertile region. The United States and France followed suit and were able to pressure China into granting concessions similar to those received by Great Britain. Under the Treaty of Wangxia, in 1844, the United States was allowed more advantages for its Protestant missionaries and granted extraterritorial privileges for its citizens in civil and criminal cases. Later that year, the French signed the Treaty of Huangpu, which secured toleration for the practice of the Catholic religion, later extended to Protestants in 1845.

In 1850, a Christian-inspired movement called the Taiping Tianguo ("Heavenly Kingdom of Great Peace"), whose core adherents were of the Hakka ethnic minority, rebelled against the Q'ing dynasty. Before that uprising was quelled in 1864, over 20 million persons had perished. Other rebellions included that of the Nian, from 1851-1868, and of the Muslims (Panthays) in Yunnan from 1853-1873. The Muslims in the northwest were also in a state of rebellion from 1862-1873.

In the meantime, a minor flag incident in Canton was exploited by Great Britain to initiate the Second Opium War (1856-1858), this time with France's collaboration. The Treaty of Tientsin, which ended that latest act of Western intimidation, forced more concessions from China, including the opening up of eleven more ports, the establishment of legations in Beijing, the allowance of trade and more Christian missions in the interior, as well as, ironically, the legalization of opium importation. In the contemporaneous Treaty of Aigun, Russia was able to acquire the territory north of the Amur River from China.

Soon after, in 1859, claiming Chinese treaty violations, given its refusal to allow foreign diplomats into Beijing, a joint Anglo-Indian and French force of 17,000 landed in northern China and marched on Beijing. During the course of the plundering that followed the army's entry into the city, the Summer Palace was torched on the orders of British General Elgin.

This barbaric act was symbolic of China's prostration. Although Great Britain took the lead in this abusive process, its interests were principally commercial, while France, in addition to having those concerns was also acting in support of its strategy in Indo-China, where it had major territorial ambitions. Russia also appeared on the scene with additional annexationist goals involving Korea and the territories along China's Northern border in Manchuria.

Notwithstanding the actions of these other European powers (and later Japan), Great Britain still remained the paramount foreign power in China, both commercially and politically. At that point in time, it controlled two thirds of China's foreign trade, which then amounted to £53.2 million, with opium still at the top of the import list and accounting for an average of £10 million per year throughout the 1880s. In comparison, textiles, which were second in commercial importance, amounted to only £3 million per year! In addition, since 1853, Britain virtually monopolized China's commercial market and had physical and administrative control of Chinese customs duty collections, thus guaranteeing China's payment of its foreign loans, most of which were owed to British banking interests.

Great Britain's predominance in China would continue through 1895, when as a result of the Sino-Japanese War, the Chinese government collapsed. This threat to Great Britain's position had a tremendous impact on its strategy and its resolve to seek an ally against encroachment by other European nations on its virtual monopoly in the economic sphere. This situation was crucial in influencing Great Britain's actions with respect to the United States during the Spanish-American War.

Meanwhile, during the Tongzhi reign of Emperor Muzong, which lasted from 1862 to 1875, there was a restoration of Q'uang control over the empire and suppression of almost all of the mid-century rebellions. Muzong's mother, the Empress Dowager Cixi, ruled in conjunction with Prince Tongzhi and certain high officials until 1873. Zeng Goufan, Zuo Zongtang, and Li Hongzhang, among others, were responsible for laying the foundation for reform. Thus, the "Self-Strengthening Movement" began, with the study of Western subjects and skills being primary goals. Arsenals and shipyards were built and equipped with machinery from the United States. When Prince Tongzhi died at the age of 18 in 1875, Empress Cixi controlled the succession in such a way that she was able in effect to continue to rule China until her death in 1908, and so became the most powerful woman of the entire Q'ing period. An infant nephew of Empress Cixi, Guangxu, was appointed to reign under the regency of an uncle, Prince Gong, all under the supervision of Empress Cixi. Guanxu only began to rule in person in 1889.

Another major Western import into China, Christian religions, was to cause almost as much internal controversy and havoc as the importation of opium. Because of concessions made under the various treaties and agreements, there was a virtual flood of religious missions into the Chinese countryside. Protestant missions alone, increased from 200 in 1864 to nearly 1,300 by 1889. A large number of these groups were from the United States. Religion and commerce seemed to go hand in hand.

In the meantime, the taking of Chinese territory continued without quarter and from all directions. In 1874, a Japanese military expedition temporarily occupied Formosa (Taiwan) in retaliation for the murder of some Ryukyu islanders, islands which Japan had claimed from China in 1872. In 1883, by the Treaty of Hué, China recognized Annam as a French protectorate, a status which was extended to Tokin two years later. In 1887, Portugal was granted an enclave in Macao. In 1895, following the Sino-Japanese War, China lost Formosa (Taiwan) to Japan, and acceded to the independence of Korea, which became a Japanese protectorate. In 1896, China granted Russia the right to build and operate the Chinese

Eastern Railway across Northern Manchuria as a link in the Russian Trans-Siberian Railway to Vladivostok. In 1897, Germany occupied Jiaozhou Bay, and thereafter received a 99-year lease and exclusive rights to develop a railroad and mines in Shandong. In March 1898, Russia extorted a 25-year lease from China for the southern part of the Liaodong Peninsula. The following month, France received a 99-year lease for Guangzhouwan and vicinity; and in June 1898, Great Britain was granted a 99-year lease for Kowloon, opposite Hong Kong.

United States interests in China were not territorial in nature. By 1897, its concerns in China included missionary, commercial and investment interests, with missionary activities being the most developed of the three with over 1,500 missionaries spread throughout China.[92] Although the onset of the Spanish-American War interrupted direct United States activities in mainland China, there is no question that China became an important part of the United States' Far East strategy in that war.

In fact, as early as seven months before the commencement of the war, Theodore Roosevelt, who was then the Assistant Secretary of the Navy, formulated what would become United States policy in this respect. The United States would attempt to retain a foothold in the Philippines, as an "American Hong Kong," to act as a commercial entrepot to the China market and as a place from which to exercise military power in furtherance of American national interests.[93]

The Japanese Empire

Japan was an isolated feudal society until well into the second half of the 19th century.[94] For several hundred years before that, it had been ruled by a decentralized oligarchy consisting of territorial feudal lords (*daimyo*) and an aristocratic cast of warriors (*samurai*). This isolation, and the unique culture that it produced, ultimately resulted in a nation that was fiercely patriotic and undeterred by the sacrifices that would be demanded of its people in the years to come. Baron Hayashi, speaking in the late 19th century, set the tone for what was required of Japan when he said,

If new warships are considered necessary we must, at any cost, build them: if the organization of our army is inadequate we must start rectifying it from now; if need be, our entire military system must be changed...[95]

An archipelago composed of numerous islands east of the Asian mainland (see Map 6), Japan is less than 200 miles from the Korean Peninsula. Its islands are mostly mountainous, with only about 20% of the land suitable for cultivation, and it is almost totally lacking in natural resources. Thus, Japan's transformation into a modern industrial nation in the span of less than two generations after the so-called Meiji Restoration in 1868, is nothing short of miraculous.

Yet this change did not come without initial resistance. Since about 1820, with the development of the whaling grounds in the northern Pacific, several Western nations, particularly the United States, sought to establish more extensive contact with the authorities in Japan to deal with the problems encountered by crews shipwrecked in Japanese waters. In 1853, after several previous attempts by U.S. naval vessels to do so, Commodore Matthew C. Perry, visited Edo Bay (present day Tokyo) with four ships and remained there for ten days. His main purpose was to deliver a letter from the president of the United States to the emperor of Japan and the feudal lords. Although his visit for the most part elicited an anti-foreign response, Perry nevertheless returned one year later, spurred by rumors that Russia and France were seeking treaties with Japan.

Perry succeeded in negotiating the Treaty of Kanghwa, whereby two ports were opened to U.S. vessels for limited trading, and Japan agreed to give better treatment to American castaways. A similar treaty was signed by Japan later that year with Great Britain and in 1855 with Russia and Holland.

In 1856, U.S. Consul General Townsend Harris arrived in Japan to negotiate a commercial treaty, which was signed in 1858. It provided for unsupervised trade and residence at five ports, the presence of an American envoy at Edo, extraterritoriality, a convention on tariffs, and an agreement prohibiting the importation of opium. Similar treaties were signed with Holland, Russia, Great Britain, and France. Notwithstanding these exchanges, anti-foreign feeling remained unabated, with a series of attacks against foreigners taking place in 1859.

That same year, the first Japanese embassy in the United States exchanged commercial treaty ratifications in Washington. Nevertheless, with the occupation of the island of Tsushima by Russia in 1861, anti-foreign violence escalated.

The following year, Japan sent its first mission to China in three centuries, thus beginning the first of its many incursions, peaceful and not so peaceful, that were to follow. That year, a British squadron attacked Kagoshima to avenge the murder of an Englishman. In 1864, a joint force of British, Dutch, French and U.S. ships silenced the forts at Shimonoseki and broke the momentum of the anti-foreign movement.

The turning point in modern Japanese history came in 1868, with the Meiji Restoration. Emperor Meiji, who had come to the throne in 1867, assumed direct control of the nation and thus ended 700 years of feudal military government under the shogun system. The Charter Oath by the Emperor promised a deliberative assembly, dissolution of the feudal system, and a decision to seek modern knowledge with which to improve Japan, regardless of the source. The capital of Japan was moved to Tokyo. The anti-foreign movement became a thing of the past as Japan's elite concluded that to avoid domination and colonization by the West it was imperative that Japan modernize. A constitution based on the Prusso-German system was approved, a legal system based on a European style civil code was established, the educational system was reformed and improved to the point that a high degree of literacy was achieved, a Western-type banking system was established, a modern navy modeled on the British navy was created,[96] and experts from the Prussian General Staff were brought in to create and train Japan's crack new army. Meanwhile the government promoted business and industrial development, thus commencing a partnership that continues to this day. There was official encouragement to developing a railway network, the telegraph and a merchant marine, as well as the establishment of basic heavy industries such as iron, steel, and shipbuilding works, much of it subsidized by government funds. Japanese exports soared, particularly in the textile industry, with silk exports becoming the largest of all Japanese exports after 1880.

Although Japan was the only non-Western country to have an industrial revolution, by the end of the 19th Century its share of the world's manufacturing output was still very modest (see Table 1). The fact is that Japan remained a nation in which, even in 1900, three-fifths of its population was employed in agriculture, fishing and forestry, i.e., non-manufacturing endeavors.

In 1872, universal military service was established,[97] a harbinger of things to come. Two years later, Japan sent an expeditionary force into Formosa (Taiwan) to avenge the murder of some Ryukyuan fishermen. Japan agreed to withdraw after China paid an indemnity, but the Japanese would soon return, a situation with long-term consequences for the Spanish (and later, American) Philippines.

Japan's propensity for international aggressiveness would become more patent when, in 1876, it forced Korea to sign the Treaty of Kanghwa, by which Korea's independence from China was recognized and Japan received extraterritorial and commercial privileges in that country. In 1894, as result of the Tonghak Rebellion, both China and Japan sent troops to Korea, actions which soon escalated into the Sino-Japanese War, and resulted in a quick and decisive victory for Japan.

The outcome was that under the Treaty of Shimonoseki, Japan, the emerging enfant terrible of Asia, annexed Formosa from China, and in addition received a £35 million indemnity. Although it also attempted to take the Liaotung Peninsula from China, France, Russia and Germany objected and made Japan return Liaotung. In exchange for this support, China then granted France mineral rights in several provinces, delivered Kwangsi and Hankow to Germany, and allowed Russia to purchase controlling interest in the Chinese Eastern Railway, which would eventually connect with the Trans-Siberian Railway in Manchuria. In 1897, Germany's turn to claim reparations came when some of its missionaries were murdered in Shantung. Germany thus received Kiachow,[98] turning it into a naval base, and a monopoly on investments in mines and railways in Shantung. Russia, not to be left behind, occupied Port Arthur, and the Liaotung Peninsula, the peninsula that had been denied to Japan two years earlier.

The Empire of the United States[99]

Long before John Louis O'Sullivan coined the term "manifest destiny," in 1845,[100] a phrase that was to become the rallying cry for American expansionists, the United States had already embarked on its own brand[101] of Darwinian imperialism,[102] –a combination of geopolitics, religious righteousness,[103] and just plain commercial entrepreneurship– to justify its territorial aggrandizement and the conquering, subjugation and absorption of other peoples.[104] In fact, this was a crusade[105] that commenced even before the United States was a nation, and certainly immediately thereafter (see Table 4 and Map 5).

By the Proclamation Act of 1763, King George III of Great Britain, the monarch that reigned over the thirteen American colonies at that time, closed to white settlers all the lands west of the Appalachian Mountains and north of streams running into the Atlantic Ocean. However, this edict was widely ignored by frontier Americans and the commercial interests that wanted to expand to the West. Although the Proclamation Line of 1763 was technically the western frontier of the United States of America when it achieved its independence from Great Britain, pursuant to the Treaty of Peace signed on February 3, 1783 (see Map 5),[106] Great Britain ceded its claims to all lands west of the Appalachians and as far as the Mississippi River, north to Canada, and south to Spanish Florida, to the new United States. This was an area larger in size (approximately 450,000 sq. mi.) than that of the original thirteen colonies (which were only about 385,000 sq. mi.) (see Map 5). The treaty with Great Britain made no mention of the Indian nations that inhabited either the original colonies or the Northwest Territory, as the newly added lands were called.

During the period of the original Confederacy (1783-1787), the states of Massachusetts, Connecticut, Virginia, New York, North Carolina, South Carolina, and Georgia all laid claim to various parts of the Northwest Territory, but these issues were resolved by the time the Constitution of the United States was finally ratified in 1788.

Not long after, in 1803, the United States made the largest of all its territorial expansions. In one stroke of the pen, it doubled the size of the country when it purchased the Louisiana Territory from France –about 800,000 sq. mi.– for $12 million[107] (see Map 5). This land had been part of the Spanish Empire, but Napoleon acquired it in the Treaty of San Ildefonso (1800) during his occupation of Spain. Napoleon's intention was to make up for France's loss of Canada to the British by increasing his presence in Louisiana. However, in 1789, the French were expelled from St. Domingue (Haiti), as result of a successful slave revolt, which was followed in 1804 by the defeat of an army sent by Napoleon to retake the island. These setbacks, when coupled with France's lack of sea power with which to maintain adequate communications with its overseas colonies, especially in the face of the continuous interdiction of French merchant ships by the British, convinced Napoleon that the sale of Louisiana to the United States was the course to follow. The U.S. resident minister in France, Robert Livingston, had been instructed to pay $7.5 million for the island of New Orleans alone, but Talleyrand offered the whole 800,000 square miles for $12 million instead! After some hesitation, considering his lack of authority, Livingston accepted on behalf of the United States.

TABLE 4
Territories Acquired By the U.S. Before the Spanish-American War [108]
(in approx. sq. mi.)

	Year	Area	How acquired
Original Thirteen Colonies	1776	385,000	War of Independence
Old Northwest Territory	1783	240,000	Cession by Great Britain
Louisiana Purchase	1803	800,000	Purchase from France
Red River Cession	1817[109]	20,000	Cession from Great Britain
Florida (and Spanish lands east of the Mississippi River)	1819	89,000	Purchase from Spain
Republic of Texas	1845	500,000	Annexation from Mexico
Oregon Country (New Northwest Territory)	1846	248,000	Claim recognized by Great Britain
Southwest Territory	1848	500,000	Conquest from Mexico
Gadsden Purchase	1852	29,640	Purchase from Mexico
Russian Alaska	1867	591,000	Purchase from Russia
Hawaii	1897[110]	6,470	Annexed by treaty with the Republic of Hawaii

The War of 1812 was the last open conflict between Great Britain and the United States. The burning of Washington, D.C., by British troops, and the Battle of New Orleans, actually won by General Andrew Jackson after the war had ended,[111] were the central events of this conflict.

This war proved to be a turning point in British-U.S. relations.[112] All else aside, after the War of Independence and the War of 1812, both of which were marginal issues in Great Britain's European conflicts, the British became convinced that they could not properly protect their interests in Europe and elsewhere while there was an unfriendly United States on its Atlantic flank. Thus began the British-American rapprochement.

In 1790, the population of the United States was 3.9 million. By 1820, it had reached 9.6 million. Meanwhile the nation's urban population increased from less than 550,000 in 1820 to 1.8 million in 1840, and by 1870, when the U.S. population had reached nearly 40 million, 10 million people already lived in urban areas. A large part of the population increase was due to immigration, however: nearly 2 million Irish immigrants in the two decades before the Civil War; 1 million from Germany; 750,000 from Great Britain and Canada. This influx of immigrants made up for a sharp decrease in the birth rate during this period, which was the case for both urban and rural populations.

In 1817, General Andrew Jackson and a force of Tennessee militia under federal orders entered Spanish Florida to avenge cross-border raids by Seminole Indians and maroons. He proceeded to haul down the Spanish flag at St. Marks and to hang two Seminole chiefs he found there. He also tried and executed two British subjects who were found guilty of espionage and aiding the Indians. Jackson then marched to Pensacola, where he ejected the Spanish governor and garrisoned the fortress with his troops. Although there was considerable fuss in Congress as a result of Jackson's highhandedness, all was forgiven after his actions convinced the Spanish government that its position in Florida was untenable, and it decided to strike a deal. The final outcome was that the Spanish government negotiated a cession to the United States of all its lands and claims East of the Mississippi for the sum of $5 million (see Map 5).

As a complement to the nation's aspiration of fulfilling its "manifest destiny," a parallel protocol was developed, which would be used by the United States to shield itself and the other newly emerging American republics from further colonial depredations by the European nations, but which in practice has allowed the United States to claim the Americas as its own informal empire. In 1823, in a message to Congress, then President James Monroe (1817-1825) announced what has become a fundamental tenet of American foreign policy: the Monroe Doctrine. This principle proclaimed that "the American continents... [would] henceforth not to be considered as subjects for future colonization by any European power," and that European intervention in the Americas would not be viewed "in any other light than as the manifestation of an unfriendly disposition towards the United States." As the Mexican War (1846-48) and the Spanish-American War (1898) clearly demonstrated, however, in announcing the Monroe Doctrine, the United States had no intention of applying its professedly noble principles to itself. In fact, intervention and invasion, particularly in the Caribbean and in Central America during the 20th century, have become standard operating procedure for the Americas' self-appointed Big Brother.[113]

In the meantime, the problem of United States-Indian nations relations, which had run the gamut from open warfare to peaceful coexistence, came to a head after efforts to maintain Indian reservations within the eastern states proved generally unsatisfactory, particularly to white American interests. Thus during the presidency of James Monroe, the United States government decided on a policy of removing the tribes from the Old[114] North West Territory and the lower South, to West of the Mississippi, a practice that began in earnest in the 1820s. Although these removals slowed some during the administration of John Quincy Adams (1825-29), who had a more humane and paternalistic attitude toward the Indians, they again picked up during the presidency of that old Indian fighter and soldier, Andrew Jackson (1829-37), especially after Congress passed the Indian Removal Act (1830).

The liquidation of Indian reservations in the Old Northwest was largely accomplished between 1829 and 1843, when the four great Indian nations of the South – the Chickasaw, Creek, Choctaw, and Cherokee – were removed, with significant suffering caused to the Indian tribes. One quarter of the Cherokee Nation died when the U.S. Army forced them to march from their lands in Tennessee and the Carolinas to Indian Territory in present-day Oklahoma. These removals took place despite the fact that the independence of the Cherokee Nation had been guaranteed by the United States by treaty in 1791, and that, if the truth be told, the Cherokee were more "civilized," by the white man's standards, than the Georgia "crackers" and "hillbillies" that coveted their lands.[115]

By 1860, the Creek nation had lost about 60% of its population. Although these eastern tribes were removed to lands west of the Mississippi, where they were guaranteed by treaty that possession of these new lands would be for "as long as grass grows and water runs," in fact soon after, the never-ending flow of white settlers again encroached on the displaced eastern tribes as well as on the western tribes. Thus between 1853 and 1856 alone, the United States would negotiate no fewer than fifty-two treaties, mostly with tribes in the Mississippi Valley or west of that river, as a result of which more than 174 million additional acres would be taken from the Indians and added to the public domain for occupation by white settlers.

In the meantime, the expansion of the American Empire proceeded in other directions. In 1821, the colonization of Texas by U.S. citizens commenced with a grant from the government of Mexico to induce their settling there. Thereafter, other grants led to the influx of large numbers of American settlers, mostly southerners, all part of the westward move-ment of the American people. By 1834, there were 20,000 U.S.-born Tex-ans, who theoretically became Mexican citizens upon moving to Mexi-can Texas, and who together with their 2,000 slaves (even though Mexico had abolished slavery in 1823) outnumbered the native Mexicans by a ratio of four to one. The outcome of this situation was predetermined.

In 1635, after a series of incidents, the Texan-Americans seceded from Mexico, and declared themselves to be the independent Republic of Texas. Thereafter, they were able to beat off Mexican attempts to reverse this fait accompli, the most renowned of these skirmishes being the Battle of the Alamo, in which the Texan garrison was wiped out by an overwhelm-ing Mexican army, giving the young Texas Republic its rallying cry, "Re-member the Alamo."

On March 3, 1837, the United States recognized the Republic of Texas. Great Britain and France followed suit. In the meantime, Texas sought annexation by the United States. After various maneuvers and diverse intrigues, mostly related to the effect that admission of a slave state would have on the political balance of the slave vs. non-slave states, Congress approved the annexation of the Republic of Texas on February 28, 1845, an act that was ratified by the Republic of Texas immediately thereafter. So Texas became the twenty-eighth state of the United States (see Map 5).

The Pacific beckoned, so the next territorial expansion was to achieve a nation that stretched "from sea to shining sea."[116] The first step in the fulfillment of this goal entailed gaining sovereignty over the Northwest, the so-called Oregon Territory, discovered by the Spanish, claimed by Russia at one point,[117] and since 1818 jointly occupied pursuant to agreement, by Great Britain and the United States. By the 1840s, however, there was such a strong presence of U.S. citizens in the Oregon Territory, most of whom had arrived by coming over the arduous Oregon Trail, that things would not long remain as they were. Following the now common expansionist pattern, in 1842 there was political agitation in Congress to annex not only the Oregon Territory but also the land that extended all the way north to the border of Russian Alaska, which if carried out would have deprived British Canada of access to the Pacific Ocean.

President John Tyler (1841-45) had started negotiations with the British seeking to acquire full U.S. sovereignty over the Oregon Territory and to establish the border with British Canada at the 49th Parallel, which would allow Canada access to the Pacific, but the British rejected Tyler's proposal outright. When James K. Polk (1845-50), a known expansionist, became president, however, things came to a head. In his annual message to Congress in December, 1845, Polk forcefully laid claim to the Pacific Northwest up to the Russian Alaska border, and he asked Congress for permission to terminate the 1818 agreement with the British, something Congress readily gave. This turn of events was enough to make the British rethink their earlier position. They concluded that it was in their best interest to reach a peaceful compromise with Tyler rather than risk an open conflict, and they proposed the 49th Parallel as the demarcation of the U.S.-Canada border. Polk already had his eye on Mexican California and wished to avoid a war on two fronts, so on June 6, 1846, already three weeks into the Mexican War, he recommended acceptance of the British offer. The Senate approved the treaty and the United States thus spanned the North American Continent " from sea to shining sea" (see Map 5).

Polk was not finished, however. After the annexation of Texas by the United States, and the flanking of California by Americans pouring into Oregon Territory over the Oregon Trail, golden California became the main prize. It was delectable and too directly in the path of America's "manifest destiny" to be ignored by the aggressive young American republic.

After Lt. John C. Fremont reported in glowing terms on what he saw and found there, President Polk knew he had to have California. He first tried to buy it, but Mexico refused. Polk next tried to promote a Texas-like revolution, with a resulting republic that could be annexed, but that also failed. All that was left was outright war. Mexico was properly baited and conveniently provided an excuse.

Mexico suspended the payment of sums owed and previously negotiated for damages caused to U.S. citizens. The installments due amounted to $3,208 at that time, but this figure was ultimately determined to only be $314.96 by a commission that later investigated the matter.[118] Polk threatened action, but then changed tactics and offered to purchase New Mexico for $5 million, saying that "money was no object" if Mexico also agreed to sell California. The offer was again refused, this time by a Mexican government that had been taken over in a military coup and which was spoiling for a fight with the United States.

Always willing to oblige, Polk ordered General Zachary Taylor to cross the Nueces River in Texas into Mexican territory, which he did, blockading the town of Matamoros. The Mexicans naturally responded, repelling what amounted to an invasion of their national territory. In a skirmish with Taylor's troops, the Americans suffered several casualties.

In his message to Congress on May 11, 1846 asking for a declaration of war against Mexico, Polk stated, "The cup of forbearance has been exhausted... Mexico has passed the boundary of the United States, has invaded our country and shed American blood upon American soil."[119] Such presidential double-speak in seeking to loose the dogs of war has a familiar ring.

In any event, the dogs were loosed and by the end of 1846, California was completely in the hands of the United States. Further south in the Mexican heartland, General Taylor captured the town of Monterrey, in Nuevo León after a three-day battle, and he asked then for reinforcements to allow him to proceed to Mexico City. President Polk, who saw Taylor as a political opponent and did not wish to build him up too much,[120] decided instead to send General Winfield Scott to outflank the Mexicans by landing in Veracruz and marching on Mexico City. General Scott did so and Mexico City surrendered to the *gringos*[121] on September 17, 1847, after several pitched battles.

Several months elapsed before any Mexican government was willing to negotiate a peace treaty. Finally, on February 2, 1848, Mexico and the United States signed the Treaty of Guadalupe Hidalgo, by which Mexico ceded Texas, with the Rio Grande as the U.S.-Mexico boundary, as well as New Mexico (including Arizona), and Upper California (including San Diego) (see Map 5). Under the provisions of the treaty the United States assumed the unpaid claims that were used as an excuse for starting this controversy, and also agreed to pay Mexico $15 million for these lands (three fifths of what Polk had authorized be paid to Mexico for these lands in 1846).

Two other territories remained to be acquired before the Spanish-American War would bring about a fundamental change in the United States national policy towards territorial expansion. The first was small in comparison to other prior expansions. By the Gadsden Purchase in 1853, the United States acquired the lands south of the Gila River in Arizona and New Mexico from Mexico for $10 million, thus setting the southern boundary with Mexico as it is today (see Map 5).

The second acquisition, however, was hardly a small item, for it involved the purchase of Alaska from Russia, some 591,004 square miles for $7.2 million (2 cents per acre) in 1867, shortly after the American Civil War ended and while Reconstruction was in full swing.

Although the present account is not a history of the United States, no chronicle of the United States during the 19th century can be considered complete without some treatment, however summary, of the American Civil War, an event whose traumatic scars and impact on the United States is without equal, and which has had lasting repercussions to this day on the character of the American people. Furthermore, the Civil War exercised an important influence on the Spanish-American War for several reasons, particularly because of its temporal proximity to that event. The Spanish-American War, being the first international conflict faced by the United States after its devastating internal one, served to unify the nation and distract it from its own recent self-destructive event.

It is difficult to encapsulate the Civil War without appearing to trivialize an event of such historical magnitude to the United States.[122] Perhaps it is best to start by stating the obvious: by this war, as in the case of all civil wars, in which the very fabric of the nation is rent by fratricidal conflict, Americans were subjected to what is probably the most scaring experience of all of man's violent confrontations. The origins and causes of the war are not directly relevant here. Suffice it to say that both sides were determined to fight to the finish on core issues of principle, and thus it was predictable that the conflict would be both bloody and prolonged.

The imbalance of resources greatly favored the Union. The North, with a population in 1860 of about 20 million whites, fielded an army which reached 1 million men in 1864-1865. The South, which had a population of only about 6 million whites, was able to raise an army of only 464,500 at its peak in 1863. In 1860, the North had 110,000 manufacturing enterprises, with Pennsylvania alone producing 580,000 tons of pig iron annually. The North also had over 22,000 miles of railroads. At that time, the South had but 18,000 manufacturing enterprises, a total annual production of but 36,700 tons of pig iron, and a mere 9,000 miles of railway track. A key component of the North's success was its navy, which allowed it to blockade southern ports and strangle the South economically. It also served to support the Union armies inland, particularly on the Mississippi-Tennessee fronts. By December 1864, the Union's navy totaled 671 warships, of which 236 were steamships built after 1861. The build-up of the American navy (though mostly dismantled after the war), would have a profound effect on the forthcoming Spanish-American War, which was principally decided on the water. All this said, however, the Union's eventual victory over the Confederacy proved to be difficult both logistically and militarily.

The war started on April 12, 1861, with the attack on Ft. Sumter, South Carolina, and lasted until April 9, 1865, almost four years to the day, when General Lee surrendered to General Grant at Appomattox Court House, Virginia. The carnage of war was greatly increased by advances in technology that allowed for increased and more accurate firepower.[123] The war produced massive conscript armies, on both sides, and drew upon the resources of mobilized war economies to create, particularly in the North, the first industrialized "total war" societies, the precursors of the prototype of such national efforts during World Wars I and II.

The casualties were massive on both sides. At the Battle of Shiloh in April 1862, the Union Army lost 13,000 soldiers out a total of 55,000 troops, and the Confederates lost 11,000 soldiers out of a total of 42,000 troops.

In the Battle of Antietam, on September 17, 1862, one of the bloodiest of the war, out of about 36,000 Confederate soldiers, 10,700 were casualties, and of 87,000 in the Union forces, only half of which were engaged, 12,410 were lost.

Five days after Antietam, President Abraham Lincoln (1861-65) announced the Emancipation Proclamation freeing all slaves in the United States.

The Battle of Gettysburg, which lasted from July 1 to 3, 1863, and was the turning point of the war, was also its bloodiest, with over 50,000 casualties on both sides. Although the Union Army won this battle decisively, it failed to capitalize on its victory, allowing Lee to escape and thus prolong the war for another two years.

It is estimated that approximately 618,000 Americans on both sides[124] lost their lives in the Civil War, out of a total U.S. population, including all races, of about 31 million in 1860.[125] This was more than the American losses in both World Wars plus the Korean conflict combined.

With the war ending at Appomattox, several things happened that affected the post-war period. The first was President Lincoln's assassination at the hands of John Wilkes Booth, on April 8, 1865, a mere five days after Lee's surrender. Had Lincoln lived, the Reconstruction Period would have been less painful for the South, for Lincoln believed that "Blood cannot restore blood, and government should not act for revenge."

At this point the South was economically and physically devastated, far worse than central Europe in 1919 or 1945. Where the armies of Generals Sherman and Sheridan had passed, the institutions of civilized life had been destroyed and the countryside laid to waste. The reestablishment of civilian government –first tried in January 1866 throughout the former Confederacy except Texas– failed when these administrations were subverted by the infiltration of former rebels bent on surreptitiously perpetuating their racial philosophies. As a reaction to these attempts, under the Reconstruction Act of 1867, the southern states were divided into five military districts, whose military governors thereafter ruled the civilian populations with a firm hand. Thus began the slow, and at times, bumpy economic and civil recovery of the South.

The freed slaves were a central focus of Reconstruction. For a time, they were wards of the Union with an undetermined status and a doubtful future. In 1865, the Thirteenth Amendment to the Constitution abolished slavery, and in 1866, the Fourteenth Amendment declared all persons born in the United States to be citizens and entitled to equal protection before the law. Under the Fifteenth Amendment, all citizens were guaranteed the right to vote, regardless of "race, color or previous condition of servitude." Of course, theory and reality were two different things, as history would soon demonstrate.

Nevertheless, by 1877, all former Confederate states were back in the Union and in charge of their domestic affairs.

Meanwhile, war broke out with the Plains Sioux when troops tried to build a road through their reservation in violation of their treaty rights. The United States thus began a concerted effort (1867-83) to destroy the buffalo, and so deprive the Plains Indians of an independent means of food and shelter outside of reservations. The influx of prospectors and settlers into the Black Hills of the Dakotas, part of the Sioux Reservations and considered sacred by them, led to an uprising in 1876. During the course of this insurgency, Civil War hero, General George A. Custer and most of his command were wiped out by the Sioux at the Battle of Little Horn under the leadership of Chiefs Sitting Bull and Crazy Horse.

By 1884, the U.S. Navy, which as previously stated, was practically dismantled after the Civil War, was down to fourteen small ironclads, mostly monitors. After much debate, in August of 1882, Congress approved the construction of two steam-driven steel cruisers, the *Chicago* and the *Atlanta*, and two more to be built in 1887, the *Boston*, and the *Dolphin*, the latter a dispatch boat. Thus began the rebuilding of the United States Navy, which would play a crucial role only twelve years later in the Spanish-American War.

In 1887, with the capture of Geronimo in Arizona, an Apache uprisings in New Mexico and Arizona dissipated, and the last of the Indian Wars ended. General Nelson Miles, who would have a prominent part in the Spanish-American War in leading the invasion of Puerto Rico, was the commander of the U.S. Army troops in that last Indian War. He had previously been in charge of the prison where Confederate President Jefferson Davis was incarcerated after the Civil War.

With the Civil War behind it, the United States was able to turn its attention to exploiting its immense resources and natural advantages towards productive ends. Its vast and rich agricultural lands; its multiple and diverse stores of minerals and raw materials, and the modern technology available to exploit them; its comparative geographical isolation, allowing for relative freedom from significant threats to its territorial integrity; its ample and productive work force; and the ready accessibility of large amounts of capital, both domestic and foreign, for the development of its industry and commerce, all combined to produce unmatched national success.

Thus, between 1865, when the Civil War ended, and 1898, when the Spanish-American War was fought, U.S. wheat production increased 256%, corn 222%, refined sugar 460%, coal 800%, steel ingots and castings from 20,000 long tons to 9 million long tons, crude petroleum from 3 million barrels to 55 million barrels, steel rails 523%, and railway tracks in operation 567%. The United States went from producing 7.2% of the world's manufacturing output in 1880 to 23.6% by 1900, surpassing Great Britain at 18.5% and becoming the world's leading manufacturing nation.

Since the Civil War, the United States had completed a transition from a predominantly agrarian society to a predominantly urban industrial nation. As in the case of Great Britain, industrialization brought with it a variety of ills and abuses. The newly arrived immigrant groups were much exploited, but with time many of these passed on to be part of the rapidly growing American middle class, the backbone of the United States particularly in the next century and an important component of American society, differentiating it from most other nations.

Unfortunately, racism, despite the Civil War and the various Constitutional amendments and laws aimed at eradicating this pervasive evil, intensified throughout the United States, particularly in the South. The Supreme Court of the United States, in deciding Plessy v. Ferguson (1895), effectively institutionalized segregation, particularly in the South, and this would be the law of the land for nearly sixty years thereafter.[126]

On the eve of the Spanish-American War, the United States, by European standards, was down to a minuscule armed force of only 39,000 men in uniform (see Table 2). But its industrial might and its experience in total mobilization –the "American way of War,"[127]– made the United States a sleeping giant, one that was about to be aroused and become a Paul Bunyan of international affairs. It is probably safe to say that of all the dynamic forces that were at large in the world toward the end of the 19th century, none would be as consistently decisive in the unfolding events of the 20th century than the United States. Thus at least half of De Tocqueville's prophesy would be validated.

In Summary

On the eve of an apparently minuscule war between an enfeebled European nation and an energized American upstart, the global scene presented a world in a vigorous state of flux. Old empires were, like old boxers, weaving and feinting, trying to survive, while rising ones were jockeying their way to position and power, intent on laying hands on all they could. One thing was certain about these interrelated events and circumstances: whatever ensued from all this turbulence, the impact would be felt not only in the immediate geographical area where the Spanish-American War took place, or directly by the participants, but would have long-lasting, global geopolitical implications.

The stakes were high and the players motivated.

NOTES

1. See generally, T.S. Ashton, *The Industrial Revolution, 1730-1830*, Oxford (1968 edition): P. Mathias, *The First Industrial Nation: An Economic History of Britain (1700-1914)*, London (1969).

2. The conflicts that did take place, the wars of German unification in the 1860s, the Austro-Prussian War of 1866, the Franco-German War of 1871, and even the more complicated Crimean War (in 1854-1856), were of short duration and fairly localized.

3. Kennedy, Paul, *The Rise and Fall of the Great Powers*, Random House, New York (1987), Table 6, at 149.

4. Id. United States picked up most of the difference, with 23.6% of the world's manufacturing output, surpassing Great Britain's 18.5%. Id.

5. Braudel, F., *Civilization and Capitalism, 15th-18th Century*, Vol. 1, London (1981-84), pp. 42 ff.

6. D. Fieldhouse, *The Colonial Empires: A Comparative Study Survey from the Eighteenth Century*, London (1966), at 178.

7. Until Japan entered the picture.

8. Rosario de la Torre del Río, *Inglaterra y España en 1898*, EUDEMA, Madrid (1998), at 13; J.M. Jover Zamora, *Teoría y práctica de la redistribución colonial*, Fundación Universitaria Española, Madrid (1979).

9. Vladimir Ilich Lenin, *Imperialism i Raskol Sosialisma Polnoye Sobraniye Sochinenii*, Politzdat, Moskow (1962), vol. 30, at 164. He also is said to have called the Spanish-American War "the first imperialist war." Quoted in *Handbuch der Vertage 1871-1964*, ed. Helmuth Stoecker, Berlin (1968), at 81.

10. J.A.S. Grenville, *Lord Salisbury and Foreign Policy: The Close of the Nineteenth Century, 1893-1902*, London (1964), at 165-166.

11. A.G.L. Shaw (ed.), *Great Britain and her Colonies 1815-1865*, London (1970), at 2.

12. A non-exhaustive list includes Canada (including Nova Scotia, Newfoundland and Labrador) in North America; British Guiana in South America; Gambia, Sierra Leone, Gold Coast, Nigeria, the Cape Province, Bechuanaland, Transvaal, Rhodesia and Nyasaland, Kenya, Uganda, Sudan, Egypt and Somalia in Africa;

Aden, India, Ceylon, Burma, Malaya, North Borneo, Sarawak and Papua New Guinea in Asia; and Australia, Tasmania and New Zealand in the South Pacific. It also had a string of strategic islands and ports throughout the world which included Bermuda in the North Atlantic Ocean; Jamaica, British Virgin Islands, the Windward and Leeward Islands, and Trinidad and Tobago in the Caribbean Sea; British Guiana in South America; St. Helena, Ascension and the Falkland Islands in the South Atlantic Ocean; Mauritius, the Seychelles, and Cocos Islands in the Indian Ocean; and Gibraltar and Malta on the Mediterranean Sea, as well as numerous islands and atolls in the South Pacific Ocean. Many of these outposts were used as naval stations or coaling ports and as links in the worldwide British cable network.

13. An example of this is the case of the Ottoman Empire in the 19th Century, which was protected by British policies from Russian, Austrian and French expansion as well from internal revolts like the one led by Muhammad Ali in Egypt, where Great Britain eventually took direct control. Another example of this informal empire is the case of 19th Century Iran, which was ruled by the Qajar dynasty but over whom Great Britain exercised indirect control.

14. Kennedy, *The Rise and Fall of the Great Po*wers, supra, at 227.

15. L.K. Young, *British Policy in China, 1895-1902*, Oxford (1970).

16. Kennedy, *The Rise and Fall of the Great Powers*, supra, Table 20, at 203.

17. Id. at 226.

18. Particularly in the Middle East after the First World War. See David Fromkin, *A Peace to End All Peace,* Avon Books, New York (1990). In Africa and India the 19th Century was mainly a period of colonial consolidation. James Lawrence, *The Rise and Fall of the British Empire*, Little, Brown and Company, London (1994).

19. Paul Kennedy, *Realities Behind Diplomacy: Background Influence on British External Policy, 1865-1980*, Fontana Paperbacks, Glasgow (1981), at 17-27. See also Lawrence, supra, at 202.

20. Germany took the lead in newer and increasingly more important industries such as chemicals and machine tools. Lawrence, supra, at 202.

21. De la Torre del Rosario, supra, at 56. See also P. Mathias, *The First Industrial Nation*, London (1969); Eric J. Hobsbawm, *Industria e Imperio. Una historia económica de Gran Bretaña*, Barcelona (1977); Charles S. Campbell, *Anglo-American Understanding. 1898-1903*, The John Hopkins Press, Baltimore (1957), at 11.

22. See generally, J.F.V. Keiger, *France and the Origins of the First World War*, London (1983).

23. R. Betts, *Tricouleur: The French Empire*, London (1978).

24. Kennedy, *The Rise and Fall of the Great Empires, supra* at 220; G. Krumeich, *Armaments and Politics in France on the Eve of the First World War*, Leamington Spa (1975).

25. Kennedy, supra, at 220.

26. Id., Table 12, at 199.

27. Michael Howard, *The Franco-Prussian War* (1961); Arden Bucholz, *Molke and the German Wars* (2001), at 6.

28. This feeling was mutual. Gordon Craig, *Germany, 1866-1945*, Clarendon Press, Oxford(1978), at 306. In a memorandum to Emperor Wilhelm dated 15 June, 1897, Admiral Tirpitz said: "For Germany, the most dangerous enemy at the present time is England. It is also the enemy against which we most urgently require a certain measure of naval force as a political factor." Id. at 309.

29. In Africa between 1883 and 1887 Germany acquired South West Africa(today's Namibia), Togoland, the Cameroons, German East Africa(today's Tanzania), and in the Pacific various Pacific islands. William Carr, *A History of Germany, 1815-1990*, Edward Arnold, London (1991) at 154.

30. Carr, supra, at 151.

31. Id. at 187.

32. Id. at 90.

33. Id.

34. By which is meant the creation of naval power.

35. Terrell Dean Gottschall, *Germany and the Spanish-American War: A Case Study of Navalism and Imperialism, 1898*, Washington State University, unpublished Ph.D. Thesis (1981).

36. Craig, supra, at 307; Alfred Thayer Mahan, *The Influence of Sea Power Upon History, 1793-1812*, New York (1890); Gottschall, *supra*, at 8. Kaiser Wilhelm ordered that a copy of Mahan's book be placed on board all of his ships "and consequently quoted" by his captains and officers. Id.

37. R. A. Kann, *A History of the Hapsburg Empire 1526-1918*, Berkley (1968).

38. D.F. Good, *The Economic Rise of the Hapsburg Empire, 1750-1914*, Berkeley, CA (1984), at 239.

39. Perhaps the closest it came to having an overseas empire was when Archduke Maximilian, Emperor Franz Joseph's brother, was enticed by Napoleon III of France

into becoming the, as it happened, ill-fated Emperor of Mexico. Unfortunately, Maximilian was executed by a Benito Juárez firing squad after the French withdrew their support and he refused to relinquish his crown.

40. The other, the United States, will be discussed separately. *See* Alexis De Tocqueville, *Democracy in America*, 2 vols. New York (1945 ed.), at 453.

41. Kennedy, *supra*, at 170-1.

42. Id. at 171.

43. J.S. Curtis, *Russia's Crimean War*, Durham, NC (1979).

44. Gregory L. Freeze (ed.), *Russia, A History*, Oxford University Press, Oxford (1997).

45. Id. at 184.

46. Id. at 188.

47. Id. at 189.

48. Kennedy, *The Rise and Fall of Great Powers, supra*, at 234-235.

49. Id. at 235.

50. Id. at 234.

51. Id. at 235.

52. Id. At 175.

53. Id. at 178-179.

54. Id. at 198.

55. Id. at 13-14.

56. See generally, Hopkick, *The Great Game*; also Note 60 post.

57. See, Bernard Lewis, *The Emergence of Modern Turkey*, Oxford University Press, Oxford (2001 rev.); *Istanbul and the Civilization of the Ottoman Empire*, University of Oklahoma Press, Norman, OK, 1963). *See also generally*, Kennedy, *The Rise and Fall of the Great Powers*, supra, at 9-13.

58. Fromkin, supra, at 30. Since the 1880s, German banks, industrial firms and railway interests had been making incursions into the Ottoman Empire. British concern over these activities were exacerbated by an extraordinary visit

by Emperor Wilhelm II to Damascus and Jerusalem in 1898, during the course of which he made inflammatory Pan-Arabic speeches. Craig, *supra*, at 314; Carr, supra, at 190.

59. Fromkin, supra, at 75. The final dismemberment of the Ottoman Empire, particularly in the Middle East and the Arabian Peninsula, would not come about until after the First World War. Sir Mark Sykes, in addressing the House of Commons had warned that "the disappearance of the Ottoman Empire [would] be the first step toward the disappearance of our own." Id. Bernard Lewis, *The Shaping of the Middle East*, Oxford University Press, Oxford (1994), at 32-33.

60. Fromkin, supra, at 28-29. Of course, it also prevented incursions by Russia into India itself, the subject of continued apprehension in Britain, at times approaching hysteria. Lawrence, supra, at 180. *See*, Peter Hopkick, *The Great Game: The Struggle for Empire in Central Asia*, Rodansian International, New York (1992); Lewis, *The Shaping of the Modern Middle East*, supra, at 129.

61. In fact, in 1913, the United States produced 140 times more oil than Persia (Iran). Marian Kent, *Oil and Empire: British Policy and Mesopotamian Oil, 1900-1920*, Macmillan Press for the London School of Economics, London (1976), at 6, and App. 8.

62. Felipe Fernández-Armesto, "Improbable Empire," at 116, in *Spain, A History*, Raymond Carr (ed.), Oxford Press, Oxford (2000).

63. Joseph Pérez, *Historia de España*, Crítica, Barcelona (2001), at 386-388.

64. Id. at 432.

65. Musicant, supra, at 38.

66. Thomas, supra, at 245-263.

67. Earl R. Beck. "The Martínez Campos Government of 1879: Spain's Last Chance in Cuba," *Hispanic-American Historical Review*, LVI, No. 2 (May, 1971).

68. Carlos Serrano, *Final del Imperio. España, 1895-1898*, Madrid (1984), at 38-47. On the political side of this equation, after the assassination of Prime Minister Cánovas del Castillo on August 8, 1897, were his successor, Práxedes Mateo Sagasta, Pío Gullón, as Minister of State (replaced in May 1898 by the Duke of Almodóvar del Río), Segismundo Moret, as Minister of Overseas Territories, Enrique Dupuy de Lome, as ambassador to the United States, Fernando León y Castillo, as ambassador to France, and the Count of Casa Valencia, as ambassador to Great Britain (replaced in January 1898 by the Count of Rascón).

69. Sagasta, Senado, Session of March 8, 1895, reproduced in Marqués de Lerma, *Cánovas o el hombre de Estado*, Madrid (1931) at 236 (translation mine). Spanish historian Carlos Serrano alleges that there is substantial evidence that Spain's

suicidal naval strategy when hostilities broke out in 1898 was a deliberate plan to lose its navy, an almost forgone conclusion in view of its inadequacy in the face of the strength and modernity of the U.S. fleet, to allow the regime to save face and thus survive losing the War to the United States. Serrano, supra, at 41-44.

70. José Martí was Cuba's preeminent revolutionary. He organized, principally from New York, the revolt that commenced in 1895 and ended with Cuba's independence from Spain. Thomas, supra, 393-310. He was killed on May 19, shortly after landing in Cuba.

71. John R.M. Taylor in *The Philippine Insurrection Against the United States*, 4 vols., Eugenio Lopez Foundation, Pasay City, Philippines (1971), Vol. II at 31.

72. At that time the parish priest was the most influential man in the community. Id. at 38. The secular clergy were all Filipino born natives, while after 1832 the regular clergy were all Spanish-born *peninsulares*. This change in the composition of the clergy caused considerable friction because of cultural differences in administrative policies, a situation further complicated by racial issues. Id. An additional aggravating factor was the fact that by the end of the Spanish occupation the Spanish religious orders, namely the Augustinians, the Recollets and the Dominicans, which were largely composed of *peninsulares*, owned 400,000 acres of agricultural land, 250,000 of which were near Manila and included some of the richest lands in the Philippines. Id. at 56.

73. Taylor, supra, at 42.

74. Id. at 46.

75. The night before his execution, Rizal wrote one of his most poignant verses: "Mi Patria idolatrada, dolor de mis dolores / Querida Filipinas, oye el postrer adiós / Ahí te dejo todo, mis padres, mis amores / Voy a donde no hay esclavos, verdugos ni opresores / Donde la fe no mata, donde el que reina es Dios." (To the Homeland that I worship, heart of my hearts / Beloved Philippines, hear my prostrated goodbye / I leave you all, my parents, my loves / I go where there are no slaves, executioners or oppressors / where faith does not kill, where God reigns...), reproduced in Horacio C. Cagni, *La Guerra Hispanoamericana, inicio de la Globalización*, Centro Argentino de Estudios Estratégicos IXBILA, OLCESE Editores, Buenos Aires (1999), at 56 (translation mine).

76. Paradoxically, the fact that the opening of the Suez Canal in 1869 made communications between Spain and the Philippines easier, and thus enabled Spain not only to oversee the local administration more closely, but, in consonance with changes in Spanish politics, to fill it frequently with *peninsulares*, most of whom lacked the local knowledge of former career colonial officers, exacerbated tensions with the native Filipino population. Taylor, *supra*, at 48-49.

77. Taylor, supra, at 35. See also, ante at n. 20.

78. In the course of an internal struggle for the leadership of the Katipúnan, the semi-secret insurrectionist organization, Aguinaldo had Bonifacio tried and shot for conspiring to murder him. Id. at 74.

79. The peace agreement provided for safe conduct to China or Japan for the leaders of the insurrection, and for the payment of 800,000 pesos to the rebels, to be made in three installments, 400,000 when Aguinaldo and his group reached Hong Kong, and two further installments of 200,000 each to those left in the Philippines, at a later date when their arms were surrendered. Id. at 84. Only the first two payments were actually made by the Spanish authorities.

80. Id. at 91-105.

81. See generally, Brian McAllister Linn, *The Philippine War, 1899-1902*, University Press of Kansas, Lawrence, Kansas (2000); J.A.S. Grenville. "Diplomacy and War Plans in the United States, 1890-1917," *Transactions of the Royal Historical Society*, Fifth Series, Vol., III, London (1961), at 3.

82. In 1759, the Ch'ing Empire controlled approximately 4.9 million square miles, compared with today's Chinese People's Republic which comprises only 3.7 square miles. Jackes Gernet, *A History of Chinese Civilization*, 2 vols. The Folio Society (2002), Vol., II, at 499. Of course, were we to go further back in history, the empire of the Grand Khan (Yuan) in the 13th Century extended even further north into Siberia past Lake Baikal and east into Manchuria to the Pacific Ocean and beyond to the Island of Formosa (Taiwan). Id., at Vol. I, p. 366-367.

83. See generally, Richard Wilhelm, *A Short History of Chinese Civilization*, trans. by Joan Joshua, George G. Harrap & Co. London (1929); John A. Harrison, *China since 1800*, Harcourt, Brace & World, New York (1967).

84. In 1644, the Manchus (also known as the Q'ing), who had been a semi-nomadic tribe from northeast China, took over Beijing from the Ming dynasty (1368-1644) and ruled China until 1911. During the first century of Q'ing rule, China gained control of Tibet, Xinjiang and Outer Mongolia, and was at its largest territorial extension except in the greatest days of the T'ang dynasty (618-907 C.E.).

85. In 1839, the official census put China's population at 410 million. Jean Chesneaux, et al, *China from the Opium War to the 1911 Revolution*, Anne Destenay (trans.), Harvester Press (1977) at 1. China's population in 2000 was estimated at 1.3 billion.

86. From the Yunnan area.

87. From present-day Sinkiang.

88. From the southwestern provinces.

89. Thomas J. McCormick, *China Market: America's Quest for Informal Empire, 1893-1901*, Quadrangle Books, Chicago (1967).

90. Lawrence, supra, at 235-241.

91. A technological inferiority that did not exist prior to the 15th Century. *See* Kennedy, *The Rise and Fall of the Great Powers*, supra, at 6-7.

92. See. William R. Braisted, "The Open Door Policy and the Boxer Uprising", at 179-180, in *Threshold to American Imperialism*, Paolo E. Coletta (ed.), Exposition Press, New York (1970).

93. McCormick, supra, at 107,117, 119, 120. 122. In the middle of the Spanish-American War, in a letter to Congress, Secretary of State Day, analyzing the world market situation, concluded that underdeveloped areas offered the best export possibilities, and that "nowhere is this consideration of more interest than in its relation to the Chinese Empire." Id. at 114. See also Grenville, supra, at 3-7.

94. For a cogent history of Japan and its rise as a modern nation, see James L. Mclain, *A Modern History of Japan*, W.W. Norton & Co. New York (2002), particularly at 283-315.

95. Quoted in R. Storry, *Japan and the Decline of the West in Asia 1894-1943*, London (1979), at 30.

96. By 1910, Japan's navy was larger than that of Russia, Italy and Austro-Hungary (see Table 3).

97. By 1900 Japan had a larger army and navy than the United States (see Table 2).

98. Occupied on direct orders from the emperor to Admiral Diederichs, the commander of the German Far East Naval Squadron, Craig, supra at 310, n.26, from whom we shall hear again in the aftermath of the Battle of Manila Bay.

99. For a detailed history of the United States, see generally, Samuel Eliot Morison, *The Oxford History of the American People,* Oxford University Press, New York (1965). Also, Paul Johnson, *A History of the American People*, Phoenix, London (1997).

100. In an article in the *Democratic Review*, of which he was the editor. *See,* Julius W. Pratt, "John L. O'Sullivan and Manifest Destiny," *New York History*, XIV, 213-234. The term "manifest destiny" was originally used to describe the "expectation that the United States, by virtue of the superior qualities of the Anglo-Saxon race [including presumably the Irish] and their democratic institutions, would inevitably absorb their neighbors." Thomas, *supra*, at 211, 206-17. *Also*, footnotes 110-112, *post*. Although originally the term encompassed mainly expansion to the Pacific Ocean and was considered a tactic for the extension of slavery, after the Civil War it was adopted by the Republican expansionist block as a slogan for overseas territorial conquest. See, H. Cabot Lodge, "Our Blundering Foreign Policy," *The Forum*, XIX, 8-17.

101. Although not totally unlike the British "white man's" burden approach.

102. Historian John Fiske wrote an article in 1885 entitled, "Manifest Destiny" in *Harper's New Monthly Magazine*, LXX, 578-590. "The general conclusion that the work which the English race began when it colonized North America is destined to go until every land on the earth's surface that is not already the seat of an old civilization shall become English in its language, in its religion, in its political habits and traditions, and to a predominant extent in the blood of its people. The day is at hand when four-fifths of the human race will trace its pedigree to English forefathers, as four fifths of the white people of the United States trace their pedigree today. The race thus spread over both hemispheres, and from the rising to the setting sun, will not fail to keep that sovereignty of the sea and the commercial supremacy which it began to acquire when England first stretched its arm across the Atlantic to the shores of Virginia and Massachusetts."

103. Congregational clergyman Josiah Strong wrote, also in 1885, in *Our Country: Its Possible Future and Its Present Crisis*: "Then this [Anglo-Saxon] race of unequaled energy, with all the majesty of numbers and the might of wealth behind it –the representative, let us hope, of the largest liberty, the purest Christianity, the highest civilization– having developed peculiarly aggressive traits calculated to impress its institutions upon mankind, will spread itself over the earth. If I read not amiss, this powerful race will move down upon Mexico, down upon Central and South America, out upon the islands of the seas, over upon Africa and beyond. And can anyone doubt that the result of this competition of races will be the 'survival of the fittest'?"

104. See generally, Julius W. Pratt, *Expansionists of 1898*, Quadrangle Books, Chicago (1936).

105. A word currently in vogue. *See*, Peter Ford, "Europe cringes at Bush 'crusade' against terror," *Christian Science Monitor*, September 19, 2001.

106. On that same day, Great Britain, France, Spain and the Netherlands signed treaties, collectively known as the Peace of Paris, ending ongoing conflicts known as the Seven Years War, which originated in Europe but had global implications, of which the American War of Independence was but a part. Under these treaties, Great Britain was to keep Gibraltar but return Minorca and the Floridas to Spain, and France received Tobago in the West Indies and Senegal in West Africa.

107. Morison, supra, at 366.

108. From 1879, the United States laid claim to Samoa (77 sq. mi.) in the South Pacific, which thereafter it held by virtue of an 1889 treaty in condominium with Great Britain and Germany until it was dissolved, in 1899, when Samoa was partitioned between the United States and Germany. The United States also laid claim to a series of islands and atolls throughout the Pacific and the Caribbean: (1) Baker Island, 1,650 mi. southwest of Hawaii, 1 sq. mi. (1856), (2) Howland Island, 1,620 mi. southwest of Hawaii, .73 sq. mi. (1856), (3) Jarvis Island, 1,300 mi. south of Hawaii (1856), (4) Johnston Atoll, 700 mi. southwest of Hawaii, 1.1 sq. mi. (1858), (5) Midway Islands, 1,300 mi. northwest of Hawaii, 2 sq. mi. (1867), (6) Navassa, 35 mi. west of Haiti, 2 sq. mi.

(1856), Palmyra Atoll, 1,100 mi. southwest of Hawaii, 2 sq. mi. (1898), (7) Kingman's Reef, 1075 mi. south west of Hawaii, .4 sq. mi. (1856) and (7) Wake Island, 2,300 mi. west of Hawaii, 3 sq. mi. (1898).

109. Rush-Bagot Agreement of 1817, ratified by the Senate in 1818. It established the 49th Parallel as the border between Canada and the United States as far as the Rocky Mountains and limited the number and size of armed ships on the Great Lakes.

110. Annexed by a treaty with the Republic of Hawaii on June 16, 1897, that was ratified by Congress in July 1898.

111. The Treaty of Ghent, which ended the war, was signed before the Battle of New Orleans. By the United States winning this battle, Great Britain was forced to recognize the validity of the Louisiana Purchase, which Great Britain and various other European nations had refused to acknowledge. More importantly, this treaty *sub silentio* accepted the United States as a legitimate international entity and a fellow in the world of nations. The United States in turn accepted the existence of a separate British Canada, while Great Britain gave the Americans carte blanche to expand westward, provided they did so south of the 49th Parallel. Under Article 9 of the treaty, the United States agreed "forthwith to restore to ...[the Indian tribes] all possessions...which they have enjoyed ... in 1811 previous to such hostilities." This the United States never did.

112. See, Paul Johnson, *The Birth of the Modern World Society, 1815-1830,* Harper Collins Publishers, New York (1991), at 41-62.

113. The Dominican Republic, which the United States unsuccessfully attempted to purchase in 1868, was occupied from 1916 to 1924 and invaded in 1970; Veracruz, Mexico, was occupied in 1914, and a punitive expedition was sent into Chihuahua, Mexico, in 1916; Haiti was occupied from 1915 to 1934; Honduras was occupied from 1924 to 1925; Guatemala was invaded in 1906; Nicaragua was occupied from 1909 to 1910 and occupied 1912-1925; Grenada invaded in 1983; and Panama invaded in 1989.

114. The Oregon Territory would be referred to as the New Northwest Territory.

115. Morison, supra, at 447.

116. Quote from the hymn, "America, the Beautiful," based on a poem written by Katherine Lee Bates in 1893 on returning from a trip to Pike's Peak, Colorado. The words are usually sung to the tune of "Materna," by Samuel A. Ward.

117. The United States and Great Britain acted in accord in pushing out Spain and France from the Oregon Territory. The Russians, who had no fleet in the area to face the British, pulled out of Oregon Territory and signed a treaty with the United States in April, 1824, setting its southern Alaskan border at 54 degrees 40 minutes North, and thereafter reached a similar accord with Great Britain.

118. Morison, supra, at 561.

119. Id.

120. The stratagem was not that successful. Zachary Taylor succeeded Polk as the next president of the United States (1849-50). Others who participated in this war and would later gain national prominence were Robert E. Lee, the future commander-in-chief of the Confederate Army, Jefferson Davis, the future president of the Confederate States, and Ulysses S. Grant, who would defeat both Lee and Davis as commander-in-chief of the Union Army, and would himself go on to the presidency of the United States (1869-77).

121. A pejorative term used throughout Latin America today to refer to U.S. citizens, which dates to this war and is derived from a popular jeer that was yelled at the U.S. troops by the Mexicans: "Greens [the color of the U.S. uniforms], go home."

122. For a more in-depth account of the American Civil War, see H. Hattaway and A. Jones, *How the North Won: A Military History of the Civil War*, Urbana , Ill.(1983); P.J. Parish, *The American Civil War*, New York (1975).

123. Rifled artillery and small arms, the Gatling gun (the precursor of the machine gun), rotating turrets on warships, the first ironclads, torpedoes and mines, steam-driven raiders, and even submarines, all made their deadly appearance.

124. The Union lost about 360,000 men and the Confederacy 258,000, about one-third in battle and the rest through disease.

125. Morison, supra, at 624.

126. Until *Brown v, Board of Education* (1954) reversed *Plessy*.

127. F. Weigley, *The American Way of War: A History of the United States Military Strategy and Policy*, Bloomington, IN (1977 ed.).

CHAPTER II

The Calm Before the Storm

Cuba

The United States had its eye on Cuba for some time before 1898. This came about originally partly at the urging of some sectors of Cuban society, mainly sugar planters, who as early as 1822 had approached official circles in the U.S. to promote annexation of Cuba as a response to Spain considering the abolition of slavery.[1] That interest was reciprocated by American slavery stakeholders in search of support for their modus vivendi, who saw the proposal as a way of adding another slave state to their ranks. The endeavor came to naught but served to whet the appetite of the "manifest destiny" adherents.

The fact is some people saw expansion of the United States in the direction of Cuba as a logical consequence of the U.S. acquisition of Florida from Spain in 1819 given that only 100 miles separated Key West from that island.[2] Thus the United States tried to follow a similar course[3] and approached Spain on three different occasions,[4] and three different presidents,[5] with offers to buy Cuba. For various reasons, those negotiations came to naught.

Thereafter, the American Civil War, the rise of the Cuban independence movement and the intervening Cuban wars for independence, in 1868-78 and in 1895, reduced the range of possibilities open to the United States in regard to Cuba. Once the independence movement got off the ground, it was clear that Cuban insurrectionists wanted nothing to do with annexation by the United States.[6]

It was the symbiotic Cuban-American commercial relationship that put the United States and Spain on an almost unavoidable collision course over Cuba. By 1895, U.S. citizens had over $30 million invested in Cuba, including ownership of such important enterprises as the Havana water works and the lighting system.[7] In the crucial sugar industry, U.S. interests had made major investments, purchasing what was then the largest sugar plantation in the world as well as acquiring other extensive holdings.[8] With these investments in land came the importation of new machinery manufactured in the United States, which was in turn installed and maintained by a large group of American technicians, generally called "Bostonians" by the Cubans, with whom they mingled and intermarried.[9]

But it was the prominent role of the Cuba-U.S. trade relationship in general[10] that interjected the United States into the "Cuban problem," eventually leading to intervention and to the Spanish-American War. Commercial interchange between Cuba and the United States, on-going since the days of the trade triangle in American colonial days, increased exponentially from the early 19th century as a substantial number of U.S. merchants established themselves in business enterprises in Havana, Trinidad, Matanzas, and Santiago.[11] Thus, maritime traffic between United States and Cuba increased tremendously, accounting for 783 of the 964 ships that entered the port of Havana in 1896 alone.[12] Later, Cuba-U.S. trade benefited greatly from U.S. tariff reform in 1890, which eliminated tariffs on raw sugar and molasses. Complementing this was an agreement reached in 1891, between Secretary of State John Foster and Spanish Prime Minister Antonio Cánovas del Castillo, by which Spain dropped her traditional protectionist policies for Cuba and Puerto Rico thus allowing the U.S. tariff reform to take effect.[13] As a result, Cuban sugar production, which had been in a slump, exceeded one million tons in 1894.

The U.S. commercial connection was highlighted by the imbalance in trade between Spain and Cuba. Cuba imported ten times more from Spain than Spain did from Cuba –which in 1894 came to only 6% of Cuba's total exports. In contrast, 87% of Cuba's exports (mostly raw sugar) were sold in the United States.[14] At the same time, Cuba's imports were almost equally divided between Spain, at 35%, and the United States, at 38%.[15] What this meant was that Cuba was no longer economically dependent on Spain, but was, in fiscal terms, viable as an independent entity that could therefore be politically separate from Spain.

As the revolution in Cuba progressed, public opinion in the United States was whipped into a frenzy in favor of a war against Spain by an unscrupulous press bent on increasing newspaper circulation and in promoting the imperialist cause.[16]

Meanwhile, in Cuba, the rebels fought an effective guerrilla war against the numerically superior and better-equipped Spanish army. Lieutenant Winston Churchill, on leave in Cuba to observe the Spanish army in action, expressed admiration for the "tough Spanish peasants" who made up the infantry, but said that he "did not think the Spaniards were likely to bring their war in Cuba to a speedy end."[17]

The issue of atrocities, attributed by the American press to the Spanish army but in fact committed mostly by irregular forces beyond the regular army's control, or by the insurgents, inflamed public opinion against Spain and brought large segments of the U.S. electorate and political establishment around to the idea of American intervention on "humanitarian grounds" to help Cuban population.

As a result of a series of brilliant victories by the insurgents, Spanish opinion demanded the replacement of the Spanish Captain-General, Arsenio Martínez Campos, and promotion of a more energetic military strategy. Martínez Campos was replaced by General Valeriano Weyler y Nicolau, who was soon to be demonized by the American press as "The Butcher."[18] Undoubtedly, Weyler was a hard case, but perhaps what made him most unpopular with the rebels and the American press was that he knew how to conduct an effective anti-guerrilla campaign.[19] His first steps were to isolate the rebel forces from each other using fortified north-south trenches or *trochas*, and to deprive the guerrillas of civilian support by concentrating the population into "military areas." This later step was the most controversial of all his actions because of the deplorable conditions of these camps and the resulting large number of civilian deaths.[20] He reorganized his troops into small mobile units to be self-sufficient in the field, and lastly, he let counter-guerrillas loose in the countryside to search for and fight the rebel forces on their own terms, with a ferocity that caused them to be more feared than the regular Spanish army.

Between the scorched-earth tactics of the insurgents and Weyler's concentration of the civilian population, the agricultural wealth of Cuba was practically destroyed. If the alleged atrocities in Cuba were the subject of public furor, the effect of the war on economic investments there received quieter but no less powerful attention within the cabals of political influence in the United States. Eighteen ninety-six was an election year in the U.S., and in November, William McKinley won the presidency on the Republican ticket. This placed the expansionists, including Senator Henry Cabot Lodge from Massachusetts and Theodore Roosevelt, in positions of influence within the new administration.

The situation continued on a substantially even keel in Cuba throughout the first year of the McKinley administration. However, with the death of the rebels' leading general, Antonio Maceo, on December 7, 1896, the Spanish army unquestionably had the upper hand. The rebels were on the defensive throughout 1897, to the point that General Weyler was recalled by Spain in an attempt to improve world public opinion about its Cuban problem.

The fact is, leaving the United States aside for the moment, on the eve of the sinking of the *Maine* and the commencement of hostilities between Spain and the United States, public opinion in Europe and Latin America generally supported Spain.[21]

Latin America

Latin America, by now fully aware of the geopolitical might of the United States and, particularly after the Mexican War, of its propensity to use force to promote its national interests, was officially and cautiously neutral before, during and after the Cuba-Spain-United States imbroglio. However, this facade could hardly conceal the strong support for Spain among the educated Creole ruling classes, especially after the U.S. military intervention in Cuba and the Philippines.[22] Nevertheless, a plea for support directed to the "peoples of Latin America" by Enrique Varona, a Cuban intellectual, had almost no official effect. The only known exception was Ecuador, whose president, Eloy Alfaro, issued a declaration to Spain supporting the rebellion.[23]

Mexico, which had recently lost large portions of its national territory as a result of the Mexican-American War,[24] was naturally more realistic. Its president, Porfirio Díaz, had his foreign minister inform the insurgents through one of their leaders, Gonzalo de Quesada, that he believed that a Spanish victory was inevitable.[25] Mexico's interests in the Caribbean were not trivial.[26] Mexico had maintained a neutral stance concerning the insurrection since 1895, a position which was officially confirmed on the commencement of hostilities between the United States and Spain in 1898.[27] This neutrality allegedly got Mexico "important concessions from the United States by way of boundary revisions, support in Central American disputes, and new treaties."[28] Thus it is nothing short of incredible that in the middle of all this the Consul-General in Havana, Andrés Clemente Vargas, made what would seem a patently absurd proposal to the Mexican Foreign Ministry, namely, that Cuba be annexed by Mexico (he called it a "Cuba Mexicana"), contending that this could be done "without confrontation with the United States."[29] There is no record of an official reply, but it is unlikely that this proposal was given any serious consideration.

Nevertheless, and notwithstanding official declarations of neutrality by Mexico, the Spanish army had an office in Mexico City to acquire food and supplies.[30] Private opinion on Cuba in governmental circles was very much divided,[31] as was the Mexican press.[32] However, public opinion generally favored Cuban independence and support was given to the cause in the form of private monetary contributions.[33]

Distant Argentina (along with Uruguay)[34] presented an interesting case of ethnic solidarity (expressed in the Spanish concept *raza*) with the Spanish cause, and there were few expressions of support for the insurrectionists.[35] A statement typical of this point of view was made by Argentine General Lucio V. Mansilla to the Montevideo newspaper, *La Razón*, in which he stated that "the cause of Spain in Cuba was the cause of all Spanish America,"[36] an extraordinary statement when one considers that the so-called "Spanish" America was practically nonexistent precisely because of insurrections such as those taking place in Cuba.

Argentine writers today claim that Argentina's close contacts with Europe led it to have a "conflictive relationship with the United States."[37] As in Mexico's case, this was not obvious from its official neutral position, but it was certainly the situation with regard to the Argentine intelligentsia[38] and the press, as echoed by the leading newspapers, *La Nación* and *La Razón* of Montevideo, and *La Prensa* and *Correo Español* of Buenos Aires.[39] Public opinion generally reflected a concern that U.S. interventionism under the aegis of the Monroe Doctrine would be extended to the rest of the Americas,[40] a point well taken.

Amazingly, the Spanish community of Argentina raised enough money to have a cruiser, the *Río de la Plata*, built in "neutral" France for the Spanish Navy.[41] That ship, with a displacement of 1,775 tons, was capable of a respectable 18 knots and had impressive armament.[42] As was to be expected, the U.S. ambassador to Argentina was less than pleased with this effort and reported the following on July 11, 1898:

> [S]ome Spaniards here believe they can manage somehow to get the ship out of France, should the war continue until it is completed, if that ever occurs, by pleading that the ship is private property. How such a visionary wild idea has ever found believers among intelligent Spaniards here I know not, but I deem it well thus refer to it and to the evidence I mention of the ship being contracted under inspection of Spanish naval officers and of it having been tenderes [sic] to accept officially by Spain, before construction began.[43]

It would seem that the objection should have been directed to France, which had declared herself neutral in the War. The Spanish were committing no illegal act by paying for the building of a warship elsewhere, nor was Argentina technically violating its declared neutrality. France, however was engaging in a material breach of its neutrality. Fortunately, this issue was never tested because the ship was not launched until September 1898, after hostilities had ended, and was not turned over to the Spanish Navy until July 31, 1899.

A further measure of pro-Spanish sentiment in Uruguay and Argentina was demonstrated when the *Río de la Plata* visited Montevideo and Buenos Aires later that year. More than 20,000 persons per day visited the vessel, and the crew was treated to much festivity in both ports.[44] The ship was similarly received when it visited Chile, Ecuador and Colombia.

Brazil, because of its Portuguese roots, was for historic reasons less sympathetic to Spain. Furthermore it had its own expansionist agenda and hopes for outdoing Argentina, which was its arch-rival in the hemisphere. Therefore, although it was technically neutral, it adopted a decidedly pro-United States stance by allowing the U.S. Navy to purchase two of its ships, renamed the *New Orleans* and the *Albany*, and allowing the United States to make use of Brazilian ports for the purpose of taking on coal and making repairs.[45]

Venezuela, involved in a major dispute with Great Britain over its border with British Guiana, which came to a head in 1897, needed the support of the United States against British pretensions, and so was not about to side openly with Spain over Cuba. Colombia, the other Bolivarian republic bordering on the Caribbean, was too entangled in its own internal problems to concern itself with the United States, which would soon take advantage of its turmoil, in 1903, to create the Republic of Panama and extract a zone across the isthmus to build a trans-oceanic canal (1914).[46]

In the meantime, the European nations, large and small, had views and took diverse actions, the nature of which depended on how they believed their geopolitical interests in Europe and elsewhere would be affected by what was happening in Cuba.

Europe

After 1895, for complex and sometimes conflicting reasons, the old world order felt threatened by the United States generally and in particular by its actions regarding Cuba.[47] This uneasiness was not relieved by statements such as that of Senator Cabot Lodge, which, although made after the Spanish-American War, reflected America's intentions to take an active part in world affairs: "The American people have decided that the United States should play its great part among the nations of the earth."[48] As events leading to the Spanish-American War unfolded, with the exception of Great Britain, the sympathies of the European nations were with Spain, a sentiment expressed in his own inimical manner by Germany's Kaiser Wilhelm II, when he referred to U.S. actions in Cuba as "the insolence of the Yankee."[49] The French warned against the dangers of the "American peril" and described U.S. actions as the "American menace."[50] There was a growing awareness that America's industrial and agricultural strength, and its obvious potential military might, could very well lead to territorial expansion at the expense of the "established" European empires, with the consequent prospect of radically affecting long-standing and emerging markets.[51]

This general European hostility towards the United States was the result of complex motivations and strategies, fueled by a variety of factors, and manifested at various levels of rationality. On the political-ideological plane, the conservatives of Europe mostly rejected the American political system and principles, and thus tended to identify themselves with monarchical Spain. Two incongruous exceptions were France and Great Britain. Notwithstanding France's usual republican sympathies, public opinion in France was vociferously anti-American. On the other hand, Great Britain, although a monarchy, was quietly sympathetic towards the United States.[52] Several factors explain these anomalies.

At least part of the growing hostility toward the United States in Europe was the product of America's loss of support among the liberal European intelligentsia. Various actions by the United States, such as the Mexican War, had caused these groups to revise their view of the United States as an anti-militaristic, anti-colonial nation committed to democratic principles.

Furthermore, on a cultural level, American intervention in Cuba was seen in some quarters in Europe as an extension of an ongoing struggle between the Latin and Anglo-Saxon "races." An important component of this assertion was religious in nature, part of the long-standing Catholic-Protestant rivalry which was still only barely below the surface in Europe. Obviously these motivations tended to have more impact in ethnically or religiously homogeneous countries, such as Italy and France. As will be seen, Germany, for other reasons, although non-Latin and mostly Protestant, joined those supporting Spain.

Economic interests were also a powerful factor in determining the stance taken, particularly when they coincided with political, cultural, or religious considerations. At that juncture, Spain itself was neither a commercial threat nor a potential market for the rest of Europe. Nor was it particularly attractive as a place in which to invest.[53] On the other hand, European producers of grain, sugar beets, livestock, and manufactured goods were feeling the bite of American competition both on the Continent and elsewhere. These commercial interests sided with Spain.

The European predilection was for a peaceful solution to the "Cuban problem," thereby opposing American military intervention and any disturbance of the international balance of power. But this solution was affected by a general climate of mutual suspicion among the Europeans and reluctance for any power to take a public initiative for fear that its doing so might be misconstrued by the United States as a hostile act.

At this point, the United States, following a national policy dating back to the time of George Washington, remained uncommitted to any political alliances in world affairs, and the European nations were particularly cautious lest they give any of their rivals an edge in establishing closer rapport with the United States.[54]

February of 1898 was an extremely bad month for Spanish-American relations. A private letter from the Spanish Ambassador in Washington, Enrique Dupuy de Lomé, to José Canalejos, the editor of *El Heraldo* of Madrid, sent in early December, 1897, in which reference was made to President McKinley as "débil y populachero" (weak and popularity-seeking) and "un politicastro" (a hack politician), was stolen by Canalejo's secretary, a sympathizer with Cuban independence.[55] He turned it over to the Cuban Revolutionary Junta in New York, which furnished it to the New York *Journal*. The *Journal* published it on February 11 under the headline: "THE WORST INSULT TO THE UNITED STATES IN ITS HISTORY."[56] The resulting furor abated somewhat when Dupuy de Lomé resigned, but the respite was short-lived.

The situation became truly critical after the *U.S.S. Maine* blew up in Havana Harbor on February, 15, 1898.[57] The American press headlined it thus: "THE WARSHIP *MAINE* WAS SPLIT IN TWO BY AN ENEMY'S SECRET INFERNAL MACHINE."[58] There was no doubt who the "enemy" was, as the aroused public soon took up the jingoistic slogan of the Hearst newspapers, which was to be the Nation's war cry in the ensuing conflict: "Remember the *Maine*! To hell with Spain!"

Austro-Hungary

The Austro-Hungarian Empire, with its several nationalities and facing unrest throughout, was generally opposed to encouraging independence movements anywhere. Several other factors coincided to bend its sympathies to favor Spain: the conservatism of Austrian society, the existence of a monarchist form of government, and the predominance of Catholicism among its ruling classes. These all worked in Spain's favor. Added to this was the fact that Emperor Franz Joseph had family ties with Queen María Cristina, who was not only an Austrian princess of the Habsburg dynasty, but an archduchess of Austria. Franz Josef also had personal sympathy for María Cristina's predicament as a young widow trying to preserve her son's throne. Many of his subjects, however, particularly those who aspired to independent nationhood, favored the Cuban separatists.[59]

Partly because of this and despite the emperor's feelings, Austria-Hungary was not prepared to take a stance that might provoke unrest at home or create a threat to its security.[60] On the other hand, Austria-Hungary was unique among the European powers in that it had no overseas empire to protect (particularly after the disastrous Mexican experience of Archduke Maximillian) and no naval or colonial ambitions to feed. So it had little to gain from active intervention in an international colonial war far from its own national interests, which lay on the continent, where for the moment they were protected in the Balkans from her main adversary, Russia, by the Triple Alliance with Germany and Italy, and in the Mediterranean by its alliance with Great Britain and Italy.

Nevertheless, Austria took the diplomatic lead in trying to diffuse the situation in Cuba.[61] It did so in early March, after a personal plea for help from María Cristina to Franz Joseph, delivered through the Austrian Ambassador to Spain, Count Victor Dubsky.[62] A reply was received on March 13 from the Austrian Foreign Minister, Count Agenor Goluchowski, who was unenthusiastic about any involvement by Austria in the Cuban-American controversy. Nevertheless Goluchowski said that Austria would be willing to join a European coalition to promote a peace initiative, if it was done in concert with the other European powers. He agreed to contact Paris and Berlin and to inform the other powers (presumably Great Britain and Russia) to ask for their support in the event that a favorable response was received from Germany and France.[63] Meanwhile, the Austrian press, including the dailies *Neue Erie Presse, Neues Weiner Journal, Neues Weiner Tagblatt, Das Vaterland,* and *Zeitung fur die Osterreich Monarchie,* criticized the actions of the United States.[64]

In early April, Goluchowski began to seek a consensus for transmittal of a collective message from the European powers to the United States, aware that it would only succeed if Great Britain joined. Thus, on April 2, the Austrian Ambassador to London, Count Franz Deym, called on the British Prime Minister, Lord Salisbury, to propose a note from the

European powers. The initiative, however, was rejected.[65] This did not deter the Austrian government from instructing its representative in Washington to meet with his counterparts from France, Germany, Russia and Great Britain and to attempt to make a joint appeal to President McKinley on humanitarian grounds, based on Spain's latest proposal, which included an offer to cease hostilities against the Cuban insurgents.

The Washington representatives of the Great Powers, including Britain, came to an agreement, and a collective note was drafted and delivered to the president on April 6.[66] At that meeting, the British Ambassador stated to the president that Europe hoped that "for humanity's sake you will not go to war," to which McKinley replied, "We hope if we do, you will understand it is for humanity's sake."[67] This was obviously not the reply that the European delegation had hoped for, but other initiatives were still making the rounds.

On April 9, the European powers in Madrid asked the Spanish Government to accept mediation by the Pope. Previously, on April 3, this proposal had been made known to President McKinley by Archbishop Ireland of Chicago. However, on that same day, the Spanish cabinet had accepted almost all the demands of the United States: an immediate and unconditional armistice, an end to the concentration of civilians, and submission of the *Maine* issue to arbitration. The deal breaker, however, was the demand by the United States that Cuba be granted independence outright, an issue that Spain proposed be decided by the autonomist governments it had just decreed for Cuba and Puerto Rico.[68]

This was transmitted to the president, who after discussing the matter with his cabinet decided to leave his scheduled message to Congress unaltered.[69] The president's message to Congress on April 11 not only made no mention of the Spanish cabinet's proposal, but failed to inform that body of the request made to him by the ambassadors on April 6. That informational gap, and the president's request for authorization "to use the military and naval forces of the U.S. as may be necessary" for the purpose of ending the hostilities in Cuba and securing a stable government for the island[70] should have been answer enough for the ambassadors. It certainly was for Spain, which saw in the approval of this resolution a virtual declaration of war, or at least a preliminary step in that direction.

On the same day of the president's message to Congress, Austria proposed to the Great Powers that action be taken in Washington on Spain's behalf. Goluchowski instructed Hengelmuller to coordinate a proposal with his European colleagues to submit the Spanish-American dispute to mediation. Hengelmuller responded to his government that in his view there was no longer any possibility of avoiding war.[71] Notwithstanding his pessimism, on April 14, he telegraphed Vienna to inquire whether it might be possible to induce the European powers to take a firmer approach and express disapproval of the aggressive attitude of the United States.[72] The British Foreign Office was informed that the Austrian Ambassador, Count Deym, had been instructed to show the proposal to Queen Victoria in confidence and to seek her views to ascertain whether Great Britain would join in such a declaration with the other European powers.[73] The reply was that Great Britain would join the other Europeans in making a statement aimed at maintaining peace, limited to expressing the hope that the declaration of an armistice by Spain would be accepted by the United States as sufficient to prevent its taking up arms against Spain. This watered-down version was presented to the president.[74]

In the meantime, the president's April 11 proposal to Congress was passed by a vote of 42 to 35 in the Senate and 310 to 6 in the House, but not before Senator Henry Moore Teller of Colorado slipped in an amendment whereby the United States disclaimed any "disposition or interest to exercise sovereignty, jurisdiction or control over [Cuba] except for the pacification thereof and assert[ed] its determination, when that [was] accomplished, to leave the government and control of the island to its people."[75] The resolution was signed by the president the next day and was taken by Spain to constitute a declaration of war, although in fact there was no actual declaration of war by the United States until April 25.[76]

On April 29, the Austrian Foreign Ministry informed the British Foreign Office that it would not declare neutrality, "as such notification would be contrary to the custom usually observed here."[77]

The Austro-Hungarian naval attaché in Washington, Lt. J. Roedler, accompanied the U.S. Army that invaded Cuba as an observer.[78] Shortly after the commencement of hostilities in the Caribbean, Austria also sent an armored cruiser, the S.M.S. Kaiserin und Konigin Maria Theresa, for the purpose of observation, not intervention.[79]

Germany

In Germany, Kaiser Wilhelm II was not only directly involved in military and naval affairs, but an active participant in the formulation and execution of Germany's foreign policy.[80] He was influenced on both matters –which in the context of the Spanish-American War went hand in hand[81]– by Bernard von Bulow, Germany's Foreign Secretary, and by Admiral Alfred von Tirpitz, the Secretary of State of the Imperial War Office. This was an unfortunate coincidence, for apart from the emperor himself, the persons who did the most to give German foreign policy a reputation in Europe for dangerous irrationality were von Bulow and von Tirpitz.[82]

Tirpitz had headed the Eastern Asiatic Cruiser Division in 1896 and is credited with influencing Kaiser Wilhelm in the choice of Tsingtao as the German base of operations in China, as well as in the acquisition of Kiachow at the end of 1897.[83] Tirpitz was an avid student and advocate of Mahan's theories and a strong promoter of the German "big navy" concept that so unnerved the British throughout this period.[84] Kaiser Wilhelm became an adherent of this philosophy early on.

The German government did little to avoid giving the impression that it had grandiose plans for naval expansion and also colonial ambitions.[85] In fact, during this period immediately preceding the Spanish-American War, Germany was hyperactive in its foreign affairs. In addition to its activities in China, in April 1894, it attempted to lay claim to sole possession of the Samoan Islands,[86] and in June, it vehemently protested the legality of the Anglo-Congolese Treaty entered into in May.[87] Later in the year, Germany quarreled with the British over recognition of the Sultan of Morocco, as well as over the boundaries of the Sudan. It also disagreed about the future of the Portuguese colonies and the policy to be adopted against Turkey as a result of the Armenian massacres.[88] In 1895, there were strong objections in the German press to claims by the United States under the Olney-Cleveland interpretation of the Monroe Doctrine, as applied to the British Guiana-Venezuelan border dispute.[89] The resolution of this dispute led to criticism by Germany because by acquiescing to the wishes of the United States, the British had in effect, accepted the existence of U.S. hegemony in the Caribbean. This disagreement was further exacerbated when thereafter (1897-1898),

German attempts to gain a foothold in this area by seeking to purchase St. Thomas (then part of the Danish Virgin Islands) and Curacao (in the Dutch West Indies) were blocked by the United States as contrary to the Monroe Doctrine.[90]

But the most serious example of Kaiser Wilhelm's (i.e. Germany's) contentious approach to diplomacy occurred during the Transvaal crisis in South Africa in 1896, after the Jameson Raid.[91] With 15,000 ethnic Germans in the gold fields alone, Germany was not about to remain passive in the face of a blatant attempt to take over the Transvaal by a mere 800 Englishmen intent on squelching the Boers, who were mostly of Dutch stock, cousins to the Germans.

Although the raid was repelled, and Great Britain had by January 1, 1896, disavowed it,[92] the German government (i.e. Kaiser Wilhelm) felt compelled to make a gesture in support of the Transvaal Republic. Unfortunately, the kaiser decided to manage the situation personally while still in a state of agitation over the status of the Military Justice Bill, so agitated in fact that the chancellor, Prince Chlodwig zu Hohenlohe-Schillingsfürst, was told by Bronsart[93] that he believed the sovereign was mentally unbalanced. Kaiser Wilhelm rambled, threatening to declare the Transvaal a German protectorate and send German troops to South Africa to fight a local war. While in this state, he sent a telegram to the president of the Transvaal Republic congratulating him on his success in repelling the raid, to which the kaiser added, "[and in] maintaining the independence of the country from without."[94] The communication caused a tremendous furor in Great Britain, where the text, particularly the added phrase, was interpreted as undue interference in British internal affairs.

This incident, together with German naval policy, had much to do with driving Great Britain and the United States closer together and further away from Germany, not only in the ensuing Spanish-American War but also during the Boer War that followed soon thereafter, and of course in the Great War that was to come. Thus, Germany succeeded in accomplishing the opposite of what it desired.

The distance between Germany and the United States was further widened with the reappearance of the Samoan issue, this time in the context of Hawaii, a republic since July 1894, in which the controlling American expatriates sought annexation by the United States.[95] In the meantime, Germany desired the withdrawal of the United States from the Samoan condominium and the neutralization of Hawaii, as in Samoa.[96] However, the main product of Germany's diplomatic clumsiness[97] was that the United States signed a treaty of annexation with the Republic of Hawaii on June 16, 1897 (finally ratified in July, 1898).[98]

In keeping with his character and ideology, Kaiser Wilhelm's first impulse as the war approached was to side with Spain.[99] In his view, Spain was a monarchy embodying conservative European values and traditions, and these needed to be defended lest Spain's downfall set off a "domino effect" among the rest of the European monarchies. There was, however, very little sympathy for Spain in Germany.[100] Only a small Catholic minority in Southern and Western Germany felt real affinity with Spain and sincerely contemplated joining her fight against the United States.[101] Furthermore, Kaiser Wilhelm's closest advisers, Foreign Secretary von Bulow, von Holstein of the Foreign Office, and Count Felipe zu Eulenburg, Germany's Ambassador to Vienna, cautioned restraint and recommended a strategy whereby Germany would be seen in Spain and Europe as sympathetic to Spain's cause and helpful in attempting to discourage U.S. intervention without unduly antagonizing the United States –Germany's second biggest trading partner after Great Britain.[102]

Count zu Eulenburg suggested that Austria be approached secretly to lead a European initiative against the United States.[103] This was the apparent commencement of the various actions, previously described, taken by the European powers before the outbreak of the war.

Conservative scholars in Germany condemned American intervention as a violation of international law because they considered Cuba to be an integral part of Spain.[104] It was the view of this sector that Spain had the unquestionable right to do with her colony as she deemed proper, and it accused the United States of trying to create new international law which was contrary to established norms. An underlying premise of this position was a widely-held view that U.S. intervention was a perversion of the Monroe Doctrine, which by its own terms was not intended to be applied to colonies that were established at the time of its announcement. The Germans, being latecomers to the colonial game, considered the Monroe Doctrine particularly offensive, because the doctrine was at odds with their own *Weltpolitik* ambitions. Furthermore, by promoting Pan-Americanism, the doctrine weakened the incursion of non-American trade and commerce into Latin America.

The Germans, like many Europeans, tended to look down on Americans culturally, often the theme of articles appearing in German newspapers and journals,[105] in which Americans were accused of disregarding European concepts of national honor and traditions. The United States' alleged ruthlessness and brutality towards Spain was highlighted, particularly later during the peace negotiations.

As part of this rhetoric the United States was depicted as the "land of the dollar," and intervention in Cuba as "the war of money bag against national honor."[106] Accordingly, American action against Spain was seen as a question solely of economic interests. Although there was much truth in this, the view held by the Germans was itself hardly based on altruistic motives.

Apart from Germany's internally expressed intentions "to fish in troubled waters,"[107] the highly influential German *Junkers* –themselves the biggest exporters of German agricultural products, mainly sugar beets, and also major promoters of derogatory anti-American bombast– were angered by the United States because they were at a serious economic disadvantage in trying to compete with American agricultural production. Throughout the 1890s, with the help of export subventions, they were able to hold their own against Caribbean sugar in the world market. In 1895, when the Cuban insurrection began and Cuban sugar production was interrupted, the Germans expected to increase their exports to the United States, the world's largest sugar consumer. They were therefore hardly interested in the pacification of Cuba. As the U.S. Ambassador to Berlin aptly put it, "Chaos is in their interest."[108]

This extravagant German rhetoric rings particularly hollow considering the views generally held in influential circles, which was that every conflict on the globe should be looked upon as an opportunity for German territorial expansion.[109] Germany was eager to acquire colonies, bases and spheres of influence whenever the opportunity arose. The Spanish colonial crisis was just such a situation. Imperial Germany, it was said, was entitled to "compensations" whenever another Great Power gained new overseas concessions. Germany's view was most cogently expressed

by the Pan-Germanic weekly *Alldeutsche Blatter* on May 29, with the Spanish-American War specifically in mind, when it said:

> The Spanish-American War shows the necessity of coal bases
> and telegraph stations for all Great Powers....Therefore we ask
> our statesmen to leave no opportunity unused to acquire such
> bases.... Certainly such opportunities will arise during the on-
> going Spanish-American War.[110]

In all fairness, although this was the view of the ruling circles, the
majority of the press and the public wanted Germany to remain strictly
neutral, and said so. Of course, it was the ruling circles that counted in
Imperial Germany when it came to establishing foreign policy.

German defenders of the U.S. action, to be found mostly among
German liberals and progressives, justified it in terms akin to Social Darwinist theory, arguing that the Spanish-American situation was part of a
historic process in the rise and fall of empires. The end of Spanish rule
was an evolutionary and necessary process whereby old and decadent
empires were replaced by younger, more efficient ones. Theodore Barth
said this in May 1898:

> A historic process of liquidation does not observe the formal
> rules of law.... I have no understanding for the political senti-
> mentality that leads to sympathies for a country which has
> proved its complete incapacity to keep its most prosperous
> colony. To my mind, Spain has forfeit its right to Cuba through
> continuous cruelty and exploitation.[111]

He defended the U.S. intervention, explaining that if someone were
to disinfect the center of an epidemic without the permission of the police, even though trespass might technically have been committed, a great
service would have still been done to the community.

Linked to these Social Darwinist views were those that saw this "Ger-
manic-Latin duel" as a "clash among races." Even German Catholic writers
saw in this encounter a decline of the Latin peoples. Alleged ethnic charac-
teristics like discipline, productivity, and power were attributed to the Americans and Germans alike, thus supposedly making them strong and health-
ful nations, while the "decadent Latin" ones were lacking in such attributes.[112]

There were also groups, mostly liberals, progressives and some so-
cialists, who saw this as a "war of liberation" and attributed unselfish
motives to the United States, arguing that it was engaging in the action
for humanitarian reasons, to relieve the sufferings of the Cuban people.[113]
These supporters sprinkled their oratory with praise for the social and
political system of the United States, thus indirectly criticizing those of
Germany, and they emphasized what they saw in America's "cultural
mission," to bring civilization to replace Spanish misrule.[114]

Commander Von Rebeur Paschwitz of the Imperial German Navy,
and the Naval Attaché to the German Embassy in Washington, accompanied the United States Army that invaded Cuba as an observer.[115]

France

Republican France joined the other continental nations, all of which
were monarchies, in adopting a decidedly unsympathetic view of American intervention against monarchist Spain. In fact, according to Louis
Sears, a search of the Library of Congress "reveals not a single utterance
by any Frenchman which could be viewed as genuinely friendly to the
United States."[116] Although it could be expected that French Catholics,
monarchists, and conservatives would have an affinity with Spain's traditional European values and traditions, that does not explain the monolithic, almost visceral anti-American stance of the French generally, a
situation that was duplicated in France over one hundred years later
during the U.S. invasion of Iraq. In both cases these uncompromising
views differed from the rest of Europe, where the opinions expressed
were somewhat more balanced.

The French press called the intervention by the United States "an act
of piracy."[117] Spain's perceived dignity and calm were contrasted with U.S.
jingoism. France was depicted as "unanimous in regarding justice as on
the side of Spain."[118] The *Journal des Débats* indicted the United States "before the conscience of mankind and ...the bar of history."[119] The U.S. Congressional Reports on the necessity for intervention were characterized as
"monuments of international bad faith."[120] Although *La Revue Socialiste*
criticized Spain for her "retrograde obstinacy...since the time of Phillip II",

it viewed McKinley's ultimatum as "a declaration of war of the new world against the old, the expression of a transformed Pan Americanism, the unlimited extension of the principles of Monroe."[121] Scholars of international law made accusations against the United States similar to those made by their German counterparts.[122]

It is worth noting that, at least during 1898, press coverage of foreign events in France was often eclipsed by the Dreyfus and Zola affairs.

In practical terms, the French were heavy investors in Spanish bonds, which were linked to income extracted from Cuba, thus there was much concern that a war involving Cuba might negatively affect them by reason of a change in sovereignty over Cuba. These views were partially counterbalanced by the fact that there were also heavy French investments in the United States. There was much concern in French agricultural sectors, traditionally ultraconservative, because of competition from the United States. Colonial interests were also worried by the projected American presence in the Caribbean, where the French had modest but strategically important interests in Martinique, Guadeloupe and French Guiana. The global implications for French colonies in Africa and Asia of a perceived rapprochement between United States and Great Britain also came into the balance.[123]

Foreign Minister Gabriel Hanotaux feared that the loss of Cuba by Spain might trigger a revolution in Spain and that the hostilities might extend across the Mediterranean if the United States intervened or if the conflict lasted too long. He thus settled on an overall strategy of containment of the controversy in terms of both geography and the actual belligerents.[124]

Major Clément de Grandpré, the military attaché to the French Embassy in Washington, accompanied the United States Army that invaded Cuba as an observer.[125]

Russia

Notwithstanding the Franco-Russian diplomatic understanding of 1891 and the formal military alliance entered into in January 1894,[126] Russia's stance regarding the United States was somewhat different from that of its French allies.

Its position was affected principally by Russia's geopolitical situation at the end of the 19th century vis-à-vis not only the United States but also its principal rival in Asia and the Far East: Great Britain. When Kaiser Wilhelm suggested defending Spain and María Cristina and establishing an economic boycott against the United States, Russia's Minister of Finance, Sergey Witte, advised Czar Nicholas against such actions, reminding him of the good relations that had existed with the United States since the days of its War for Independence.[127] The czar agreed with Witte, and thus Europe's most autocratic government in effect sided with the world's democratic prototype. Foreign Minister Count Mikhail Muraviev reasoned thus: "We find it very convenient to make use of the Monroe Doctrine, especially if this most popular theory in America is against the interests of our opponents,"[128] i.e., Germany and Great Britain. Conservative Russia considered Cuba to be within the United States' sphere of influence and held the view that its claim to hegemony in the Americas was convenient for Russia's own assertions of such rights to Asian primacy. Nevertheless, because Russia's interests in the Far East and Pacific could be affected by the redistribution of Spain's colonies in the area, Russia hedged to the extent that it was supportive, in principle, of collective European action that might prevent armed U.S. intervention in Cuba.[129]

To the extent that newspapers could be relied upon to express public opinion in czarist Russia, in the spring of 1898 there was not much published that could be called anti-American in content or that varied substantially from the official position of the government. The biggest daily newspaper, *Novoye Vremia*, with a conservative but independent bent on foreign affairs, warned Spain in its March 15 editorial not to expect Russian support, as "European countries have a lot of things to do even without that."[130]

Although Lenin is alleged to have called the Spanish-American War "the first imperialist war,"[131] before the commencement of hostilities the liberal press on the whole supported the position of the government, but for their own ideological reasons, looking upon the United States as the ideal they wanted to achieve in terms of political organization, democracy and freedom of economic relations, and viewing favorably what they perceived as America's noble mission of freeing the Cuban people from Spanish oppression.[132]

Both public and private perceptions changed with the declaration of war by the United States.

Great Britain

Great Britain engaged in a truly remarkable balancing act with respect to the Spanish-American War and the international scenario surrounding this conflict.[133] Britain's far-flung imperial and commercial interests determined the attitudes it held and the actions it took in connection with this encounter.

Although in the ten-year period before 1895, as part of its goal to have an unbroken empire from Cairo to the Cape, Britain had acquired Kenya and Somalia, it faced opposition to the completion of its trans-African plan from the Boers in the Transvaal and Natal, from the Germans in Mozambique and Angola, from the French in the Sudan, and from the Italians in Abyssinia. Meanwhile, in Central Asia, Britain's traditional rival Russia loomed in Persia and the Hindu Kush, while in China, Great Britain's dominance was challenged not only by Russia but also by Germany, France and Japan.

In the Mediterranean, Spain's policy of international isolation was advantageous to Great Britain's interests, thus it followed a strategy of avoiding pushing Spain into an alliance with a continental power such as Germany or France, which might endanger Britain's Gibraltar-Suez-India route. In 1894, a controversy arose over Spain's announcement of plans to fortify Algeciras Bay, contiguous with Gibraltar. This would have put both Gibraltar and the strait within Spanish artillery range. However, that crisis was satisfactorily resolved by appropriate diplomatic maneuvering and the Spanish desisted from this endeavor.[134]

The Anglo-American relationship had been gradually improving since the 1870s.[135] The movement of these two continental plates towards each other began on the British side, for it was Great Britain, pressed on all sides and around the globe by French, German and Russian expansions, that was in dire need of an ally, particularly in China.

The growing closeness between Great Britain and the United States was put to a test in the 1895 dispute over the Venezuela-Guiana border.[136] After some indecorous saber rattling by President Cleveland's

Secretary of State, Richard Olney, which Great Britain wisely ignored, the British agreed to arbitration (in which they prevailed in October 1899). A more important outcome of this incident, however, was the permanent arbitration treaty between United States and Great Britain, the Olney-Pauncefote Treaty, which, though never ratified by the U.S. Senate, was another indication that the two nations were headed for a closer relationship.[137]

After the Venezuela controversy subsided, British policy and goals in the Americas focused on the protection of its existing possessions and dependencies (Canada, British Guiana, British Honduras, Jamaica and other smaller Caribbean islands) and on avoiding confrontation with the United States. It did so by recognizing the United States' paramount interests in the Americas, and more specifically in the Caribbean. Great Britain's willingness to accept President Cleveland's expanded interpretation of the Monroe Doctrine was a clear signal that Anglo-American relations were becoming closer. That was also the precursor to other similar actions related to the Spanish-American War, which in turn would set the stage for a major rapprochement between the two nations, and these would be still more pronounced by the turn of the century,[138] flourishing throughout the entire 20th century and on into the present.

In the meantime, in the period before the commencement of hostilities in the Spanish-American War, the British made a half-hearted attempt not to alienate Spain, but it was obvious where their real sympathies lay.[139] The common culture and language, the large number of Americans of English descent, the similarity of legal and religious traditions, and the undeniable fact that Great Britain was the United States' most important trading partner, undoubtedly had overwhelming influence in the corridors of British power.[140]

The views of the governmental actors, however, were divided as the conflict loomed. The pro-Spanish lobby included Queen Victoria, the British Ambassador in Madrid, Sir Henry Drummond Wolff, and the Under Secretary of State, Sir Thomas Sanderson. Arthur Balfour, representing Prime Minister Lord Salisbury,[141] who was ill, was in favor of neutrality, while the ambassador to Washington, Sir Julian Pauncefote,[142] and the Colonial Secretary, Joseph Chamberlain, were openly in favor of the United States, as were the overwhelming majority of the British public, to judge by commentary in the press.[143]

Given the lack of British interest in official involvement in any diplomatic initiative to curb U.S. actions, on March 17 María Cristina appealed to Queen Victoria for help as she had previously done with regards to Emperor Franz Josef, seeking intercession on her behalf in getting Great Britain to cooperate with the other European powers in pressuring the United States to stop its aggressive actions against Spain.[144] Although Queen Victoria's sympathies were with Spain, or perhaps more accurately with María Cristina[145] and her son, political decisions on these matters were ultimately the business of the British Cabinet. As was to be expected, following Lord Salisbury's lead, the decisions were not favorable to Spain.[146]

Great Britain's participation in the European effort was lukewarm.[147] Suffice it to say that when rumors of intervention began to circulate, the Foreign Office gave explicit instructions to Ambassador Pauncefote to be guided by the wishes of the American government before associating himself with any collective action by the foreign envoys in Washington.[148] Following this directive, Sir Julian consulted the draft of the April 7 proposal to the president with Secretary of State William Day before it was submitted to the president. Day suggested changes acceptable to the United States which were incorporated into the final version.[149]

Pauncefote's moves were equally self-effacing in all the diplomatic maneuvers that followed before war broke out. This in turn acted as a restraint upon the actions of Austria-Hungary, France, Germany, Russia, and Italy during this period.[150]

Things were more complicated in the Far East and the Pacific. The British government was agreeable to honoring United States' designs regarding the Philippines, but was opposed to any European nation, or Japan, gaining a foothold there.[151] Great Britain hoped that this would lead to American support of its Far East interests, especially regarding mainland China.[152]

Meanwhile, conditions in the United States were propitious for the establishment of closer relations with Great Britain. In the period preceding the Spanish-American War, political power was in the hands of a new class of millionaires who came to think of themselves as an American aristocracy and who were aware that new markets were needed as outlets for the surpluses in agricultural and industrial goods that the United States was producing, particularly since the Civil War had ended.

These, together with the big-navy theorists and proponents, known as the "Large Policy"[153] exponents, who favored overseas expansion by the United States, led to a shift towards the British camp, which had similar concerns, particularly with respect to the great Far Eastern prize, the China market. In this respect, British and American interests coincided and complemented each other.

Great Britain pinned her hopes on the China market above all others, for in the 1890s, one sixth of her total international commerce was with China (worth £33 million annually). Furthermore, British ships carried three-fourths of China's international cargo and over one-half of her coastal trade.[154]

Britain could hold her own against other international competition, provided that the Chinese door was left open to free commerce by all nations. It was the threat of that door being closed that brought the United States and Britain together, for both stood to lose from the exclusive systems which Germany, France and Russia sought to impose on the decaying Chinese Empire.

It was thus to counteract this possibility that on March 7, 1898, Ambassador Pauncefote was instructed by the Foreign Office to find out what Washington thought about an Anglo-American accord for a joint policy and action with respect to China. However, he was politely turned down, allegedly because of the imminent war with Spain, but that possibility was definitely left open for the future.[155]

Notwithstanding the lack of a formal alliance concerning the China situation, that circumstance gave Great Britain a compelling reason to support the United States when the War with Spain commenced barely one month after China yielded Kiachow to Germany and Port Arthur to Russia. The inclination to support the United States was further buttressed by the passage of the German Naval Bill on March 28, 1898, making it crystal clear to the British that with a German challenge to Britain's sea lanes becoming a looming reality, an important component of the empire might be in jeopardy, and that having the United States as an ally had become vital.[156]

To accomplish this goal, Great Britain's strategy was (1) to maintain the status quo in the Mediterranean, and (2) to give the United States a free hand in the Caribbean and the Pacific, provided British interests were not affected importantly.

Others who played less significant roles

There were several other countries and jurisdictions that played less significant roles with relation to the Spanish-American War. These included Italy and the Vatican, as well as the Netherlands, and Portugal.

Italy and the Vatican

The Italian and Vatican influences on the Spanish-American War present a different set of circumstances and intrigues, dominated by religious rather than political or economic considerations. But Italy was also concerned lest the conflict alter the balance of power in the Mediterranean, either through outright concession of territory, such as by Spain ceding some of its Morocco interests to France or another European power in exchange for support against the United States, or through naval or military operations spilling over into this area, which could have unpredictable consequences.

As might be expected, there was strong sympathy for Spain, a seasoned defender of the Faith for 500 years, among Italy's monarchists, traditional Catholics, and Pan-Latinists. None of these groups, however, were by themselves in any position to do more than make vague declarations of encouragement to Spain, although the Italian government did join in some of the European initiatives. But there was also a considerable group of Italians, who favored the U.S. position and rejected Spain's treatment of the Cubans,[157] if only on ideological grounds.

The decade preceding the Spanish-American War was one of dramatic change for Italian society. In 1896, its army had suffered a disastrous defeat in Abyssinia, at Adua, which meant a temporary pause in the advancement of its colonial ambitions in Africa. Shortly before that, Italy had itself consolidated territorially and politically, and had stripped the Pope of his temporal powers outside of Vatican City, an area of only a few hundred acres in Rome. Pope Leo XIII responded with the 1891 encyclical, *Rerum Novarum*, urging Italian Catholics to not participate in politics.[158] These events were accompanied, in fact, were intermingled, with the political ferment unleashed by the *Risorgimento*.[159]

And it was then that the Roman Curia, led by the Jesuits,[160] spoke out on the "perils of Americanism" as a looming danger to the Church, a "specter" which spilled over into the Italian political arena. In a religious context, "Americanism" referred principally to the Catholic clergy in the United States –its relationship to Rome and to the government of the United States– but also to American Catholics generally. The issues largely concerned the American model of government and style of life, a difficult, dynamic and self-centered society, which was hard to control, particularly from distant Rome. The very fact that there was a relatively harmonious separation of Church and State in the United States –in contrast to the acrimonious confrontations between the Church and State in Italy– made the conservative establishment that controlled the Vatican very uneasy. In fact, Pope Leo XIII had stated the Vatican's position on this issue when he promulgated the encyclical *Longinqua Oceani*,[161] on January 6, 1895, which was specifically directed at the American Catholic community, unequivocally stating that it was wrong to infer from the American case that Church and State should be separated as a matter of principle. His urging that American Catholics give "spontaneous and complete obeisance" to the Catholic hierarchy and to the Pope was not likely to be well received by Americans, Catholic or not.

But it was the American Catholic clergy that caused the most serious concern. It had a strong nationalist bias, and was also perceived to be too independent on matters of faith and not strictly obedient to the will of the Roman hierarchy.[162]

On the other hand, the *conciliatori* and the Christian-Democrats generally favored Americanism. This was an important consideration for the Vatican. The Pope, aware of the implications of Americanism not only in the United States, but more importantly at that juncture in Italian history –the possibility of its having an influence on the Italian scene– attempted to squelch Americanism with the encyclical *Testem Benevolentiae*, issued on January 22, 1898.[163]

There is no evidence that the timing of this edict was specifically intended to influence the approaching Spanish-American War, but its religious consequences and its political implications should not be overlooked. First, it stirred the conservative press to further attacks against the United States. Typical of this view was an article that appeared in the

December 29, 1897, issue of *La Tribuna*, entitled "Repubblica decadente," in which the United States was described as having "the most corrupt, most contemptible of all forms of government and the most susceptible to abuses resulting from egotism and unconfessable [sic] private interests."[164] The *Osservatore Romano*, the Vatican's official voice, had since February 1898, been voicing sympathy "with generous and patriotic Spain" in its tremendous struggle to oppose "the brutal, violent, intimidating force of the United States."[165] Apart from the fact that this position was an affront to the American clergy, who sincerely supported their country's cause, it revealed a considerable lack of knowledge, and perhaps arrogance, regarding the impact that these diatribes would have on American Catholics: they made up more than half of the U.S. army, and over 200 of them had been killed when the *Maine* was destroyed, including their Catholic chaplain.[166]

With an estimated ten million American Catholics out of a total population of eighty million,[167] the Vatican could ill afford its biased stance. It thus decided to engage in a strategy of mediation, which had in fact been urged by some of the European powers. There was much to commend the Vatican's choice as its American intermediary, John Ireland, the Archbishop of St. Paul, Minnesota, in that he was a close personal friend of President McKinley and had access to the top echelons of American officialdom.[168] However, he was also the leading "Americanist" in the Catholic hierarchy of the United States, and he championed a religious version of American "Manifest Destiny" –the theory that the United States' mission under the "God of Nations" was "to bring liberty to the world."[169] In any event, Bishop Ireland's activities were not successful, principally because they came too late.[170] What is more, a public statement by Bishop Ireland in which he contrasted the free and civilized manner of American Catholicism with the allegedly medieval Catholicism of the Spanish friars,[171] cannot have endeared him to the Vatican's Secretary of State, Cardinal Rampolla, who already had misgivings about the choice of Ireland as intermediary. This episode simply confirmed the cardinal's fears that Bishop Ireland's agenda was different from Rome's, and led to his dismissal.[172] Thus ended Italian and Vatican intervention in the period before the commencement of hostilities.

Portugal

Portugal had its own version of Spain's 1898 disaster with the United States. This took place in 1890, in what came to be known as the "the crisis of the Ultimatum," when Great Britain forced Portugal to withdraw from what was eventually to become Rhodesia (now Zimbabwe). This crisis, which was seen in Portugal as a national humiliation, resulted in the long term destabilization of the Portuguese monarchy.[173] During the course of this, Spain had tried to help her Iberian neighbor by initiating consultations with other European powers.[174] Other than bringing Spain and Portugal into a closer relationship, there were no positive results, but both monarchies felt the need to cooperate against "republican subversion,"[175] particularly after Brazil declared itself a republic in 1889.

Even so, there was an underlying distrust of the Spanish by the Portuguese, fueled by a long history of invasions, military interventions and wars –and the fear that Spanish frustrations after a humiliating defeat by the United States might, in the end, cost the Portuguese independence or territory.

As tensions mounted between Spain and the United States, Portugal became concerned that it would be dragged into the conflict by circumstances beyond its control. It was disquieted by the possibility that its colonies might be exposed to the ongoing colonial redistribution roulette.[176] This was particularly so when a fleet of U.S. naval vessels arrived in Lisbon in late January and stayed through mid-March 1898. The fleet included the cruisers *Helena, Machias, Bancroft,* and *San Francisco,* all fast ships armed with numerous quick-firing guns.[177] It was apparent that the arrival of these vessels was not coincidental, but was timed to prevent Spain from sending all her Atlantic fleet to Cuba for fear of leaving her own coasts and outlying islands unprotected.[178]

At that point, the Spanish Torpedo Boat Squadron, consisting of three modern British-built destroyers and three powerful torpedo boats, was getting ready to sail to Cuba from Cadiz. This coincided with the explosion of the *Maine* in Havana, and both then-Assistant Secretary of the Navy Theodore Roosevelt and Admiral Sampson, the ranking U.S. admiral, took the arrival of the Spanish Torpedo Boat Squadron in Cadiz to be a *casus belli* under international law. They thus recommended an attack on the Spanish fleet in Cadiz, without further warning or delay.[179] However, Secretary of the Navy John D. Long and the president resisted, although other naval operations, namely the blockade of Cuba, did eventually precede the declaration of war.

On March 13, word was received that the Spanish fleet had sailed from Cádiz. Shortly thereafter the U.S. vessels left Lisbon, with the *San Francisco* headed for Great Britain to join the *Amazonas* and *Topeka*, recently purchased from Brazil, while the rest of the squadron left in search of the departed Spanish fleet.[180]

Portuguese concerns regarding the possibility of accidental involvement in the Spanish-American controversy were not over. After a brief stop in the Canary Islands, the Spanish fleet headed for the Antilles, but two of the torpedo boats suffered heavy damage due to bad weather and were forced to pull into the Portuguese Cape Verde Islands. There they were eventually joined not only by the rest of the Torpedo Boat Squadron but also by Admiral Cervera's cruiser fleet consisting of the *Oquendo, Vizcaya, Infanta María Teresa,* and *Colón.*[181] With the help of the Portuguese authorities, the fleet provisioned as best they could and prepared for a long campaign. Admiral Cervera, a valiant naval officer but aware of the deplorable condition of the Spanish fleet, opposed its being sent to the Caribbean where, it was likely to suffer almost certain destruction. Unfortunately he was unable to dissuade the central government in Madrid from taking this step.[182]

On April 25, upon the declaration of war by the United States,[183] international law required a statement of Portuguese neutrality. Nonetheless Portugal withheld its declaration of neutrality until April 28, which allowed Admiral Cervera to delay his departure until April 29 in compliance with international norms.[184] Therefore, despite their concerns regarding Spain and involvement in the war, the Portuguese did all they could to help its sometimes ungrateful neighbor.

In the meantime, Portugal was preparing to stress its neutral stance by sending ships and troops to Cape Verde, the Azores, and Madeira, and by placing artillery in forts and batteries in Lisbon, where its most important cruiser, the *Adamastor,* was moored.[185] At the same time, the *Jornal de Comercio* expressed the general public's sentiment in condemning the violence against Spain, claiming that it arose from the same brutal Anglo-Saxon mercantilist spirit of which Portugal had been the victim in 1890.[186]

In fact, Portuguese neutrality was violated by the entry of a squadron of Spanish torpedo boats into Faro on July 7, on their way from Cádiz
to Vigo.[187] And on July 4, the British battleship *Illustrious* had arrived at
Lisbon, followed on July 17 by the Italian cruiser *Piamonte*, both allegedly
to oppose the entry of an American squadron into the Mediterranean.[188]

After the war ended two worrisome threats remained for Portugal
from opposite sides of this conflict. The first was expressed by the Portuguese ambassador to Washington, Santo Thyrso, who said, "Nobody
who has lived in Spain is ignorant of the fact that the national ideals of
that country covet Portugal...[and] if the circumstances lead to a concentration of political and military forces in Spain [because of the loss of all
its colonial possessions], we shall be faced with a life of anxiety and even
conflict."[189]

The second source of Portuguese concern came from the United States
and was expressed by U.S. Senator McEnery during the debates over the
annexation of Hawaii in June, 1898. At that time he stated, "This annexation of Hawaii, too, will be only the beginning of the extension of our
territory.... Very shortly we shall have an excuse to wrest the Azores, the
Madeiras and Cape Verde Islands from Portugal."[190]

The result of these dual threats was to drive the Portuguese back
into their traditional alliance with the British. Thus on October 14, 1899,
they reached an agreement with Great Britain, in what became known
as the Treaty of Windsor, whereby Great Britain guaranteed the security
of all Portuguese colonies and islands. This accord was entered into notwithstanding Portuguese awareness of Great Britain's diplomatic double-
dealing with Germany during this time regarding Portugal's territories
in Africa.[191]

The Netherlands

Ever since their own wars of independence, the Dutch had been adversaries of Spain on both political and religious grounds. It is thus not
surprising that initially they had a negative view of the "Cuban problem" as it deteriorated from 1895 to 1898, perceiving it as just another
proof of Spanish backwardness and colonial misrule. But the problem did
not stop there. Like Portugal, the Netherlands, a small European nation

with large colonial holdings spread throughout the Far East and the Caribbean, viewed the approaching conflict with trepidation, as the possible source of a domino effect that might lead to a general redistribution of territories at the expense of the smaller colonizing nations such as itself.

The very fact that neither Portugal nor the Netherlands was included in the circle of European countries engaged in the maneuvering that preceded the outbreak of hostilities bode ill for these smaller nations. But the fact was that the Netherlands, although traditionally a seafaring nation, lacked a navy sufficient to protect its colonial empire, a classic flaw pointed out by Mahan. It thus opted for strict neutrality,[192] as it had done during the Franco-Prussian War in 1870 and the Russo-Turkish War ("Crimean War") of 1877.

It gave evidence of this decision by sending a warship to Curaçao in the West Indies. This was a move that actually aided the Spanish cause, as it prevented the Cuban rebels from being supplied with Dutch ships and kept them away from Dutch territory.[193]

In the Far East, the Dutch went a bit further.[194] In the Dutch East Indies, which bordered on the southern islands of the Philippine Archipelago (see Map 11), they had, since 1873, been "rounding off" their empire by attempting to subdue Aceh, on the northern coast of Sumatra. The governor-general of the East Indies not only prohibited the export of arms to the Philippines, but kept the Spanish consul in Batavia informed of such shipments to other countries.[195] This was also done in the Netherlands proper, as the Spanish minister in The Hague had complained about arms smuggling from Belgium.[196]

The Netherlands also pressed both Great Britain and Germany to get guarantees from Spain and the United States that they would not sanction the use of privateers. These had already been prohibited by the Treaty of Paris of 1856, but neither Spain nor the United States were signatories. Nevertheless, they both agreed to comply with these provisions of the treaty.[197]

Shortly after the commencement of hostilities, Admiral Cervera and his fleet arrived in Curaçao, requesting fuel and provisions. The Dutch, in strict accordance with neutrality rules, allowed two of the ships to enter and take on 200 tons of coal, sufficient for them to reach the nearest Spanish port, which was San Juan, Puerto Rico.[198] This did not prevent the U.S. ambassador at the Hague, Stanford Newel, who was not fully informed of what actually happened, from filing a protest for alleged violation of neutrality by the Dutch. He eventually relented when the true facts were made known to him.[199]

The Dutch press, although ideologically diverse, largely followed the general European trend of criticizing American intervention.[200] An exception was the liberal protestant *De Standaard*,[201] which at first defended American intervention, although it cooled its defense considerably as annexationism came into the picture.[202] It was thought that the Monroe Doctrine might be extended by the United States to promote ejection of all the colonial powers from the Americas.[203] Because the Dutch considered themselves "enlightened colonialists," they thought that the Monroe Doctrine should not apply to them.[204] Several of the papers derided the Pope's mediation efforts, and one of them, the *De Nederlandsche Spectator*, a literary-oriented weekly journal, published a cartoon of Leo XIII under the title "An impartial (?) arbitrator."[205]

There was much interest in the Dutch press in the Philippines, where it was noted that the insurgents were supported by an increasing number of the local population.[206] There were also a number of East Indies newspapers which, although of relatively small circulation by European standards, kept up a lively but ideologically monolithic discussion of events, mostly from the viewpoint of the Dutch planters,[207] that was definitely anti-insurrectionist. At least one paper deplored the inadequate size of the Dutch navy and its inability to protect its colonial interests in the Far East.[208]

The Dutch thus sat out the War and its aftermath in nervous expectation.

Japan

In contrast, Japan looked upon the coming War in a state of expectant anticipation. Of all the major countries other than the United States with the island of Cuba very close by, no other nation had the Spanish-American conflict closer to its home territory, or to its natural sphere of influence, than Japan. The Philippine Islands were in Japan's back yard (see Map 6), just as Cuba was in that of the United States (see Map 7). Formosa (Taiwan), over which Japan had recently acquired sovereignty from China, is about the same distance across the Luzon Straits from the Northern Philippine Island of Luzon,[209] as Cuba is from Key West across the Florida Straits, a bare 75 miles. In the late 19th century and later, Japan embarked on its own version of Manifest Destiny, viewing expansion as an attribute of national greatness.[210]

Although Japan was interested in acquiring the Philippines,[211]and as we shall see, actively interested, it had no intention of precipitating a conflict with the United States while it had other more pressing issues pending. It was willing to bide its time as long as the United States did not impede its agenda on the Asian mainland.[212] And Japan was willing to give assurances to the United States and the European powers that it would adhere to an "open door" policy in China. Towards this end, Japan looked for support from Great Britain, with whom it later signed a treaty of alliance in 1902.

This is not to say that Japan-U.S. relations did not have some worrisome moments during this period. These in fact presaged major future confrontations. The first serious Japanese-American crisis occurred in 1897 over the issue of Hawaii. After the Hawaiian Revolution of January 1893, there was a strong movement there, led by U.S. expatriates, for annexation by the United States.[213] This was blocked by President Cleveland in 1893, but nevertheless, American expansionists both in Hawaii and on the mainland, continued to press for annexation.

In the meantime, sugar growers in Hawaii had been importing large numbers of Japanese citizens to work the fields, to the point that by the mid 1890s there was an ominously large Japanese population in Hawaii, causing controlling American interests there much uneasiness, particularly after the Japanese victories in China. Thus in 1897 these American interests attempted to stem the flow of immigrants from Japan, to the chagrin of the Japanese government which proceeded to dispatch a warship to the islands and to file a strong note of protest.[214] Theodore Roosevelt, then the Assistant Secretary of the Navy, wanted the U.S. Navy to seize the Islands immediately, and in May 1897, he asked the Naval War College to plan for a conflict that would involve the simultaneous defense of Hawaii against Japan, and the liberation of Cuba from the Spanish Army.[215] He also instructed the commander of an American cruiser visiting Hawaii at the time to declare a provisional protectorate if Japan attempted to use force.

Influenced in large part by this situation, [216] in June 1897, President McKinley submitted a treaty of annexation to the Senate. Japan strongly protested this action and attempted to draw the European powers into the dispute, but without success. Nevertheless, Japan informed the United States that annexation would upset the status quo in the Pacific and endanger its perceived rights in Hawaii. Japan reluctantly withdrew its protest after receiving vague assurances from the United States.

The calm before the storm was about to end.

NOTES

1. Thomas, supra, at 100-101.

2. One outgrowth of this geographic proximity was the establishment of semi-permanent colonies of Cuban political exiles in Florida, particularly in Key West and Tampa, fleeing Spanish persecution. These eventually became the nucleus of the Cuban Revolutionary Party, which worked out of New York under the leadership of José Martí, and fueled the last war for independence that started in 1895.

3. On June 2, 1818, after his unauthorized and undeclared war with Spain over Florida, which Congress accepted as a *fait accompli* without so much as a reprimand, then General Andrew Jackson wrote President Monroe. "I will ensure you Cuba in a few days", but this was a bit too much and he was refused the frigate that would have made this possible. Jackson to Monroe, June 2, 1818. Robert V. Remini, *Andrew Jackson and the Course of American Empire, 1776-1821*, New York (1977), at 364.

4. Actually there was a fourth occasion if we consider that in 1808 President Thomas Jefferson made some preliminary overtures in this respect. Id. at 88.

5. In 1847 under President Polk, *id.* at 209-17, in 1854 under President Pierce, *id.* at 213, in 1857 under President Buchanan. Id. at 221-223.

6. Id. at 298.

7. Id. at 290.

8. Id. at 290, and 306-307.

9. Id. at 289. The movement of United States citizens to Cuba was not a new phenomenon. In 1819 alone 10% of the immigrants to Cuba came from the United States, the third in number after Spain and France. Id. at 98. Also in the period between the two wars for Cuban independence, a substantial number of Cubans sought the protections awarded by U.S. citizenship by becoming naturalized. Luis A. Perez, Jr., *Cuba Between Empires (1870-1902)*, University of Pittsburgh Press, Pittsburgh, Pa.(1983), at 28.

10. In addition, of course, to the activities of José Martí and the Cuban Revolutionary Party, as well as Spain's incompetence in resolving the "Cuban problem."

11. Id. at 98.

12. Id. at 194.

13. Id. at 288-289.

14. Id.

15. Id.

16. Joseph Erza Wisan, *The Cuban Crisis as Reflected in the New York Press (1895-1898)*, Columbia University Press, N.Y., New York (1934).

17. Winston Churchill, *My Early Life: A Roving Commission*, Oldhams, London (1930) at 78-87.

18. Thomas, supra at 336-337; Wisan, supra, 153, 199, 203. At the same time the press repeatedly glossed over the excesses committed by the insurgents. For example, while on the one hand the *Journal* reported with obvious satisfaction that rebel leader Máximo Gómez had ordered his troops to "leave nothing undestroyed" in the towns and villages, it condemned Weyler for allegedly wanting "to quench his thirst with American gore." Thomas, supra, at 337.

19. Thomas, supra, 328-331.

20. This was a technique copied by the British in the Boer War that was soon to follow the Spanish-American conflict.

21. Marcus Manley Wikerson, *Public opinion and the Spanish-American War: A Study in War Propaganda*, Louisiana State University Press, Baton Rouge, LA (1932).

22. Joseph Smith, *The Spanish-American War: Conflict in the Caribbean and the Pacific, 1895-1902*, Longman, London (1994), at 228. *Cf.*, *El Caribe y América Latina. El 98 en la coyuntura imperial*, 2 Vols.; María Teresa Cortés Zavala, Consuelo Naranjo Orovio, y José Alfredo Uribe Salas (coordinadores), Instituto de Investigaciones Históricas, Michoacán, México (1998). See also, *El 98 y su impacto en Latinoamérica*, Leopoldo Zea y Adalberto Santana (compiladores), Instituto Panamericano de Geografía e Historia, México (2001) (hereafter cited as *El 98 y su impacto*); Mónica Quijada, "Latinos y anglosajones: el 98 en el fin de siglo sudamericano," *Hispania*,196 (1997).

23. Thomas, supra, at 333.

24. The fulfillment of its "manifest destiny" by the United States within the confines of the continent is undoubtedly one of the reasons for its setting its sights offshore in both the Caribbean and the Pacific. See, Johnson, supra at 621-624. *Cf.*, Pratt, *Expansionists of 1898*, supra.

25. Id.

26. Its eastern coast line, of course, bordered on the Caribbean Sea. It also had considerable commercial interchange throughout the region as witnessed by the fact that it had consular offices in Puerto Rico, the Dominican Republic, Jamaica, Martinique, St. Thomas, and Cuba, in which it had consulates in Havana and five other cities. *México frente al desenlace del '98: La Guerra Hispanonorteamericana*, José Alfredo Uribe Salas, María Cortés Zavala y Consuelo Naranjo Orovio (coordinadores), Colección Estudios de Historia Mexicana 6, Morelia, Michoacán, México (1999), at 49 (cited hereafter as *México Frente*).

This was an unusually large number of consular offices considering that only about 200 Mexican citizens lived in Cuba at the time. Id. at 55.

27. Id. at 41.

28. *México y el mundo. Historia de sus relaciones internacionales*, Senado de la República, 9 Tomos, México (1990), at 71-75, cited in *México Frente*, supra, at 49 n.9.

29. María Margarita Espinosa Blas, "Cuba en la correspondencia consular mexicana, 1895-1900", in *México Frente*, at 52.

30. Laura Muñoz Mata, "México ante la cuestión cubana, 1895-1898", in *México Frente*, at 67.

31. Id. The substantial number of Spanish and Cuban *emigrés* in Mexico led to lively public relations and support campaigns representing both sides of the Cuban situation. Leticia Bobadilla González, "La opinión pública en México frente a la guerra hispano-cubano-norteamericana de 1898", in *México Frente*, at 133 159.

32. Id. at 73. R. Figueroa Esquer, "El *Correo Español*: la prensa españolista mexicana y el 98", in *Cuadernos hispanoamericanos*, Agencia Española de Cooperación, Madrid. Monográfico, Núm. 577-578, julio-agosto (1998) (hereafter *Cuadernos*), at 87-89.

33. Id. at 76.

34. María Emilia Pérez Santacieri, "El 98 español visto desde Uruguay", in *Cuadernos*, supra, at 129-159. The Uruguayan writer, José Enrique Rodó, in his work *Ariel*, published in 1900, implicitly likened the United States to "Caliban", a monster respected for its energy and strength but feared for its insensitivity and apparently unquenchable appetite for material expansion. José Enrique Rodó, *Ariel*, Dormache & Reyes, Montevideo (1900).

35. For a more detailed coverage of Argentinean attitudes and actions, see Horacio C. Cagni, *La Guerra Hispanoamericana. Inicio de la Globalización*, Centro Argentino de Estudios Estratégicos IXBILIA, ODLCESE Editores, Buenos Aires (1999), at 69-78.

36. *La Nación*, Montevideo, 3 May, 1898, at 1, reproduced in, Rodrigo González Natale, Carolina López, y Patricia Orbe. "El 98 en Cuba: génesis de una nueva dependencia continental vista desde la Argentina", in *El 98 y su impacto*, supra at 47.

37. Id. at 40.

38. Roque Sáez Peña and Paul Groussac strongly denounced the actions of the United States, Id. at 42-43.

39. Id. at 41.

40. Id. at 46.

41 Adriana Rodríguez, Natalia Fandussi, and José Marciles, "El crucero *Río de la Plata* como símbolo de 'Común-Unión' 1898-1902", in *El 98 y su impacto*, supra, at 67.

42. Id. at 68 n 2.

43. Id. at 68-68.

44. Id. at 71.

45. Smith, supra, at 228.

46. See, David McCullough, *The Paths Between the Seas*, Simon & Schuster, New York (1977).

47. See generally, *European Perceptions of the Spanish American War of 1898*, Sylvia L. Hilton and Steve J.S. Ickringill (eds.), Peter Lang, Bern (1999) (hereafter *European Perceptions*) at 9-32.

48. Speech given on November 23, 1900, cited in William C. Widenor, *Henry Cabot Lodge and the Search for an American Foreign Policy*, Berkeley, California (1980), at 120.

49. Cited in Ernest R. May, *Imperial Democracy: The Emergence of America as a Great Power*, New York (1961), at 196.

50. Joseph Smith, *The Spanish-American War: Conflict in the Caribbean and the Pacific, 1895-1902*, Longman, London (1994), at 227.

51. *European Perceptions*, supra, at 9-10.

52. Although internal opinion was divided. Queen Victoria was decidedly supportive of Spain, principally out of personal sympathy toward Spanish Queen Regent María Cristina and her infant son, as were Sir Henry Drummond Wolff,

the British ambassador in Madrid, and Sir Thomas Sanderson, the Under Secretary of State. On the other hand, the government's position of official neutrality was expressed by Prime Minister Salisbury, as well as by his deputy when he was ill, Arthur Balfour, as well as by Joseph Chamberlain, the British ambassador to the United States, who openly supported the U.S., as did the overwhelming majority of the British public. *European Perceptions*, supra, at 22.

53. An exception were the French, who had extensive holdings in Spanish bonds. This was a major factor, together with others mentioned, for French opposition to US intervention in Cuba, as Spain's income from Cuba provided a large part of the moneys needed for the interest payments on these bonds.

54. William Langer, *The Diplomacy of Imperialism, 1890-1902*, 2d ed., New York (1951); Richard Langhorne, *The Collapse of the Concert of Europe. International Politics, 1890-1914*, MacMillan, London (1981); Andrew Porter, *European Imperialism, 1860-1914*, MacMillan, London (1994).

55. Thomas, supra, at 360.

56. *Journal*, February 11, 1898.

57. For a balanced analysis of the Maine's sinking, *see* Admiral Hyman G. Rickover, *How the Battleship Maine Was Destroyed*, U.S. Naval Institute, MD (1977); also, José Cervera Pery, *La Guerra Naval del '98*, Editorial San Mateo, Madrid (1998).

58. Thomas, supra, at 356-366.

59. Josef Polisensky, "La guerra hispanocubanoamericana de 1898 y la opinión pública checa," *Historica*, 7, Prague (1963), at 99-113, showing that Czech newspapers largely favored Cuban independence. See also, Luis Álvarez Gutiérrez, "Los imperios centrales ante el progresivo deterioro de las relaciones entre España y los Estados Unidos," *Hispania*, LVII/196 (mayo-agosto, 1977), at 435-478.

60. Id.

61. See generally, Nicole Slupetzky, "Austria and the Spanish-American War," in *European Perceptions*, supra, at 181-194.

62. Id. at 182.

63. Id. See also, John L. Offner, *An Unwanted War: The Diplomacy of the United States and Spain over Cuba, 1895-1898*, University of North Carolina Press, Chapel Hill/London, (1992), at 159-176. See also generally, Carmelo Rosario Natal, *Puerto Rico y la crisis de la Guerra Hispano-Americana, 1895-1898*, Ramallo Printing Co., San Juan (1975).

64. Slupetzky, supra, at 182, in *European Perceptions, supra*.

65. Id, at 184; *Public Records Office, Foreign Office*, 115/1087 fol. 62 v (hereafter PRO, FO).

66. Slupetzky, supra, at 185, in *European Perceptions*, supra.

67. Thomas, supra, at 373.

68. Id.

69. Id. at 374.

70. Id. at 375.

71. Slupetzky, supra, at 188. in *European Perceptions*, *supra*.

72. Id. at 188.

73. Id.

74. Id.

75. Thomas, supra, at 376. This pronouncement has a familiar ring. See President Bush's declaration of May 1, 2003 at http://www.cbsnews.com/stories/2003/05/01/printable551946.shtml

76. Id. at 376-377.

77. *Correspondence Respecting the War between Spain and the United States (1898-1899)* (Confidential Print, 7267, Foreign Office, March, 1900) (hereafter *CPFO*), No. 310, at 174.

78. E. Ranson, "British Military and Naval Observers in the Spanish American War," *Journal of American Studies*, 3 (1969): 33-56.

79. Rene Greger, "The Austro-Hungarian Navy and the Spanish-American War of 1898," *Warship International*, 1, (1980), at 61-67.

80. Craig, supra, at 244.

81. Gottschall, supra.

82. Craig, supra, at 303.

83. Id. at 305.

84. "The military situation against England demands battleships in the greatest possible numbers," Tirpitz. *Id*. at 309. In a marginal note to a July 31, 1897, telegram reporting the denunciation by Great Britain of the Anglo-German Treaty,

the Emperor commented: "Now that superiority of German industry is recognized, Albion [Great Britain] will soon make efforts to destroy it, and she will undoubtedly be successful, unless we quickly and energetically forestall the evil by building a strong fleet." *GDD* at 487. XIII. 33 (July 31, 1897).The *real* threat, of course, was Britain's overwhelmingly superior *financial* strength, which was created by its enviable geopolitical position. Craig, supra, at 310 n. 24.

85. But it is a mistake to think that there was a lack of public support in Germany for these notions of *Weltpolitik*, in which German energy and culture were to play an important role. They were in fact greeted with enthusiasm not only by those who stood to profit from overseas commerce and investment, but also by patriotic groups like the Colonial Union and the Pan-Germanic League, and by ordinary citizens who saw their individual images projected in a vision of their country's greatness. Id. at 249. Some major German thinkers, such as Fredrich Nauman and Max Weber were also caught up in this euphoria, as was Paul Rohrbach, who authored *The German Thought* and *Onward to the Position of a World Power* in support of *Weltpolitik*. Id.

86. *German Diplomatic Documents, 1871-1914*, 4 Vols., selected and translated by E.T.S. Dugdale, Barnes & Noble, New York (1969) (hereafter *GDD*), Vol. II, at 278-294. Since 1879-1881, there had been rivalry for control of these islands between United States and Germany. In 1889, a tripartite treaty was entered into by Great Britain, United States and Germany establishing a condominium to oversee them. *See* George Herbert Ryden, *The Foreign Policy of the United States in Relation to Samoa*, Yale University Press, New Haven (1928). In 1894, the Germans were under the impression that the United States was going to withdraw from the treaty, whereupon Kaiser Wilhelm indicated that if that was so, Germany would no longer be bound by it, "and we are to try to press our claims to Samoa in their fullest extent with England." *GDD*, supra, VIII. 426 Vol. II at 290-291. The Germans did not believe that the United States would go to war over Samoa. Id. at VIII. 435. At this time von Bulow was not yet foreign secretary and Chancellor Count von Caprivi was directly involved. The condominium was finally dissolved in 1899 and Samoa was partitioned between United States and Germany.

87. Craig, supra at 242. This was an attempt by the British to evade the Anglo-German Agreement of 1890, which provided for a common border between German East Africa and the Congo State. Instead the Anglo-Congolese Treaty gave the British a corridor separating them and thus assured the British of a continuous overland route between Cairo and the Cape. Id. at 243.

88. Id.

89. Id. at 16.

90. Id. at 17.

91. Carr, supra, at 191; Craig, supra, at 245. Although the Transvaal was an independent state, by agreement with the British government in 1884, it could not enter into accords with foreign governments without British permission.

For Britain, the Boer Republics stood in the way of the consolidation of its interests in South Africa. However, Germany had considerable investments in the Boer Republics, 20% of all foreign capital there being German –including control of the national bank, the water supply, and the whisky and dynamite monopolies– and German enterprises were the principal importers of iron, steel, chemicals, machines and utensils. Id.

92. Id., supra, at 245.

93. Id. at 246.

94. Id.

95. GDD, at 483-484.

96. Id. at 483, XIII. 28 (July 18, 1897).

97. As well as problems with Japan, to be discussed more fully below. *See also* T.A. Bailey, "Japan's Protest against the Annexation of Hawaii," *Journal of Modern History*, III, 46-61.

98. Pratt, supra, at 317.

99. *European Perceptions*, supra, at 16. Luis Álvarez Gutiérrez, "La diplomacia alemana ante el conflicto hispano-norte americano de 1897-1898: primeras tomas de posición," *Hispania*, LIV/186 (enero-abril 1994), at 201-256.

100. Id. See also, Markus M. Hugo, "'Uncle Sam I Cannot Stand, for Spain I have No Sympathy': An Analysis of Discourse about the Spanish-American War in Germany, 1898-1899," in *European Perceptions, supra*, at 71-93. For a different opinion, *see* Lester B. Shipee, "Germany and the Spanish-American War," *American Historical Review*, XXX/4 (July 1925) 754-777, at 763-764.

101. Id. at 92.

102. GDD, at 496, XV.3 (Cipher telegram. Very secret. September 29, 1897).

103. Id. at 487 (XV.4, September 30, 1897; XV.5, September 30, 1897).

104. Hugo, supra, at 78, in *European Perspectives, supra. Cf.*, W.W. Goodrich, "Questions of international law involved in the Spanish War," *American Law Review*, 32 (1898): 461-500, at 493-495.

105. Hugo, supra, at 80.

106. Id. at 81.

107. Post at n. 109.

108. Hugo, supra, at 82 n. 43. German resentment and distrust of the United States generated during this period had longer lasting effects on German-American relationships. In debates in the Reichstag in February 1899, the Conservatives predicted that "the United States within a short time [would] reach an alarming predominance over old civilized nations in Europe, not only in industrial and commercial terms, but also in regard to their political power." Id.

109. As the Emperor himself so aptly put it, "The aim is to fish in troubled waters." *GDD*, at 513, marginal note in XV. 28 (April 22, 1898).

110. Hugo, supra, at 83.

111. Id. at 87.

112. Id. at 89. Emperor Wilhelm himself was heard to say that "all Latin nations are in a state of decay." Id. at 89 n. 68.

113. Id. at 89-90.

114. Id. at 90.

115. Ranson, supra, at 33 n. 3.

116. Louis M. Sears, "French Opinion of the Spanish-American War," *The Hispanic-American Historical Review*, 7 (1927): 25-44, at 25. *See also*, Serge Ricard, "The French Press and Brother Jonathan: Editorializing the Spanish-American Conflict," in *European Perceptions*, supra, at 133-149.

117. *Journal des Débates*, March 2, 1898.

118. Id., March 2, 1898.

119. Id., April 3, 1898.

120. Id., April 15, 1898.

121. Paul Louis, "Apropos de la Guerre Hispano-Américane," in *La Revue Socialiste*, May 1898, at 606, 608.

122. *Journal du Droit International Privé et de la Juriprudence Comparés*, XXV, 432-433; "Chronique Internationale" in *Annales des Sciences Politiques*, XVL, 643-645.

123. *European Perceptions*, supra, at 19.

124. Id. at 20. France's two great rivals in Europe, Great Britain and Germany, were neutralized by France's alliance with Russia in 1894. This allowed France to proceed with her plans elsewhere. In 1895-1896 it annexed Madagascar and tried to go into the Upper Nile and create a Sudanese empire, which led to a stand-off with the British in Fashoda in the autumn of 1898. Id.

125. Ranson, supra, at 33 n.3.

126. Consolidated by Czar Nicholas's visit to Paris in 1896, which was followed by that of Foreign Minister Count Mikhail Muraviev, in January 1897, and that of President Faure to St. Petersburg at the end of August of that year.

127. Ludmila N. Popkova, "Russian Press Coverage of the American Intervention in the Spanish-Cuban War," in *European Perceptions*, supra, 111-132, at 111.

128. Id.

129. L.S. Vladimirov, *La diplomacia de los Estados Unidos durante la Guerra Hispano-norteamericana de 1898*, Foreign Language Editions, Moscow (1958) (Spanish translation); Blas Noel Pérez, "Visión rusa de la guerra hispano-cubano-norteamericana," *América Latina*, La Habana, (diciembre, 1998), at 62-65.

130. Id. at 112.

131. Lenin, supra, at 164.

132. *Popkava*, supra, at 112-113.

133. See generally, Rosario de la Torre del Río, *Inglaterra y España en 1898*, UDEMA, Madrid (1988), at 67-97.

134. De la Torre del Río, supra, at 248-292, 285.

135. Charles S. Campbell, Jr., *Anglo-American Understanding, 1898-1900,* The Johns Hopkins Press, Baltimore (1957). America's bitterness over Britain's and Canada's aid to the Confederacy during the Civil War, the actions of the Irish-Americans and their combative organization, the Fenians, British championing of the gold standard opposed by the Free Silver zealots in the United States, as well as recurring fishing disputes in Newfoundland and the Bering Sea, were all stumbling blocks preventing closer relations between the U.S. and Great Britain before 1898. Id. at 1-4.

136. J.A. Sloan, "Anglo-American Relations and the Venezuelan Border Dispute," *Hispanic American Historical Review*, Vol.18 (1938), at 486-506.

137. N.M. Blake, "The Olney-Pauncefote Treaty of 1897," *American Historical Review*, Vol. 50 (1945), at 228-243. For a view that this accord and other apparent signs of Anglo-American rapprochement during the McKinley administration "resulted more from American blackmail than from kindly transatlantic feelings," see, Charles S. Campbell, Jr., "Anglo-American Relations, 1897-1901," in *Thresh old to American Internationalism, Essays on the Foreign Policies of William McKinley*, Paolo E. Coletta (ed.), Exposition Press, New York (1970), at 250, 251.

138. *See*, Thomas J. Noer, Briton, *Boer and Yankee, The United States and South Africa, 1870-1914*, Kent State University Press, Kent, Ohio (1978). During the

Boer War, in late January, 1900, in the course of a debate in the U.S. Senate to consider a Democratic proposal favorable to the Boer cause and against the British, Senator Henry Cabot Lodge reminded his colleagues of British support for the United States during the Spanish-American War. The Democrat's proposal was eventually defeated. *Congressional Record*, 56th Congress, 1st Session, Pt. 2, at 1250-54.

139. de la Torre del Río, supra; Robert G. Neal, *Great Britain and United States Expansion, 1898-1900*, Michigan State University Press, Lansing (1966); Alec E. Campbell, *Great Britain and the United States, 1898-1903*, Longmans, London (1960); Braford Perkins, *The Great Rapprochment: England and the United States, 1895-1914*, Victor Gollancz, New York (1969).

140. Perhaps a more subtle but important factor were also the numerous trans-Atlantic marriages by American women (many of whom were rich heiresses) to Englishmen in high places, more than seventy by 1903. Campbell, *Anglo-American Understanding*, supra, at 9. *See also*, Johnson, *The Birth of the Modern*, at 49-50.

141. Salisbury had told Wolff that the United States-Spanish dispute over Cuba was not Great Britain's business and that although he did not like to see Spain humiliated, Great Britain would stay out of it. R.G. Neal, *Great Britain and United States Expansion, 1898-1900*, Michigan State University Press, Lansing (1966), at 3.

142. Ambassador in Washington from 1889 until his death in 1902. When he died, President Roosevelt ordered the U.S. flag at the White House flown at half mast, an unprecedented honor for a foreigner. R.B. Mowat, *Life of Lord Pauncefote, First Ambassador to the United States*, London (1929). See also, Campbell, *Anglo-American Understanding*, supra, at 26-27.

143. The *Daily Chronicle* went so far as to advocate a "demonstration" in Havana by the British North American Squadron and the sale of British warships to the "cousins across the ocean." *Daily Chronicle*, April 7, 1898. J.H. Mcminn, "The Attitude of the U.S. press during the Spanish-American War," Ph.D. thesis, Ohio State University,1939; Geoffrey Seed, "British Reactions to American Imperialism Reflected in Journals of Opinion, 1898-1900," *Political Science Quarterly*, 73/2 (1968), at 254-272.

144. *The Letters of Queen Victoria*, Series III (1886-1901), George Easle Bucke (ed.), London, (1930-1932), vol.3, at 236, 237. See also, R.G. Neale, supra, at 6-7.

145. The Queen Regent was Queen Victoria's niece. Buckle, supra, vol. 3, at 236-7, 244.

146. Id. at 239; Neal, supra, at 7.

147. *See also*, Campbell, *Anglo-American Understanding*, supra, at 25-40; see generally, Neal, supra, at 1-42.

148. Id. at 31 and 31 n.20; Foreign Office to Pauncefote, March 28, *PRO, FO* 115/1087.

149. Campbell, *Anglo-American Understanding*, supra, at 32.

150. Id. at 32-36.

151. Geoffrey Sneed, "British Views of American Policy in the Philippines Reflected in Journals of Opinion," *Journal of American Studies*, 2/1 (1968), at 49-64. Cf., Alec E. Campbell, "Great Britain and the United States in the Far East,1895-1903," *The Historical Journal*, 1/2 (September 1958), Cambridge, at 154-175. Cf. the Spanish newspaper, *La Época*, which speculated that Great Britain in lieu of the United States acquiring the Philippines, might favor Japan "which has had its sights on the Philippines for some time." *La Época*, April 8, 1898.

152. de la Torre del Río, supra, at 65; Campbell, *Anglo-American Understanding*, supra, at 12-23.

153. See J.W. Pratt, *Expansionist of 1898, The Acquisition of Hawaii and the Spanish Islands*, Quadrangle Books, Chicago (1936).

154. Campbell, *Anglo-American Understanding*, supra, at 12.

155. Id. at 19.

156. Brooks Adams, "The Spanish-American War and the Equilibrium of the World," *The Forum*, Vol.25 (1898), at 645.

157. See generally, Daniela Rossini, "The American Peril: Italian Catholics and the Spanish-American War, 1898," in *European Perceptions*, supra, at 167-179; Fernando García Sanz, "El contexto internacional de la guerra de Cuba: la percepción italiana del '98 español," *Estudios de Historia Social*, Madrid (1988), at 295-310.

158. Rossini, supra, at 172.

159. The political, social and military events that resulted in a unified Kingdom of Italy in 1861.

160. Id. at 172. Italian Catholics were divided into *gli intransigenti* (the uncompromising), led by the Jesuits, the *i conciliatori* (the conciliators), who favored reconciliation between the Church and the modern scientific spirit, and the Christian-Democrats, who were basically promoting social programs. Id. at 172-3.

161. Published February 16, 1895 in Latin and Italian in *Civiltá Cattolica*, No. 1072, at 385-410.

162. G.P. Fogarty, *The Vatican and the American Hierarchy from 1870 to 1965*, Anton Hiersemann, Stuttgart (1982), at 143-190.

163. Rossini, supra, at 173.

164. Id. at 170 n. 8.

165. *Osservatore Romano*, February 11-12, 1898; March 21-22, 1898; April 2-3, 1898.

166. Rossini, supra, at 175.

167. Id. at 177.

168. John L. Offner, "Washington Mission: Archbishop Ireland on the Eve of the Spanish-American War," *Catholic Historical Review*, LXXIII/4 (October, 1987), at 247-289.

169. Rossini, supra, at 179.

170 The anti-clerical Republican press in Spain was highly critical of the Vatican's last minute mediation efforts, ascribing self-interest to the Church's attempts to its secure properties and the freedom to conduct Catholic activities in the United States if the latter won the War. *European Perceptions*, supra, at 18-19. They also accused the Church of being responsible for the discontent of the Filipinos, caused mainly by the discriminatory manner in which the religious orders operated there. Id. at 19.

171. Id. at 179.

172. Luigi Bruti Liberati, *La Santa Sede e le origini dell'impero americano: la guerra del 1898*, UNICOPLI, Milan (1984), at 23.

173. D. Jesús Pabón de Suárez de Urbina, *El 98, Acontecimiento Internacional*, Ministerio de Asuntos Exteriores, Escuela Diplomática, Madrid (1952), at 31; Agustín Rodríguez, "Portugal and the Spanish Colonial Crisis of 1898," in *European Perceptions*, supra, at 151-165. *See also*, Joao Medina, "A crise colonial dos anos novemta em Portugal e Espanha e as suas consecuencias para os dos paises ibéricos (1890-1898). Estudo de historia comparada," in *Portugal, España, y Africa en los últimos cien años. IV Jornadas de estudios luso-españoles*, U.N.E.D., Mérida (1992), at 17-27.

174. Agustín R. Rodriguez, "España ante la crisis del Ultimátum (1890-94)," in *La historia de las relaciones internacionales: una visión desde España*, C.E.H.I.R.S., Madrid (1996), at 496-510.

175. Julio Salom Costa, "La relación Hispano-portuguesa al término de la época iberista," *Hispania*, 25 (1965), at 219-159.

176. Rodríguez, supra, in *European Expectations*, supra, at 160.

177. Id. at 156.

178. Id. at 155.

179. John L. Offner, *An Unwanted War: The Diplomacy of the United States and Spain over Cuba, 1895-1898*, University of North Carolina Press, Chapel Hill (1992), at 129-130.

180. Rodriguez, supra, in *European Perceptions*, supra, at 157.

181. *Colección de Documentos Referentes a la Escuadra de Operaciones de las Antillas*, Editorial Naval, 5a Ed., Madrid, 1986, at 76.

182. Id. at 97.

183. Although the actual U.S. declaration of war was dated April 25, it indicated that a state of war had existed since April 21, when the U.S. Navy began its blockade of Cuba.

184. Id. at 158.

185. Id. at 159.

186. Id. at 159.

187. Id. at 162.

188. Id.

189. Id. at 163.

190. Id.

191. Great Britain and Germany agreed in the secret annexes of August 30, 1898, to the Anglo-German Convention that the Portuguese colonies south of the equator, including most of the Atlantic Islands, were to be parceled out between them. Id at 161. See also, José María Jover Zamora, *1898: Teoría y práctica de la redistribución colonial*, Fundación Universitaria Española, Madrid (1979), at 19-23.

192. Nico A. Bootsma, "Reactions to the Spanish-American War in the Netherlands and the Dutch East Indies", in *European Perceptions*, supra, at 37.

193. Id.

194. Id.

195. Id.

196. Id.

197. Id. at 38. Spain reserved the right to engage in privateering. *CPFO*, No. 124 (24 April, 1898).

198. Id. at 39.

199. Id.

200. Id. at 40.

201. Id.

202. Id.

203. Id.

204. Id.

205. Id. at 42.

206. Id. at 41.

207. Id. at 43-46.

208. Id. at 46.

209. "[F]rom one of the islands through which the northern line of the Treaty of Paris runs, situated only a pleasant morning's journey in a launch due north of Aparri, the northernmost town of Luzon, you can see, on a clear day, with a good field glass, the southern end of Formosa, some 60 or 70 miles away. *Japan can land an army on American soil at Aparri any time she wants to, overnight....* James H. Blount, *The American Occupation of the Philippines, 1898-1912*, G.P. Putnam's Sons, New York (1912), at 329 (italics in the original).

210. McClain, *supra*, at 312-315: Charles E. Neu, *The Troubled Encounter: The United States and Japan*, John Wiley and Sons, New York (1975), at 32-33.

211. Payson J. Treat, *Diplomatic Relations Between the United States and Japan, 1895-1905*, Stanford University Press (1938), at 55.

212. Grenville, supra, at 13. The fact was, as demonstrated during World War II, that the United States could not have held the Philippines against a Japanese incursion. Even with the Panama Canal in operation, which of course had not yet been built in 1898, it would have taken 68 days for a U.S. fleet to reach the islands, while the Japanese fleet was only 8 days' cruise away. Id. at 16. Without the canal, it would have taken 104 days for U.S. relief to arrive in the Philippines from the East coast, where the main U.S. naval forces were concentrated. Id.

213. See generally, Pratt, supra, at 74-145.

214. Id. at 34.

215. Id. at 35.

216. Id.

THE AMERICANS

Alfred Thayer Mahan.

Henry Cabot Lodge.

President William McKinley.

THE SPANIARDS

Alfonso XIII, King of Spain.

Queen María Cristina.

Práxedes Mateo Sagasta.

General Arsenio Martínez Campos.

General Valeriano Weyler.

General Ramón Blanco.

THE CUBANS

José Martí.

General Calixto García.

General Máximo Gómez.

Officers of General Gómez' Army at Remedios, Cuba.

THE FILIPINOS

José Rizal.

Emilio Aguinaldo in uniform.

Emilio Aguinaldo and his chief aides.

IMPORTANT OTHERS

Kaiser Wilhelm II.

Queen Victoria.

Lord Salisbury.

Joseph Chamberlain.

The Emperor of Japan.

Archbishop John Ireland.

CASUS BELLI

U.S.S.Maine entering Havana Harbor.

Maine wreck, Havana Harbor.

THE WARRIORS

John D. Long, Secretary of the Navy.

Lieutenant Colonel Theodore Roosevelt.

Admiral George Dewey.

Admiral Pascual Cervera.

Admiral Montijo.

The Spanish Commandant of Manila.

American commanders against the Filipino insurgents.

The Filipino insurrection, 1899.

General Nelson A. Miles.

THE OBSERVERS

English, Russian, German, Austrian, Japanese and Swedish military attaches with the American Army at Santiago de Cuba.

ACTION STATIONS

Bombardment of San Juan, Puerto Rico.

Entrance to harbor at Santiago de Cuba.

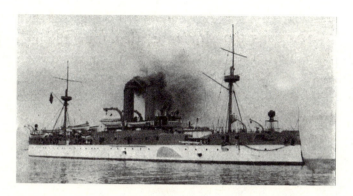

Armored cruisier.

American troops on ramparts at Manila.

Dewey's Flagship *Olympia*.

Battleship *Pelayo.*

Cristóbal Colón armored cruiser wrecked.

THE PEACEMAKERS

William Rufus Day.

Signing of the peace protocol of the Spanish-American War.

SENOR MONTERO RIOS, PRESIDENT

GENERAL R. CERERO.

SENOR J. DE GARNICA

SENOR W. Z. DE VILLAURRUTIA

SENOR BUENAVENTURA ADARZUZA

THE SPANISH PEACE COMMISSIONERS.

Spanish peace commissioners.

Signing of Treaty of Paris.

Jules Martin Cambon.

President McKinley presenting Admiral Dewey.

CHAPTER III

The Spanish-American War Commences

Following his message to Congress on April 11, 1898, President McKinley requested that Congress issue an ultimatum to Spain, the principal conditions of which were its recognition of Cuba's independence and the immediate withdrawal of its armed forces from the island. Spain was given until April 23 to agree to the demands.[1] On April 21, Congress issued a joint resolution containing the president's request, which the Spanish authorities refused to accept proceeding instead to sever diplomatic relations with the United States.[2] Thereupon, on April 25, Congress formally declared "That war be, and the same is hereby, declared to exist, and that war existed since the 21st day of April AD, 1898, including said day between the United States of America and the Kingdom of Spain."[3] The retroactivity of the war declaration, the subject of criticism particularly by European experts in international law, was due to the fact that U.S. naval forces had been enforcing a naval blockade of most of Cuba since April 22[4] in search of Admiral Cervera's squadron and to prevent reinforcement of the Spanish garrison.[5] Under international law such actions by the United States constituted acts of war and thus a de facto state of war.

So began this brief (120-day) but global spanning war, important not only to the combatants but also to the not-so-innocent non-belligerent bystanders.

This conflict could very well be seen as America's debut in the big leagues of international politics. Although the United States had previously engaged the several nations of the world in various ways, this war led to more complex and longer lasting relationships and entanglements than any in its previous history, in places distant from the American mainland, and involving peoples of very different races, cultures and

103

backgrounds. Perhaps even more important, as a direct consequence of the Spanish-American War, the United States broke with its past radically by becoming an openly colonial nation.[6] Lastly, as we shall see, this period marks the beginning of a strategy of globalization[7] whereby the United States would engage in a course of conduct to justify its beginning a war, and *sub silentio,* to support global economic goals. As will become evident, these actions would be precursors of similar conduct taken with regards to its present conflict in Iraq.

Business as usual

On April 23, the warships of three non-belligerent nations entered Havana harbor. Each demonstrated by their actions where their true feelings lay in this conflict. As the Italian cruiser *Giovani Baussan* passed the El Morro fortifications at the entrance to the port, the ship's band played the Spanish royal anthem and its crew dressed ship and hurrahed Spain.[8] On shore, the Italian captain publicly bragged about how much he had enjoyed outrunning the American blockade given his ship's superior speed. When they arrived, they found the French cruiser, *Fulton,* which had also cheered the Spanish on entering the harbor shortly before the Italians.[9] The British cruiser *Falbrot* was the third to enter the Havana harbor. In passing the blockading fleet, the crew dressed ship and cheered and waived the Union Jack. The ship's band on the *U.S.S. New York* reciprocated by playing "God Save the Queen."[10]

It is fitting that these somewhat innocuous but telling interchanges should take place on the water, for it was on that element that the Spanish-American War was decided. The two most important naval actions – they should not really be called battles, they were so one-sided – were at Manila Bay in the Philippines, on May 1, and in Santiago, Cuba, on July 3, 1898.[11]

On the same day that war was declared by the United States, Secretary Long sent a cable to Hong Kong, on the Chinese mainland. It was delivered shortly thereafter by the U.S. Revenue Cutter *McCulloch* to Admiral Dewey, whose ship was anchored in Mir Bay outside British waters. The message read: "War has commenced between the United States and Spain. Proceed at once to the Philippines."[12]

Admiral Dewey arrived in Manila (see Maps 10 and 11) shortly after midnight on May 1, and opened fire on the Spanish fleet anchored off Cavite at 5:22 A.M., with the now famous command to the captain of his flagship: "You may fire when ready, Gridley."[13] By 7:35 A.M. the Spanish fleet lay sinking or in flames, and most of the shore batteries had been silenced.[14] All were victims of Spanish incompetence and unpreparedness and of Dewey's overwhelmingly superior force (see Map 12). The United States fleet suffered only minor damage and casualties.[15]

In the United States, the victory was hailed as the greatest in naval history and Admiral Dewey was held to be the equal of Nelson.[16]

Bombast aside, Manila Bay was important, not only as the first victory of the war, with all the psychological boost that such a result entails, but as a fairly accurate reading of what could be the expected outcome of this uneven contest.

Perhaps more subtle, but most important, were the geopolitical implications of the Manila Bay "turkey shoot." A war that before its commencement was focused on events developing in the Caribbean started instead thousands of miles away in the Far East (see Map 6). The possibilities that had previously been considered only in theory, were now a reality to be dealt with in the immediate future not only by the combatants, but also by those who had a stake in that region and thus would be most affected by a change in the balance of power there: Great Britain, France, Germany, Russia, Japan, and of course the United States.[17] The later suddenly found itself in possession of a trump card in the strategic game for the China market, the ultimate goal of the several players.

The events in the Philippines did not end with the Manila Bay naval engagement: several important incidents took place in regard to the nonbelligerents in the Philippines, which will be discussed presently. And the land war in the Philippines would evolve into the Filipino War that lasted into 1903,[18] in which U.S. troops would suffer considerably more casualties than during the entire Spanish-American conflict.

In the meanwhile, after the Manila Bay episode but before the Santiago, Cuba naval engagement, the U.S. Atlantic Fleet under Admiral Sampson arrived off San Juan, Puerto Rico (see Maps 7 and 9) on May 12, in the hope of coming on Admiral Cervera's squadron.[19] They did not find it there. Nevertheless, Admiral Sampson proceeded to shell the fortifications at the entrance to the harbor. The firing was over by 9:00 A.M., with Sampson's ships mostly hitting the city proper, resulting in 113 casualties, almost all civilians.[20]

The search for Admiral Cervera continued, and on May 30 the squadron was located anchored inside the harbor at Santiago, Cuba (see Map 8). It was in reality a paper fleet. By now Cervera's ships had foul bottoms, were desperately short of coal and provisions, and several of his capital ships had inoperative or missing heavy guns, having been forced to leave Spain prematurely.[21] Probably more important, the Spanish fleet was bottled up in an untenable tactical situation (see photograph of the entrance to Santiago Harbor). The entrance was so narrow that the Spanish ships would have to leave in line, one at a time. This allowed the blockading American fleet to bring all of its guns to bear, enabling it to concentrate its full fire power on each Spanish ship as it left the harbor, while preventing the Spanish fleet from returning fire from more than one ship at a time. But Admiral Cervera's squadron had been placed there against his expressed wishes,[22] by reason of political decisions made by politicians, allegedly to save Spain's "honor," and thus the Monarchy.[23]

Upon seeing the *Cristóbal Colón* anchored in the harbor next to the *Almirante Oquendo*, Admiral Schley, commanding the Flying Squadron, turned to a reporter and said, "We've got them now, Graham, and they'll never go home."[24] The fate of the Spanish Empire was about to be sealed, for in losing its fleet, Spain would not only be left without an indispensable strategic and tactical asset for the conduct of an intercontinental war (while their Atlantic fleet was still able to roam, the Eastern Seaboard of the United States could theoretically be bombarded and Spain's coast could be defended), but her armies in Cuba and the Philippines would be deprived of supplies and reinforcements, and thus any land campaign was doomed to attrition and failure. Mahan's theories were vividly proven at that point in history: naval power and control of the seas were essential to any nation aspiring to be in the first ranks of international status. Naval strength was the equivalent of today's control of the skies.

At 9:35 A.M. on July 3, following orders[25] from his government,[26] Admiral Cervera and his decrepit squadron filed out of Santiago Bay and into a semi-circle of awaiting U.S. Navy ships (see Map 13). By 1:00

P.M., after a firefight in which the Spanish ships were picked off one at a time without much difficulty, Cervera's fleet was no more.

The Austro-Hungarian cruiser, *Kaiserin María Theresa*, arriving unannounced to observe the action, came close to being fired upon by the *U.S.S. Indiana* before she finally identified herself as a neutral, at a range of only 3 miles.[27]

The naval victory at Santiago was a good Fourth of July present for the American public which had just started to receive the casualty list from the El Caney and San Juan Hill engagements on the outskirts of Santiago. These land skirmishes were the product of landings by the U.S. Army at Daiquirí, west of Santiago, commencing June 22 and involving approximately 17,000 troops.[28] Accompanying these troops was an interesting collection of foreign observers. These included military observers from Great Britain, Russia, France, Japan, Sweden, and Norway, and naval observers from Austro-Hungary, Germany, Japan, Great Britain, Sweden and Norway (see photographs in "The Observers" section).[29]

The hopeless situation of the Spanish garrison in Santiago was apparent after the loss of Cervera's fleet on July 3. Santiago was already practically encircled following the El Caney and San Juan Hill skirmishes on July 1. These were much-touted American victories largely because of an ongoing publicity campaign by Theodore Roosevelt and his "Rough Riders." There is little doubt that Roosevelt was already thinking of his political future. In fact, it took some 4,000 U.S. troops several days to dislodge 521 ill-armed Spaniards from atop San Juan Hill.[30] On July 16 Santiago capitulated.[31]

Thereafter the rest of the land campaign in Cuba went from slow to slower and was soon caught up in the peace process. Hostilities were officially suspended on August 14, 1898.[32]

Before that, however, General Nelson Miles, of Indian Wars fame, headed for Puerto Rico with a modest-size expeditionary force. Although the invasion of Puerto Rico had been considered in the early planning stages of the War,[33] these plans did not come off the shelf again until after the naval situation had been decided and Santiago had been secured.[34]

After considerable dissent and discourse both within and outside Miles' command, on July 25, U.S. troops landed at Guánica on the southwestern coast of Puerto Rico (see Map 9). They encountered light resistance from the Spanish army, who suspected that the war was already lost. Nevertheless the invading army received a delirious welcome from the civilian population.[35] General Miles issued a proclamation, one which has a familiar ring, to the effect that the United States was engaged in a war "in the cause of liberty, justice, and humanity,"[36] and he cabled the War Department to send as many American flags as could be spared, as they had run out of the ones they had with them, because the troops were giving them to the municipalities.[37]

From the southwest, Miles' troops moved slowly toward the capital city, San Juan, on the north coast, fighting small skirmishes along the way with contingents of the Spanish forces. They were halfway to San Juan when the hostilities were suspended on August 14.

Great Britain's intrigues

With the declaration of war by United States and Spain, Great Britain announced her neutrality on April 24, 1898,[38] and also agreed to represent U.S. interests in Madrid during the war. The commencement of hostilities led to a series of situations which caused Spain to accuse Great Britain of breaching her declared neutrality by taking action in favor of the United States.[39]

One of the most egregious of these incidents was related to the issue of what material or cargo was considered to be contraband in time of war. Almost all materials that could be used by a nation at war were classified as contraband and thus not normally allowed to be supplied by neutrals to belligerents . A critical item in this respect was coal, which at the time was needed to power most of the ships in commerce and naval warfare. The war was, after all, being fought at least in part because of the need of the Great Powers to have coaling stations in strategic places throughout the world.

Considering the importance of this question, it was not surprising that on March 28 the British Admiralty raised the issue with the Foreign Office, contending at the same time that it considered "that the character of the coal [i.e., whether or not it was contraband] should be determined by its destination."[40] On April 21, when this matter was raised for discussion in Parliament, the Government left its options open by taking the position that it "[could] not lay down any general principal as to whether coal is contraband."[41]

A major international incident soon arose concerning a neutral provisioning a belligerent when Spain attempted to send a relief squadron to the Philippines through the Suez Canal in June, 1898. From May of that year, a Spanish naval squadron had been preparing in Cadiz to render aid to the beleaguered Spanish garrison and population in the Philippines[42]. This was a fact that was most assuredly known to the former U.S. Consuls in Spain, who upon commencement of hostilities simply moved to Gibraltar from Jerez de la Frontera (Vice-Consul Hall) and Cádiz (Consul Carroll). There they continued their spying activities, a fact that was known but quite obviously tolerated by the British authorities.[43] This was only one of several situations that gave credence to Spanish claims regarding subtle, and not so subtle, violations by Great Britain of its allegedly neutral status.

In any event, on June 15 Admiral Cámara, the head of the relief squadron, received orders to leave for the Philippines the following day via the Suez Canal.[44] The squadron that left Cadiz on the 16th was composed of the armored cruisers *Pelayo* and *Carlos V*, the former being the flag ship, accompanied by the auxiliary cruisers *Patriota* and *Rápido*, each loaded with 3,000 tons of coal. These four ships were supposed to travel all the way to the Philippines. A second group, comprised of three torpedo boats, the *Audaz*, the *Osado,* and the *Prosperina*, were to go only as far as Port Said. They were in such poor condition that they had to be towed or sailed most of the way. It is thought that they were taken along mainly to impress the crowd that saw the fleet off at quay side in Cadiz.[45] Several ships –the *Buenos Aires*, the *Isla de Panay*, the *Colón*, and the *Covadonga*– were loaded with troop reinforcements. Two mail ships, the *San Agustín* and the *San Francisco*, which had been converted into colliers, also joined the relief flotilla.[46] Another group of ships left at the same time, also to impress the public, but headed for Cuba. Several days later, two more ships recently launched for mail service but also converted to colliers for the trip, left Cadiz to meet the fleet at Port Said. These were the *San Ignacio de Loyola* and the *Isla de Luzón*.

On 23 June, that is, three days before the Spanish squadron arrived in Port Said, the U.S. consul general in Egypt went to see the British governor general, Lord Cromer, to seek his aid in impeding the procurement of coal and supplies by the Spanish fleet.[47] The consul-general proposed that Lord Cromer approach the Egyptian authorities and convince them to apply the same neutrality rules as would be enforced in a British port under international law.

At this point in time, that is 1898, Egypt was still technically part of the Ottoman Empire having been returned to the empire in 1802 after Napoleon's invasion. But things were not as they appeared, for after a revolt in 1882 by Arabi Pacha, the British had occupied Egypt and established a de facto protectorate. Although Egypt was theoretically governed by the Khedive under the authority of the Sultan in Constantinople, the real power was wielded by the British governor-general.

There were two other factors to be taken into account. First was the fact that Turkey had not declared its neutrality,[48] and second, the Suez Canal was internationalized by virtue of the Treaty of 1888,[49] Article 4 of which prohibited canal authorities from rendering assistance to the warships of belligerent nations except under strictly limited circumstances. Nor could ships of belligerent nations remain in Port Said or use its road except in cases of *force majeure*.

Unfamiliar with the legal implications of what was being asked of him by the Americans, Lord Cromer immediately notified the Foreign Office and sought instructions.[50] He was promptly informed to advise the Egyptian government to refuse coal to the Spanish ships if they declared their intention to proceed to the Philippines.[51]

As expected, the Spanish squadron arrived at Port Said on June 25 and requested berths from the Suez Canal authorities.[52] On the following day Lord Cromer telegraphed Lord Salisbury:

> Acting upon my suggestion, and after taking legal advice, the Egyptian Government has issued orders to the effect that, for the present, no coal is to be furnished. The fact of the coal contractors being French increases the difficulty of the situation, as a question of rights conferred by the Capitulations has to be considered in addition to that of the obligations of a neutral state...in a case of this kind the Capitulations must give place to the laws of neutrality.[53]

Meanwhile, the judicial adviser to the Egyptian Government stated that, in his opinion, the Spanish fleet should be given only enough coal to reach a place of safety.[54]

Lord Cromer telegraphed Lord Salisbury that although the Spanish Admiral had asked for three to six thousand tons of coal, "he was inclined to think that the Spaniards would in reality be rather glad to be delayed and hindered in their voyage...[it] being merely a demonstration in order to satisfy public opinion."[55] The French, he reported, were of the opinion that the Spaniards should be given the coal.[56]

In the meantime, the American consul-general was pressuring the British/Egyptians to give notice to the Spanish that they were to leave the Canal ports immediately.[57]

On the other side of the globe, the Spanish consul in Hong Kong was protesting to the British authorities that Philippine insurrectionist Emilio Aguinaldo and 17 other rebels had been taken from British territory in Hong Kong to an awaiting U.S. naval vessel, the *U.S.S. McCulloch*, just inside Chinese territorial waters, for transportation to the Philippines to lead an insurrection against the Spanish.[58]

Back in Egypt, the Spanish decided to move their vessels to waters outside of the Egyptian three-mile territorial limit to take on coal from barges. Upon learning of this stratagem, Lord Cromer informed Lord Salisbury, "I have warned the Egyptian Government not to allow coal carriers and barges to go outside and assist."[59] On July 4th, the Spanish fleet, its attempts to take on coal in the open seas having been frustrated, moved back into Port Said.[60]

The Spanish Minister of Foreign Affairs filed a formal complaint with Great Britain protesting the treatment given the Spanish Squadron in Suez.[61] At the same time, an internal Foreign Office minute attached to a confidential communication referred to "the *rapprochement* or *entente cordiale* which has come about between the United States of America and this country."[62]

The result of these maneuvers was that, on July 9, the Spanish squadron abandoned Suez and returned to Spain.[63]

What is sure is that, if one of the requirements of neutrality as understood in 1898 was impartiality,[64] it cannot be said that Great Britain, based on its own records, acted as a neutral throughout the Suez incident.[65]

This seems to have been a recurring problem with British actions, even before the beginning of the commencement of hostilities. On April 21, 1898, the Spanish torpedo boat, *Audaz*, was forced to enter Cork, Ireland, to carry out repairs. The authorities kept an eye on its activities while in port but decided to go no further as there were three U.S. warships in Hong Kong at the time and it did not want to be compromised in their regard by any action against the *Audaz*.[66]

At the same time, a situation arose with regard to the transit through Canadian waters of four U.S. vessels, two of them belonging to the U.S. Coast Guard, after the commencement of hostilities.[67] On April 6, the U.S. Government requested passage for the two U.S. Coast Guard ships and the other two U.S. vessels, then still under construction, from Lake Ontario through the St. Lawrence River and into the Atlantic. Permission was granted that same day, but due to ice in those waterways they were not able to move until several days after the war had commenced. In view of this, on April 23, the Canadian government asked the Colonial Office for instructions, indicating that it did not want to create bad feeling with the Americans. On that same day, Colonial Secretary Chamberlain requested an opinion from the Law Offices of the Crown, but without waiting for a reply it informed the Foreign Office that he wished to honor the approved transit permission as he did not want to antagonize the United States by an "unfriendly interpretation against them of the neutrality laws."[68] Notwithstanding Chamberlain's concerns, the Law Offices promptly (also on April 23) issued the opinion that passage of the U.S. vessels through Canadian waters would constitute a violation of Great Britain's neutrality.[69]

Nevertheless, the Foreign Office decided on April 25 to reconfirm authorization for the passage, and instructed its ambassador in Washington so to inform U.S. authorities, indicating that the permission was subject to the vessels taking on no more coal in Canadian ports than was needed to reach a U.S. port, not taking on additional crew or equipment, and providing they would proceed directly to U.S. territory without engaging in intervening hostile acts against the Spanish. These conditions were accepted and they were communicated to the captains of the ships on May 1 before their departure.

In the meantime, the Spanish Consul General Bonilla Martel in Montreal learned about the situation through the Canadian press and proceeded to protest not only this incident but a similar one involving the cruiser *U.S.S. Gresham*.[70] By this time, however, the matter was moot, as all the U.S. vessels had transited the St. Lawrence and cleared Canadian waters.

Another point of contention was the use of British communications facilities by the belligerents. One of the first hostile acts by the United States against Spain in Cuba was the cutting of underwater telegraph cables that led to and from Cuba. This was repeated in the Philippines. Thus, the only cable communication with Europe in the vicinity of the two theaters of war were in British territory, in Jamaica in the case of Cuba (see Maps 7 and 8), and in Hong Kong in the case of the Philippine Islands (see Map 11). The British took the position that their cable facilities were available for use by the belligerents, provided their transmissions did not involve military or naval operations but were limited to giving news of the progress of the conflict.

The first case in contention arose when the Spanish troopship *Alfonso XIII* arrived in Barbados on May 2 on its way to Havana. The U.S. consul there was prevented from cabling this information to Washington, which led to a protest by the United States.[71] The Legal Office of the Crown advised that the Governor of Barbados had acted wrongly, because the impediment only applied when a belligerent ship attempted to communicate information, but not when a consul was transmitting the same information from his station, an extraordinary interpretation indeed.[72]

Interestingly, in similar circumstances, the Governor of Jamaica received an altogether different opinion when on June 7 he reported that the U.S. Admiral in Cuba was sending his naval dispatches to Jamaica for transmission from Kingston to Washington.[73] Chamberlain advised that "no action [was] required unless [a] complaint [was] received from the Spanish Government."

The situation in the Philippines was more complex, as was reflected in the inconsistent British solution to the problem. At the beginning of the conflict, after the cable from Manila to Hong Kong was cut by Dewey's forces, the cable company in Hong Kong decided it would accept for transmission all communications brought to Hong Kong by either of the belligerents. On May 12, the Spanish government put a stop to that by informing the cable company that there would no longer be such a service to both sides, an action which it could take because it was the owner of the cable concession between Manila and Hong Kong. As a result, the United States requested that it be allowed to lay its own cable to Hong Kong, a petition which was rejected by the British. Meanwhile, in Cuba, U.S. ships flying the Spanish flag attempted to get close enough to the shore to cut the cable from Guantanamo to Spain, which caused the Spanish press to urge retaliation by severing the cables from the United States to Europe,[74] but that action was not carried out. The situation back in Hong Kong remained unclear, with British cable companies at times refusing to transmit Spanish traffic[75] and at other times doing so.

One case above all others demonstrates the double standard of the British in dealing with the United States and Spain during the 1898 conflict. This was the so-called Carranza-Dubosc affair,[76] which can be compared to that of the U.S. spy/consuls operating out of Gibraltar to which we have already referred. When hostilities began, in April, two of the members of the Spanish legation in Washington, the First Secretary, Dubosc, and the naval attaché, Lieutenant Carranza, went to Montreal, undoubtedly to keep an eye from there on what was transpiring in the United States. This was made clear as a result of a letter published in the June 6, 1898 edition of the *Washington Post*, allegedly written by Lieutenant Carranza and sent from Montreal to a José Gómez Ismay, making reference to an espionage network against the United States, organized and directed by Carranza from Canada. What followed is best described as high comedy rather than tragedy, with the parties resorting to melodrama as needed.

Already, on June 2, the U.S. government had called the matter to the attention of the British government,[77] which referred to the incident in an internal memorandum as "a flagrant abuse of neutral territory", demanding that Lieutenant Carranza be asked to leave Canada "with the least possible delay." Carranza then filed an accusation against a person named Keller for allegedly stealing the letter, but the charge was dismissed by a Canadian magistrate for lack of evidence. Thereafter, on June 7, Keller turned around and filed criminal and civil libel charges against Carranza and Dubosc, and was able to convince the Supreme Court of Quebec to issue an order detaining Carranza and Dubose to assure their presence at trial.[78] On that same day, the Spanish Foreign

Minister Rascón filed a protest with the Foreign Office, which promptly replied through its second in command, Sanderson, that the matter was outside the control of the British executive branch and would have to be dealt with directly by the Spanish consul-general in Montreal.

Meanwhile, in London, Lord Salisbury concentrated his efforts on trying to find proof of the alleged spy ring as the case escalated into a cause célèbre and was discussed in Parliament. Ambassador Pauncefote in Washington, in search of evidence that the letter was not a forgery as claimed by Carranza, was shown what was purported to be the original document, which according to the U.S. Secret Service was purloined by one of its agents from Carranza's room in Canada. The letter was on the official stationary of the Spanish Legation in Montreal, and was written in Spanish. In it, Carranza stated that he was engaging in *vigilancia* of the activities of the United States, which properly translated means that he was "watching," but which instead was interpreted by Washington, through incompetence or bad faith, as "engaging in a spy-system."[79] Notwithstanding that crucial point and the fact that the apparent breach of neutrality (as well as the crime of burglary) was committed by an agent of the United States, not by Lieutenant Carranza, Lord Salisbury decided to end this embarrassing incident by ejecting both Carranza and Dubosc from British territory. To the suggestion that Carranza's prosecution be continued based on the information provided by the U.S. Secret Service, Salisbury replied:

> If we prosecute the man on confidential information given us by the United States Government, we must not expect to receive confidential information ever again. I would certainly drop the matter.

Drop it they did. But Dubosc did not, for in his case there did not appear to be any reason for his expulsion. Although there was a half-hearted protest by the Spanish Minister of State, and Dubosc filed a civil action in London, neither avenue was pursued for long, probably out of exhaustion, if for no other reason.

Overall, there appear to be valid grounds for concluding that British non-belligerency was decidedly biased in favor of the United States during the Spanish-American War.

Germany's bellicose behavior

Germany's actions during the period of hostilities were the most aggressive, militarily speaking, of all the non-belligerents. It is probably fair to say that they were an extension of the hyper-active foreign policy in which Germany engaged during the latter part of the 19th century.

As regards the Spanish-American War, the most serious incidents were those between Germany's Far East Squadron, under the command of Admiral Otto von Diederichs, and the U.S. Pacific Fleet, under Admiral Dewey, in Manila Bay. Rather in the nature of a cold war,[80] they could easily have escalated into a shooting war because of actions that, even with the passage of time and the contemporaneous denials of Admiral von Diederichs,[81] appear to have been deliberate provocations on the part of the Germans.[82]

On May 2, 1898, the day after Dewey's destruction of the Spanish fleet at Manila, the first of several non-United States naval vessels –the British gunboat *Linnet*[83]– arrived in that port. It was joined on May 8 by the British armed cruiser *Immortalité*, commanded by Captain Edward Chichester, an officer who would play a crucial role in defusing the events that followed.[84] Although in the ensuing weeks Manila would be visited by warships from France,[85] Japan,[86] and Austro-Hungary,[87] and other British ships,[88] none would be involved in incidents like those brought about by Germany's Admiral von Diederichs. Russia was the only major European power not to send a warship to the Philippines, most likely because she welcomed the American invasion as a possible distraction from her with regards to her main Far East competitors, Great Britain and Japan.[89]

In response to an order issued by Kaiser Wilhelm II on April 28 to protect German nationals in the Philippines, the second class cruiser *Irene* and the third class cruiser *Cormoran* arrived in Manila on May 6 and 9, respectively.[90]

On entering Manila Bay, the *Irene* ignored the blockade, forcing one of the U.S. blockading vessels to fire a shot across her bows, which caused her to come to a stop. Later her captain claimed not to have been aware that a blockade was in effect.[91] Nevertheless, when the *Cormoran* arrived two days later in the middle of the night, a similar incident occurred requiring a shot from the *U.S.S. Raleigh* and boarding by a U.S. naval officer, who thereafter assigned her an anchorage at Cavite.[92]

Several days later, Prince Henry of Prussia, then commanding the Asiatic Squadron, cabled German Foreign Minister von Bulow from Hong Kong to inform him that a German merchant from Manila has stated in a way most worthy of credence that a rebellion was justified in the Philippines and would succeed; that the natives would gladly place themselves under the protection of a European power, especially Germany.[93]

A few days later, another cable arrived, this time from the German consul in Manila, Friedrick von Kruger, purportedly corroborating the information contained in the telegram to Prince Henry and indicating that the insurgents did not believe they could manage a republic but would be best off as a kingdom, and that

> Existing indications are that the matter will probably termi- nate with an offer of the throne to a German prince. Ought the thing be allowed to develop freely, or should it be waived aside?"[94]

Von Bulow advised Wilhelm that Admiral von Diederichs be sent to Manila, where he could observe the situation first hand and report on the sentiments and position of the natives. Thus on June 2, the Kaiser ordered von Diederichs, who was in Japan refitting his ship, the *Kaiser*,

> to proceed to Manila in order to form personally an opinion on the Spanish situation, mood of the natives, and foreign influence upon political changes.... Also protect with the Squadron German interests in the West-Caroline Islands, Palaos Islands. Send a ship [there] as soon as the Americans do the same.[95]

In my view, this and other actions by the Germans all demonstrate that Germany was not such an innocent bystander in the Manila Bay incidents as she later claimed, but rather was executing substantive plans directed at gaining a foothold in the Archipelago.[96] Von Bulow was forthcoming when he stated on July 1, 1898, that "His Majesty the Emperor deems it a principal object of German policy to leave unused no opportunity which may arise from the Spanish-American War to obtain maritime fulcra in East Asia."[97] It would seem that the German presence in the area was part of these policies of opportunistic imperialism,[98] in this case also aimed at containment of the expansionist designs of the upstart "Yankee Republic."[99]

Von Diederichs arrived at Manila Bay on June 12 aboard the first-class cruiser *Kaiserin Augusta*. When he entered Manila Bay, von Diederichs was stopped at Corregidor by a blockading vessel and assigned anchorage at Cavite. Despite this, he proceeded directly to Manila, where he fired a 21-gun salute with the Spanish flag flying at his mainmast. He then crossed the Bay to Cavite, where he fired a 13-gun salute as he passed Dewey's flagship, which Dewey did not answer. Von Diederichs sent an officer to Dewey's ship requesting an explanation for Dewey's apparent breach of naval etiquette, to which Dewey responded that he should have been saluted first considering that he was in command of the bay and holding it under strict blockade.[100] There was no apology or gun salute, and German-American relations only deteriorated thereafter.

From the outset, there was a marked difference in the actions of the Germans from those of the British who had preceded them. If the British, who were the biggest foreign investors in the Philippines, were conspicuously friendly towards the Americans, the Germans' contacts with the Spanish were equally extensive, although, in fairness to von Diederichs, he tried to discourage reports, spread mostly by the Spaniards, that the Germans were in Manila Bay to help Spain against the United States. Nevertheless, the Spanish governor general proposed to von Diederichs that the neutral powers take Manila *in deposito*, a proposal which was rejected outright by von Diederichs as being beyond his warrant.[101]

There were also rumors of the Germans assisting the Spaniards in improvising torpedo boats on the Passig River (adjacent to Manila), leading to a German launch nearly being sunk by U.S. gunfire when she approached the *Olympia* without lights in the middle of the night.[102]

Admiral Dewey was decidedly nervous[103] at the arrival of the Germans and at their repeated refusal to abide by the rules of the blockade set down by the blockading country, the United States. On the day after von Diederichs's arrival at Manila, Dewey cabled the Navy Department:

The German Commander-in Chief arrived today. Three Germans, two British, one French, one Japanese man-of-war, now in port; another German man-of-war is expected. I request the departure of the *Monadnock* and *Monterey* be expedited.[104]

The two ships referred to were both heavily armed monitors (each with two twelve-inch and two ten-inch guns).

Although Dewey's own force of six cruisers and two smaller craft was superior to von Diederichs' at that point, the situation changed with the arrival on June 18 of the German cruisers *Kaiser*, and two days later, *Prinzess Wilhelm*. The German fleet was now 20% stronger than Dewey's, with the *Kaiser* at 7531 tons, the only fully armored vessel in either fleet, and *Kaiserin Augusta* at 6331 tons, both outclassing Dewey's largest ship, the *Olympia*, at 5800 tons.[105] The size of this fleet, when compared with the commercial interests of Germany in the Philippines would appear to be not only out of proportion, but seemed unduly provocative, particularly in the tense atmosphere before the fall of Manila and the possible arrival of the relieving Spanish fleet still attempting to transit the Suez Canal. Von Diederichs' after-the-fact explanation about the strength of the German naval contingent in Manila[106] was that the concentration of the German fleet in Manila coincided with the arrival of a German relief ship with replacement crews.

Incidents involving the Germans continued to build up tension with the Americans. Apparently under German supervision, the Spanish 10-inch batteries in front of Manila where backed by a high embankment to protect the city from shells aimed at the battery.[107]

Although there is no evidence that it was anything but coincidental, shortly after news was received of Cámara's squadron reaching the Suez, von Diederichs moved his ships from their assigned anchorage to Marivele at the entrance to Manila Bay, across the Boca Chica from Corregidor. This would have been the probable place of entry to the Bay of Cámara's squadron. Furthermore, while at Marivele, von Diederichs proceeded to hold landing drills and moved his quarters ashore into the abandoned residence of the Spanish colonel. He caused Dewey even more stress by having German troops take over an abandoned Spanish hospital and to proceed to establish their barracks there.

Admiral Dewey came over in the *McCulloch* personally to check this situation and he took note of the absence of the *Irene*.[108] The next day, information was received that the *Irene* was at Subic Bay, trying to prevent Filipino insurgents from capturing the Spanish Garrison at Isla Grande. The *Raleigh* and *Concord* were dispatched, and as they arrived, the *Irene* left in hurry, giving them a wide berth. The situation ashore was as reported, and the *Raleigh* took over the Spanish garrison and transported it on parole to Manila.[109]

Meanwhile, public opinion in the United States –having been fed truths, half-truths and outright fabrications throughout the War by a yellow press– was aroused by reports of the presence of the large German fleet in the Philippines and of its activities there. The German press, in turn, took exception to the criticism of German actions appearing in the American press.[110]

The Subic Bay incident brought to a head what Admiral Dewey believed to be the Germans' deliberate violations of its neutrality, and he thus decided on a course of action to confront Admiral von Diederichs. Consequently, on July 7, he sent Lieutenant Thomas M. Brumby to von Diederichs' ship with a summary of the U.S.'s complaints since the commencement of the blockade. The German admiral expressed surprise at the allegations and "disclaimed any intention of interfering in the least with Admiral Dewey's forces or plans of operation."[111]

On July 10, von Diederichs formally replied through Flag-Lieutenant Hintze, who visited Admiral Dewey aboard the *Olympia*. Lieutenant Hintze had instructions from von Diederichs to register a counter-protest by bringing up the issue of the *Irene* being stopped and boarded on June 27 off Corregidor. Dewey's response was explosive, according to Lieutenant Hintze's own account:

> Why, I [Dewey] shall stop each vessel whatever may be her colors! And if she does not stop I shall fire at her! And that means war, do you know, Sir? And I tell you if Germany wants war, all right, we are ready. With the English, I have not the slightest difficulty, they always communicate with me, etc. Admiral Dewey became more and more excited. When the phrases, "If Germany wants war," etc., began to recur, the flag lieutenant [Hintze] left.[112]

Von Diederichs apparently realized that Dewey was under great strain and that he had pushed him further than was wise. Dewey in the meanwhile cooled off and replied to Diederichs in writing on July 11, stating that as commander of a blockading power he had the right to stop any vessel and make "such inquiries as are necessary to establish her identity."[113] This was interpreted by von Diederichs to mean that Dewey was claiming the right to board any vessel, whereupon he communicated with the other warships in the harbor seeking their interpretation on this point. Those that gave definitive answers to his inquiry, and these included Captain Chichester, agreed that ordinary rules of visit and search did not apply to men-of-war, even in a blockade.[114]

On July 14, Dewey backtracked to the extent of writing that by "inquiries" to "establish identity" he did not necessarily mean to board and search, but rather to seek such information through ordinary means of communication between ships, and this led von Diederichs to accept the principle that Dewey might board his ships at night when identification was otherwise difficult.[115]

This had been a critical period in German-American relations in the Philippines, for von Diederichs had given explicit orders to repel any boarding, even with the use of force, except at night, and any misstep on either side could have led to an armed confrontation and degenerated into war.

The full impact of Captain Chichester's presence in Manila Bay as a calming influence must not be underestimated. It went beyond his good offices. Undoubtedly von Diederichs suspected that, in the event of an outbreak in hostilities, it was probable that the British would side with the Americans, in which case the Germans would be greatly out gunned.

Dewey's own position was strengthened considerably by the news of the destruction of Cervera's fleet on July 3, and of Cámara's recall from Suez on July 5. Furthermore, on June 30, the first of four troop transports arrived in Manila together with the cruiser *Charleston*, which carried much needed ammunition aboard. These arrivals were soon followed by the departure of the German *Irene* on July 9, and the coming of the second (on July 17) and third (on July 31) U.S. transports, and of the monitor *Monterey* on August 4th. With these reinforcements, Dewey had for the first time clear-cut naval and military superiority over the Germans in Manila Bay.

Although relations between the two fleets improved, in part because these altered circumstances gave the Germans pause, there was still one last episode to come.

On August 7, Dewey notified all non-U.S. ships anchored off Manila proper that the battle to capture Manila by the U.S. forces was about to begin, and that they should move out of the line of fire by the 9th. The British and Japanese moved to Cavite, eight miles across Manila Bay, with their respective refugee-laden steamers. At the same time, the two French cruisers, as well as their three civilian-laden vessels, moved past the mouth of the Passig River, to the north of the city. Three of the remaining German men-of-war also moved there. The fourth, the *Cormoran*, was left in charge of their four steamers laded with civilians at Mariveles Bay, 20 miles south of Manila.

On August 13, Dewey's fleet left Cavite to bombard Manila's defenses in preparation for taking the City. As the U.S. fleet passed the *Immortalité*, the British ship's band struck up the *Star-Spangled Banner*. That vessel, and then the *Iphigenia*, followed the Americans to Manila, where they found that the Germans had stationed themselves in a location that was inconvenient for the U.S. fleet's operations. To prevent further friction, the two British vessels proceeded to anchor between the German and American fleets. Once more, Captain Chichester acted as a moderating force between the two antagonist forces.[116]

By late afternoon of August 13, Manila had fallen. Immediately thereafter, the cruiser *Kaiserin Augusta* left the harbor for Hong Kong, carrying aboard the Spanish governor general and his family. When they arrived, the U.S. protested the action. The captain of the German ship answered that the Americans had consented to the departure of the Spanish captain-general, but no record exists of this "consent."[117]

Between August 14 and 15, all naval ships returned to their anchorages at Cavite. As the *Immortalité* passed the U.S. flag flying over Manila, it fired a 21-gun salute, much to the discomfiture of the Germans.

Thereafter, on August 16, von Diederichs received his marching orders and left the Philippines never to return.

Germany's actions in the Philippines, more than those of any other nation connected with the Spanish-American War, had disastrous long-term consequences. Its clumsy diplomacy and its attempt at gaining a foothold in those islands not only proved unsuccessful, but they failed at the cost of alerting the American public to Germany's opportunism and of creating ill-will towards Germany. At the same time, they contrasted with British attitudes and actions, which served to foster a sense of gratitude to and closeness with Great Britain. In the long run, for Germany this was a most unfortunate consequence.

Germany's meddling during the Spanish-American War, the highest point of which was its interference in Manila, was to prove pivotal in German-American political relations before the First World War.[118] They undoubtedly would have a permanent negative influence on the American public's perception of Germany.

On the other hand, the German public was kept in the dark about the actions of its government in Manila. This was partly because the overwhelming majority of the German press adhered to the official version that Germany had acted within the bounds of strict neutrality. In fact, it denied that there had been any German-American tension in the Philippines. Count von Bulow even asserted that "communication between our naval officers and the American naval officers was free from any kind of tension, and guided by a spirit of mutual courtesy."[119] So the German public remained largely unaware of the deeply negative impression that German conduct in Manila had on their American counterparts, an impression that was fueled by the American press.

On the other hand, German officialdom used the Spanish naval and military disasters in both Cuba and the Philippines to support their arguments for building up their naval programs. Admiral von Tirpitz argued in the Reichstag: "The Spanish-American War has proven in a frightening manner the consequences for a nation which has important naval interests but no means to defend them."[120] To which, Rosa Luxemburg, then a recent arrival at the German political arena responded:

> According to our Government, what has promoted the idea of further fleet enlargement in Germany since 1898? Its just amazing: The Spanish-American War! A war in which a dissolute, worthless, and bankrupt government lost its decadent, exploited colonies; from this war Germany learned that it needs to double its fleet for defense of her colonies? With revelations of this kind, our Government has lost the last of any confidence that remained.[121]

The fact is that, for the first time in history, the United States was regarded as a serious naval power by the major European countries, and thus, shortly after Rosa Luxemberg's caustic speech, the German Imperial Naval Office began planning for a naval war against the United States.[122]

Japan becomes a Pacific adversary to be watched

Japanese activity during the Spanish-American War was directed principally at the Philippine Islands. It included both overt and covert actions.

As previously indicated, the Japanese Army and Navy both had observers with American troops in Cuba. Coincidentally, although it is not generally known, several Japanese sailors were killed aboard the *Maine* when it exploded in Havana, although these were part of the ship's complement as mess boys.[123] The Japanese also had observers in the Philippines who, as will be shown presently, did more than just observe.

Although Japan declared its neutrality on May 2, 1898, it proceeded to send four cruisers to Manila "to watch operations and protect Japanese subjects."[124] With only seven Japanese subjects in Manila at the time, this worked out to one cruiser for every two Japanese nationals!

The fact is that Japan was herself interested in gaining a foothold in the Philippines.[125] There was obviously much logic to this (see Map 6): the southward projection of the Japanese island chain leads directly to Formosa (Taiwan), which Japan had just acquired in 1895, and if the projection is extended further south, one ends in Luzon, the northernmost island of the Philippine Archipelago.

However, Japan was not yet ready to engage the U.S. in a major challenge,[126] having already had recent confrontations elsewhere in the Pacific with the United States.[127] This strategy of avoidance was partly because Japan needed U.S. support, or at least its acquiescence, to Japan's, China and Korea ventures. Japan was also aware that Great Britain favored the United States in its war against Spain, and did not want to antagonize Great Britain at a time when it also needed British backing to continue its activities on the Chinese mainland. This strategy bore fruit in 1902 with the signing of the Anglo-Japanese defense treaty needed by Japan to neutralize France in the event of a Russo-Japanese war (which came in 1905).

Baron Hayashi's words in mapping out Japan's strategy in its rise to power were not only prophetic but were mirrored in Japan's actions at this time:

> At present Japan must keep calm and sit tight, so as to lull suspicions nurtured against her; during this time the foundation of national power must be consolidated; and we must watch and wait for the opportunity in the Orient that will surely come one day. When this day arrives, Japan will decide her own fate.[128]

This strategy notwithstanding, the Japanese engaged in a series of *sub rosa* acts which were clearly in violation of its avowed neutrality and were indicative of its desire to expand southward. In fact, these could very well have been classified as belligerent acts against the United States.

Apart from Japan's national interests, these activities were fueled by the America's initial ambivalence and equivocation as to its intentions regarding the Philippines. This hesitancy was caused by the intense public debate in the United States as to the fate of the Philippines.

There had been a connection between Japan and the Philippines dating back at least to the days of the Filipino insurrections against the Spanish. In fact, in 1896, Andrés Bonifacio unsuccessfully attempted to induce Japan to aid in the Filipino revolt.[129] Later, Japan again came into the picture when a settlement of the revolt was proposed, which included deporting the rebel leaders to Japan or mainland China.[130] As previously discussed, they chose to be exiled in Hong Kong.

And in 1898 after the Spanish-American War started, Emilio Aguinaldo and most of the Filipino Junta that had been exiled to Hong Kong, were transported from Hong Kong to the Philippines by the U.S. Navy to help the United States in their efforts against Spain.[131] Aguinaldo and his people expected that independence would follow Spain's defeat,[132] and thus joined the fight against Spain on the U.S. side. The Americans were less than forthright as to the quid pro quo to be given in exchange for this help.

If the Americans were hesitant on this issue, Aguinaldo sought to prepare the ground: on May 24, 1898, he issued the first of a series of independence declarations indicating his intentions regarding the war against Spain and his motives for joining the Americans.

In the meantime, no decision had been reached in official Washington as to the future of the Philippines, and the United States continued to equivocate. It was during this period of uncertainty that indications began to appear that Japan was engaging in questionable activities regarding Aguinaldo and his movement.[133]

Relations between the United States and Aguinaldo's forces were exacerbated with the arrival of large numbers of American troops in preparation for the assault on Manila. Aguinaldo correctly concluded that with the presence of these large contingents on Filipino soil, there was a heightened possibility that the United States intended to remain after the hostilities with Spain ended. He decided to prepare for this possibility.

Aguinaldo did two things. First, he sent two representatives to Japan, Mariano Ponce and Faustino Lichauco, with instructions to contact authorities there and seek aid. Second, he ordered Felipe Agoncillo, the Junta's representative in Hong Kong, to purchase arms with the money that remained on deposit there from the agreement ending the insurrection against Spain in 1897.[134]

Captured insurgent papers[135] establish July 8, 1898, as the first documented contact between the Japanese and insurgent representatives, although it is probable that there were earlier undocumented exchanges. On that date, there was a brief message from Teodoro Sandico, the Junta's secretary, to a Captain Faquisa of the Japanese Consulate in Manila setting up an appointment to meet.[136]

Elsewhere, on July 17, Ponce and Lichauco met in Yokohama, Japan, with Colonel Fukushima, the chief of military intelligence for the Japanese General Staff, and provided him with the answers to questions he had asked previously regarding the status of Aguinaldo's forces, particularly in Luzon.[137]

On July 20, Agoncillo, using the code name "Respe," replied to a message from Aguinaldo that had been taken to Hong Kong on a Japanese cruiser.[138] In it, he reported about a communication from the Junta's representatives in Japan informing him of a meeting in Yokohama with the "superintendent" of that city and the vice-president of "the Mikado." The later indicated that Japan would support the independence movement and had placed 200,000 rifles at its disposal. There was to be a meeting with Fukushima to arrange for delivery. It also reported that the Japanese believed that "the Americans are thinking of keeping the Philippines."

On August 9, Teodoro Sandico reported to Aguinaldo that "the Japanese Captain" had given him letters of recommendation to the Japanese consul in Hong Kong and to his chief in Yokohama, where the question of arms and other matters of interest was to be discussed.[139] The Japanese captain also told him that the attack on Manila was to take place in three days. He also stated that he did not think the American soldiers and men were worth much, and that it appeared that the Americans had "lost their good feeling towards [Filipinos]." Last, the captain told him about a valuable topographic map that was in the hands of a certain Almonte, who lived at No. 36 Saludo Street, and that he was offering it to the highest bidder. He recommended that they "take it or buy it," so that it would not fall into the wrong hands.

On July 15, a Captain Y. Tokizawa, an artillery officer with the Japanese General Staff,[140] was sent by Sandico to Aguinaldo. Sandico reported to Aguinaldo that "the Japanese captain...advises us to avoid conflict until [the Spanish-American] peace is declared." The captain assured the insurgents that a desire to recognize Philippine independence prevailed in Japan. From observing the Americans during the attack on Manila, the Japanese captain was of the opinion that "Americans are not courageous and that they are badly disciplined." He also advised the Filipinos to fight in large numbers of from 1,000 to 2,000 men at a time.

On August 20, Agoncillo gave his first negative report about Japanese support, stating that judging from what was said by the insurgents' representatives in Japan, he did not think that they would get any help from Japan against the United States, but probably would get such support against Spain.[141]

An undated letter to Aguinaldo from Sandico, delivered to him by the Japanese captain's interpreter, informed Aguinaldo that in a few days he would be visited by a high ranking Japanese official, who wanted to consult with them and would appear incognito.[142] The note also indicated that "[t]he Japanese Admiral and Captain wish me to tell you that it is advisable to take Manila at all costs and also to send forces to the Islands of Mindanao and Visayas before these are taken by the Americans."[143]

The next few communications give a glimpse into the nefarious world of international arms dealing.

On August 20 Ponce and Lichauco wrote "Mr. W. Jones," the code name for Apacible in Hong Kong, discussing ongoing negotiations in Yokohama with an arms dealer named Mr. Robertson for the purchase of 40,000 Werndle rifles, used by the Austrian army, and 200,000 rounds of ammunition.[144] They recommended that Mausers be purchased instead.

On that same day, Ponce and Lichauco wrote Agoncillo in Hong Kong informing him that the Japanese did not want to take a "definite step of any kind as long as America has not clearly defined its decision with reference to the Philippines [because]...they do not wish to break with America, for that country brought them their present civilization and progress." They reported to Agoncillo that the Japanese were aware of the "spirit of the [Peace] Protocol" signed on August 12 in Washington between the American Government and the French Ambassador representing Spain, in which the future of the Philippines was left to further negotiations. The letter went on to analyze the internal politics of Japan, where elections had just been held, indicating that "these politicians are occupied with internal problems," including a deficit of "thirty millions," which the new chief of the government, Count Okuma, was opposed to covering by new taxes. All of these problems, Ponce and Lichauco indicated, were factors that worked against their receiving aid from Japan.

Additional letters dated May 23 and 24 were dispatched to "Mr. Jones" in Hong Kong, in which the rejection of the Werndle rifles was acknowledged and a new proposal was made for the purchase of 30,000 Mauser rifles at $10 apiece, delivered in Yokohama or some other Japanese port such as Kobe or Nagasaki. A nebulous Englishman, a Mr. Nortman, "an old friend of the Filipinos" who was the editor of the Japan *Gazette* and the correspondent of various periodicals in London, New York and Bombay, would be used to transport the rifles to their ultimate destination in the Philippines. He had reportedly lived in Japan for twelve years.[145] A Mr. Castro is also mentioned as having found several individuals who would guarantee the success of the expedition, including a Mr. R. Bauld, representing Vickers Sons and Maxim, both arms manufacturers, in London, as well as a General Merly, "of the Chinese Infantry," and Messrs. Tegle & Co., "importers of firearms" – a motley crew indeed.

The May 24 letter revises the May 23 offer, indicating that 20,000 Mausers could be had for $7.50 apiece delivered in Yokohama, or $9 per piece at "any point within the Philippines that may be designated," but no responsibility would be accepted for the risks that might occur in Philippine waters nor in landing the arms. If 30,000 rifles were purchased the price was reduced to $8.83 apiece delivered in the Philippines. "Mr. Jones" was informed that "[t]he parties making the offer are importers of arms for the Japanese Government, belonging to an English firm."

On August 30, "Mr. Jones" is given an update on how things were going in Japan. Colonel Fukushima advised the Filipinos to make known to his government all that the Philippine Provisional Government desired of Japan.[146] The colonel indicated that he believed the expedition was entirely feasible and that it might be possible to purchase Japanese Murata rifles directly from the Government arsenal at $10 apiece. Colonel Fukushima assured them that the expedition would be "un-officially" permitted by the Japanese Government. The letter then entered into a detailed analysis of Japanese politics and how public opinion was forming against the disposition of the Philippines in the Paris negotiations without participation by Japan. Further intrigues by former French Minister of Foreign Affairs, Messr. Moret and the Austrian Ambassador to Madrid, Count Dubsky, were also discussed.

In an undated letter to Aguinaldo, Sandico reported on a meeting with "the commander of a Japanese war ship and other officers" regarding their views on Filipino independence. They were non-committal.[147]

A September 4th letter from Lichauco and Ponce to "Mr. Jones" deals with new offers from the arms dealers of the Japanese Government regarding the Gras rifle which at $12 per rifle and $6 per 100 cartridges was deemed excessive. The writer also comments "that as it is possible to purchase from the government itself the arms they are at presently using, everything else being equal, it would be better to purchase from the government."[148]

On September 4, Sandico informed Aguinaldo that the Japanese consul in Manila had received telegrams from his government indicating that it was very favorably disposed towards the insurgents and their agent assured him of the secret aid that would be forthcoming from Japan.[149]

A letter dated September 13 from the insurgents' representatives in Japan to Apolinario Mabini,[150] indicated that

> the Japanese Government is much inclined to favor our cause, only fearing the possibility of a conflict with a friendly nation like the Yankee one. This has not prevented them, however, from giving us permission to buy arms from their factories to be used in our revolution.[151]

Another letter dated September 16 to Mabini extolled the Mutata rifle and talked about "a man who promises to deliver them to our coasts," for which it was recommended that a schooner be purchased for about 10,000 or 15,000 pesos. The man who made these arrangements was Colonel Fukushima.[152]

On September 18, Faustino Lichauco was replaced by Francisco Rivera in Japan and sent to Hong Kong.[153] The delegates were given general instructions regarding their negotiations with the Japanese Government, recognition of their status as belligerents under international law, and validation of Philippine independence.

A communication dated September 25 from a "J.A. Ramos" in Yokohama to a "Gonzalo" made reference to a meeting with high officials in Tokyo to which neither Ponce or Lichauco had access, in which "Ramos" was told that the Japanese would provide "all sorts of arms and all munitions of war" that the Filipino's needed, but that they should "put no confidence in the good treatment and promises of those who do their utmost to deceive [them]." The Filipinos were advised to "accept nothing but complete independence."[154]

On October 4, Apacible informed Aguinaldo that he was sending Gregorio Agoncillo to Japan with $200,000 to purchase arms.[155]

The captured records contain an undated copy of a letter from Aguinaldo to the Emperor of Japan, presenting him with "a saber and military decoration of Spanish origin."[156] There is no record that this gift was actually received by the emperor or anyone on his behalf.

On October 31, Sandico reported to Aguinaldo regarding a banquet given at the Japanese consulate in Manila and attended by the whole Japanese colony. There prevailed a spirit of "friendliness of the Japanese towards the Filipino people" and their desire for independence.

The dining room was decorated with crossed Japanese and Filipino flags made by Consul Takiwana himself and distributed by him afterwards to those present. The numerous speeches by the Japanese present ended all with a cheer of "Long live the Independence of the Philippines."[157]

On that same day, Secretary of State Rufus Day announced the intention of the United States to annex all of the Philippines and to pay a sum to Spain as compensation.[158]

On November 10, Ponce wrote Apacible that the expected fall of the Japanese cabinet was a serious setback to the insurrectionists' aspirations. However, he gave somewhat conflicting information when he reported that Ramos had been called to Tokyo by Colonel Fukushima, who explained the situation and introduced him to Count Katsu, an influential politician in the court. Katsu indicated that the new cabinet would be dominated by "the military element, which sympathizes with us." Ponce reported that the Japanese government had brought the Filipino delegation into contact with Lung Tai Kuan, the secretary of the Chinese Reform Party, which was in exile and planning a revolution to restore the deposed Emperor Kwang Hsu. The Japanese took the view that Chinese reformers and Filipino revolutionaries might be able to aid each other.[159]

A letter dated November 28 reports on the arrival from Manila of Captain Tokizawa who would supposedly report favorably on the insurgents and their movement in the Philippines. Colonel Fukushima indicated that he saw no objection to the assignment of Captain Tokizawa to the insurgent army, who he thought would be of great help since he spoke Spanish and was sympathetic to the Filipino cause. But the request had to be made immediately, before Captain Tokizawa was posted elsewhere.[160]

On December 1, Ponce wrote Apacible in Hong Kong regarding the need to have the funds available from the letter of credit in the amount of 200,000 pesos, as Colonel Fukushima had informed him that the Cabinet was about to approve the sale of the arms. Arrangements had been made with a Mr. Suzuki, an Osaka merchant who was a friend of Count Aoki, the Minister of Foreign Affairs, who had a steamer which he offered for hire.[161]

On December 5, Rivero wrote Aguinaldo that the Japanese would not negotiate the 200,000 peso draft on a Hong Kong bank and that

Agoncillo was on his way to Hong Kong to attempt to personally fa-
cilitate the transaction. He also informed Aguinaldo that the Japanese
authorities were refusing to deal directly with the representatives of
the Filipino insurgency; they would only negotiate with José Ramos,
whom they held in high regard and to whom they gave "an allowance of
$40 a month." Ramos was called to Tokyo on an almost daily basis to be
consulted on Filipino affairs.[162]

On December 6, Ponce and Rivero again informed Apacible that they
could not negotiate the Hong Kong draft, and that a bill of exchange
must be sent on the Yokohama Species Bank Limited, as the Japanese
did not want any foreigners to know about the transfers of money. Ramos
was again called to Tokyo, where he was told that the Japanese Government had authorized the sale of 5,000 Murata rifles and ammunition.
The Junta representatives in Japan also recommended taking advantage
of the Japanese merchant's offer of a steamship, as "[l]ater when the
enemy's ships surround our coasts, it will be very difficult and very dangerous to find vessels."[163]

On December 7, Aguinaldo wrote Ponce instructing him to proceed
to negotiate a deal to purchase 10,000 Murata 5-shot rifles (at 13 pesos
each, or 130,000 pesos), 5 million cartridges (for 250,000 pesos), equipment to manufacture more ammunition (with Japanese instructors), and
inquire as to the cost of a mountain battery (with Japanese instructors
willing to serve with the Filipino army). He also asked Ponce to recruit
Japanese army officers to serve in units of artillery, cavalry, infantry, and
on the general staff and administrative corps. In a post script, he further
asked Ponce to inquire about "fixed and movable torpedoes, sub-ma-
rine (sic) mines, dynamite guns and Maxim guns, ten pieces with
2,000,000 cartridges and an intelligent (sic) personnel."[164]

Considering the limited funds at the disposal of the Junta in Hong
Kong, and what remained of the money that Spain had paid to Aguinaldo
and the *insurrectos* back in 1897, which at this point was only about 400,000
pesos, it is difficult to fathom what Aguinaldo was thinking about with
such grandiose schemes, particularly since not even the Junta's 200,000
peso check was being honored by the Japanese. It may be that he was
considering the possibility of exacting money in the way of "taxes" from
areas controlled by his movement.

Meanwhile, on December 10, a momentous event occurred that affected the insurgents fundamentally: the Peace Treaty was signed in Paris between Spain and the United States, in which, among other things, Spain ceded sovereignty over the Philippine Islands to the United States in exchange for payment of $20 million.[165] We will turn to the events surrounding the treaty presently, but it must be said here that the Filipinos were totally excluded from the treaty negotiations, a situation that merely added fuel to a fire that was already burning. Nevertheless the Treaty of Paris did have a major effect on the ongoing negotiations between the Junta and the Japanese.

Apacible wrote Aguinaldo on December 13 informing him of the finances of the Junta and recommending that Rivero be relieved of his post in Japan for some unspecified misconduct.[166]

The following day Apacible wrote Aguinaldo again concerning the purchase of 2,000 single-shot rifles at $11.50 each and 5,000,000 cartridges at $4.00 per 100 from a contact in Shanghai.[167] Apparently the Junta was hedging against the possible effect the Paris Treaty might have on their dealings with Japan, since a war against the United States now seemed a foregone conclusion.

Nevertheless, on December 14, Aguinaldo authorized Ponce to seek permission from the Japanese to allow "the necessary Japanese officers to enter the Filipino Army."[168]

On January 9, Emiliano Riego de Dios reported on a private dinner attended by Mr. Aski, the Minister of Foreign Affairs, Mr. Miura, a former consul in Manila, as well as Colonel Fukushima and a Major Akasi of the Japanese General Staff, in which there was discussion of the changed situation in the Philippines, which impeded Japan from aiding the insurgents.[169] A similar communication was sent by Ponce to Apacible on January 11.[170]

Notwithstanding these events, which reflected the official position of the Japanese Government, on January 27, Ponce wrote Apacible introducing Captain Mageno Yoshitora, a Japanese army officer who was recommended by Colonel Fukushima to serve in the Filipino army.[171] This was followed up by a communication dated January 31, in which Ponce indicates that he had decided to send Captain Yoshitora, who had been in Formosa and was highly recommended, not only by Colonel Fukushima but also by Major Akashi, to join the insurgent forces at Malolos (a town 20 miles North of Manila).[172] Ponce indicated that he had advanced $220 to Yoshitora for his trip, and that, although he spoke only Japanese, he had a letter directed to the Japanese consul in Manila with instructions that he be supplied with an interpreter. If he was not hired once he got there, Yashitora had indicated that he intended to stay as he was very enthusiastic about the Philippine cause. This would suggest, together with his connection with Colonel Fukushima and the fact that he was purportedly going against his government's expressed policy, that perhaps he was being sent to the Philippines in more than one capacity, i.e., as a double agent.

On the night of February 4, 1899, open warfare finally broke out in Manila between Aguinaldo's Army of Liberation, estimated at anywhere between 15,000 and 40,000 members, and the approximately 20,000 U.S. troops in the Manila area.[173] It would be a dirty three-year war of "pacification," in which American casualties would exceed by several thousand those suffered by the U.S. in the entire Spanish-American War proper, and in which the losses on the Filipino side would rise into the tens of thousands and large areas of the Philippines and its economy would be devastated.[174] The similarities between this conflict and that resulting from the present invasion of Iraq by the United States are too important to be overlooked and shall be commented upon in more detail presently.

Meanwhile, in a letter dated February 20, Ramos introduced Captain Yuchi Tokizawa, a Japanese artillery officer, to Antonio Luna[175], the insurgents' chief of operations, indicating that he was going to the Philippines to observe the insurgents as he had done during the campaign against the Spaniards.[176]

A March 27 letter to Apacible from Ponce reported on a meeting with Mr. Nakamura, reputedly one of the richest men in Japan, and a member of its parliament. Nakamura stated that he had decided to aid the Filipinos. He was allegedly preparing an expedition to the Philippines and was expecting to ship "everything" through Formosa. He also promised to provide some Japanese officers who were eager to join the Filipino cause. The communication also reported that the Japanese press was reputedly in favor of the Filipino cause.[177]

A July 4 cable in cipher to "Kant" (Apacible) from "Sampere" stated that "Serge [code name for the arms] sailed yesterday for east coast via Formosa."

A letter from "Paula Pardo" to Sra. Rosalía Magdalo [cover name for Aguinaldo], dated August 23, reported the arrest of various Japanese by U.S. police in Manila, aided by Filipino informants, but it indicated that they had arrested the wrong Japanese. The actual Japanese agents were warned and were able to get away.[178] This communication was followed by a letter from Batienlin (an assumed name) to Aguinaldo on August 26, indicating that he had given a letter to the Japanese consul from the Secretary of Foreign Affairs of the insurgents.[179]

A General Mascardo in the Filipino army sent a request dated 1 September, asking "for an interpreter to enable him to utilize the services of the Japanese officers attached to [his staff]."[180] An undated letter from a Z. Macapagal to Padre Blas Reyes says that Madame Aguinaldo, in Taralao, had stated that the insurgent army was well officered by Japanese officers.[181]

A document dated October 11 records the discussion between Lieutenant General Mariano Trías, one of the leading Filipino officers, and the Japanese Consul, S. Hojo, in which, in addition to discussing various supply issues, it was suggested on several occasions that Gen. Trías journey to Japan "to negotiate for a voluntary contribution of arms and concerning the future of the Archipelago."[182]

Three calling cards found with Gen. Trias' papers were from a Captain S. Narahana, the military attaché in Manila accredited to the U.S. Government there, from a T. Hojo, the chancellor to the Consulate in Manila, and from a J.A. Ishikawa, Captain Narahana's roommate, who claimed to be an English teacher but whose real employment was unknown.[183]

The above evidence leaves little doubt that Japanese officials engaged in numerous and continuous breaches of the rules of neutrality during the Spanish-American War. In all fairness to the Japanese, it is difficult to determine with certainty whether these actions where sanctioned at sufficiently high levels to implicate their government. Of course "plausible deniability" is not an unknown technique of governments when engaging in *sub rosa* activities. On the other hand, there is no question that officers of the Japanese General Staff actively encouraged and aided the insurgents, that Japanese officers served with those forces, that arms in the possession of the Japanese Government somehow passed into the hands of the insurgents[184] by way of Formosa, where transshipment could have taken place only with the connivance of Japanese officials there, and that a Japanese officer and the chancellor of the consulate in Manila, entered into negotiations with representatives of the insurgent government regarding varied belligerent activities.

Rumors of these activities were rife. The American authorities sought the cooperation of Viscount Aoki when they learned of arms deals in the making by Filipino agents in Japan (i.e., Ponce and Lichauco). Viscount Aoki reported that after investigating the matter, no evidence was found as to these allegations.[185] In fact, when Dr. Ponce was invited to address the Tokyo Club, where he appealed for help for the Filipino cause from the press and the people, the member who had arranged for his appearance was expelled from the club.[186]

Nevertheless, there is at least one documented case of a gunrunner which left Japan, the *Nunobiki Maru*, and sank in a storm off China on July, 21 1898. That vessel left from Kobe for Formosa on July 13 and stopped at Nagasaki. The *Nunobiki Maru* had belonged to an allegedly reputable Japanese firm until July 5.

General Trias' meeting with the chancellor of the Japanese Consulate in Manila became the subject of a protest to the Japanese Government by the United States, which asked that a rigorous investigation be made. The chancellor was recalled and subjected to close examination, which according to the Japanese Government revealed only a chance encounter with insurgent leaders in which the secretary to the chancellor made some unauthorized remarks. That was the end of the matter.[187]

The bottom line was that, although officially the Japanese government reacted cautiously to U.S. territorial advances into East Asia, its leaders had hoped for no change in the status of the Philippines. But if change did occur, Japan preferred, at least at that period in time, to have the United States in control of the Philippines rather than a European power such as Germany.

Of course, this was not the last that would be heard from Japan regarding the Philippines.

France, the "éminence grise"

Once hostilities actually began, France, despite its vitriolic attacks against the United States during the pre-war period, did not engage in any acts that could be termed as outright violations of its announced neutrality.[188] However, in terms of public opinion and the internal governmental stance, the pro-Spanish bias remained unabated.[189]

Out of 52 newspapers that appeared in Paris on the morning of April 23, 1898 when the Spanish-American War commenced, only three were favorable to the United States.[190]

The French government's official intervention during the Spanish-American War to attempt to end the conflict was in effect a continuation of the joint European efforts to prevent it, although in its more recent actions, France had acted on its own at the request of Spain.[191] Two different foreign ministers were involved, Gabriel Hanotaux, until June 28, 1898, and Théophile Declassé, thereafter. Hanotaux was a known sympathizer with the Spanish cause and was trusted by the Spanish authorities. Declassé was a promoter of French expansionism, particularly in Africa and especially in Morocco. Both Hanotaux and Declassé used the French press extensively to influence, and in effect to announce, French domestic and foreign policy. This practice reached the point that one of the leading newspapers, *Les Temps*, was regarded by many as the unofficial spokesman of official governmental policy.[192]

When Declassé became foreign minister, he lacked experience or background in either United States affairs or Spanish-American War issues. He thus relied heavily on the advice of the French Ambassador to the United States, Jules Martin Cambon (in Washington from December, 1897), with whom he had worked closely on prior occasions when Declassé was Minister of Colonies and Cambon was Governor of Algeria. Cambon's views on the United States and on the War were critical to the determination of French policy in this regard.[193]

In a letter to Declassé when the he first took office, Cambon summed up his views of Americans generally: "[T]hese people love no one; they envy the English; they distrust the Germans; since 1871 they scorn us."[194] As Cambon saw it, the war with Spain was like a second American revolution in which the United States was projecting itself not only into global politics, but extending U.S. imperialism beyond its continent and into a new historical period. If the war continued, it might affect the Western Pacific, the Canary Islands, and even the Mediterranean. Great Britain, he said, sought to interpose itself between Europe and the United States, and given the ignorant and brutish nature of the later (the way he saw Americans), it could very well lead to a continental conflagration. Cambon urged Declassé to work with the other European powers to try to prevent a formal Anglo-American alliance –and here is the real concern– to keep the United States out of the Mediterranean, which France looked upon with proprietary interest.[195] The war was also affecting its commerce, and French holders of Spanish and Cuban bonds were losing money.

The first contact to attempt to end the war came on May 1, 1898, shortly after the Manila Bay debacle, when Hanotaux approached Horace Porter, the U.S. Ambassador in Paris and inquired as to the United States' intentions regarding the Philippines. Without consulting Washington, Porter replied that the United States opposed expansionism. This information was passed on to the Spanish, and to France's ally, Russia, with the latter urging a quick end to the war to prevent a takeover of that archipelago by the British.[196]

The United States rejected early Spanish attempts to open peace discussions directly between Spain's Ambassador to France, Fernando León y Castillo, and U.S. Ambassador Porter, as well as strongly rebuffing European attempts to interject themselves directly into any peace negotiations. This was a position vehemently held by the United States throughout the war and during the ensuing peace process.[197] Thus, on July 18, Spain turned to France as an intermediary, a logical choice since France had not only taken over Spain's interests in Washington upon the declaration of war, but had handled Spanish blockade shipping cases and provided prisoner of war support. The French were asked to allow Ambassador Cambon to deliver a message to President McKinley on behalf of Spain, asking for a suspension of hostilities to be followed by final peace negotiations.[198] Through a series of mishaps, it took eight days for the French to authorize Cambon's intervention, by which time Puerto Rico had been invaded, thus eliminating one of Spain's objectives in seeking an expeditious cease-fire.

From this point on, the French Government, which was supposed to act only as a post office in the transmission of messages between the two belligerents, not only violated its status as a neutral by actively counseling and assisting the Spanish in their negotiations with the United States, but placed itself in a serious conflict of interest predicament. It was clear before long that the French were actively looking to protect their own interests in the Eastern Atlantic and North Africa, interests which did not necessarily coincide with those of Spain.

For these reasons, France wanted a quick end to the war. Thus, from the very beginning, Cambon warned Madrid that to obtain an armistice Spain would have to agree to McKinley's demands.[199] However, Spain initially hoped that in exchange for the surrender of Havana, and its agreement to transfer sovereignty over Cuba to the United States, the latter would withdraw from Puerto Rico and the Philippines.

On July 26, Cambon, accompanied by the first secretary of the French embassy, Eugéne Thiébault, serving as translator, met with President McKinley and Secretary of State Day to present Spain's proposals. Thiébault read the Spanish note, which only referred to matters related to Cuba and made no specific mention of Puerto Rico or the Philippines. Thereafter, Cambon made an impassioned plea to McKinley with reference to the sufferings of the mothers of the American and Spanish soldiers serving in Cuba (nothing was said about Cuban mothers), to which McKinley answered in equally emotive terms. On a more realistic note, Secretary Day asked whether Spain was just talking about peace for Cuba or was interested in peace on all fronts, to which Cambon replied that Spain wanted a comprehensive peace.[200] The president agreed to consider the Spanish proposal and to give a prompt reply.

Cambon reported to Declassé about the meeting, adding that "McKinley's impressions are fleeting because he is weak," and that he was subject to cabinet pressures in an election year. Cambon further believed that Secretary Day and the American public were distrustful of diplomacy and that Spain should be prepared to lose Puerto Rico.[201]

McKinley met long into the night with Day, Secretary of the Navy John Long, Secretary of War Russell Alger, Secretary of the Interior Cornelius Bliss, Secretary of Agriculture James Wilson and Postmaster General Charles Smith. After the meeting concluded, the president wrote a memorandum embodying the consensus reached:

> As a condition to entering negotiations looking to peace, Spain must withdraw from Cuba and Puerto Rico and such adjacent islands as are under her dominion. This requirement will admit of no negotiation. As to the Philippines, I am of the opinion, that with propriety and advantage, they can be the subject of negotiation, and whenever the Spanish gov't desire it, I will appoint commissioners to that end.[202]

Opinions on what to do about the Philippines were so divided that no general agreement could be reached among those attending the meeting.[203]

McKinley met formally with his cabinet next day and indicated that the United States would seek a protectorate over Cuba and annexation of Puerto Rico, but again no agreement could be reached as to the Philippines.

Declassé in the meantime met with León y Castillo in Paris and urged Spain to prepare its own terms for peace, and to propose that negotiations continue in Paris. It is difficult to see what Spain had left to bargain with at this point, having lost practically all of its navy, the U.S. Army being in virtual control of Cuba, Puerto Rico and the principal city in the Philippines, and a U.S. naval squadron under Admiral Watson about to sail for Spanish waters to shell and possibly land marines on Spain's coasts.

A second meeting between Cambon and the American president was held on July 30, at which time President McKinley indicated the intention of the United States to demand that Spain cede Cuba for eventual independence, and to annex Puerto Rico and Guam, with the issue of the final disposition of the Philippines to be left for negotiation as part of the peace treaty to be entered into in the future. No indemnity would be demanded from Spain. Although Cambon indicated that Spain wanted an immediate end to hostilities, McKinley stated that this could not take place until Spain agreed to negotiate a treaty based on the American proposal. Cambon was most disturbed about the U.S. position regarding the Philippines.[204]

Cambon reported the outcome of the meeting to Declassé, asserting that in his opinion, McKinley was immovable in his demands. Spanish reaction to the U.S. proposals was almost surreal, as demonstrated in the suggestion by Foreign Minister Almodóvar to the effect that Cuba be made to pay for the military costs incurred in the fighting, and in his refusal to be reconciled to the loss of Puerto Rico.[205]

At a third meeting in Washington on August 3, Cambon, following instructions from Spain, proposed that Puerto Rico be exchanged for some other island, a point which President McKinley was not even willing to discuss. Cambon again brought up a proposal previously made to the effect that Cuba's fate be submitted to a plebiscite, to which the president replied that Cuba was being acquired by force of arms and that he wanted to bring the Island under direct control of the United States for the granting of independence in the future. McKinley added that the only proposal subject to negotiation was the fate of the Philippines. Cambon's last proposal was that the peace negotiations be moved to Paris, which was met with the answer that the matter would be considered.[206]

The next day, Secretary Day informed Cambon that the United States was agreeable to the treaty negotiations taking place in Paris, hinting to American expectations that France would be completely neutral in these proceedings. Day also demanded the immediate removal of Spanish troops from Cuba and Puerto Rico as soon as the armistice went into effect, which Cambon claimed was a new demand and contrary to custom. Day said that the United States would be flexible, allowing that the commissioners be given discretion as to the actual departure date of the troops, but he insisted on this point.

Cambon transmitted the U.S. demands to the Spanish, and in a personal letter to Declassé said to him, "One cannot imagine what it is to deal with Americans when one is defeated; they have the blood of Indians in their veins."[207] He again warned Declassé that any delay in making peace could result in U.S. incursions into Africa or the Mediterranean, which would be to the detriment of France's interests. This comment highlights France's obvious conflict of interests in purporting to present Spain's views or in keeping a neutral stance as an intermediary.

The Spanish answer was read by Cambon to McKinley on August 9. It was argumentative and assertive, blaming the United States for the war, and while accepting McKinley's proposal, it indicated the need to convene the Cortes to seek its approval, as required by the Spanish Constitution when a cession of Spanish territory was involved. An acrimonious discussion ensued during which Day forcefully expressed the view that the United States should withdraw its proposal and continue with the war. Nevertheless, it was finally agreed that a brief note be prepared stating the agreed proposal, and that Cambon would seek authorization from the Spanish Cabinet to sign it. The parties would sign the note, and the need for approval by the Cortes and the U.S. Senate would be postponed until a treaty was negotiated and entered into. The withdrawal date of the Spanish troops from the West Indies would in the meantime be negotiated.

The Spanish cabinet met and authorized Cambon to sign the protocol, whereupon it was signed in a ceremony at the White House at 4:00 P.M. on August 12, 1898. President McKinley immediately issued a peace proclamation and ordered the cessation of hostilities by the United States forces.[208]

France continued to play an important if conflicting role during the course of the peace negotiations in Paris which started on September 26.

NOTES

1. Musicant, supra, at 183-188.

2. Id. at 187; DEEU, at 9-18.

3. Musicant, supra, at 190. See also, 55th Cong., ch. 189, 30 Stat. 364 (1898).

4. DEEU, at 31-2.

5. Musicant, supra, at 189.

6. Juan R. Torruella, *The Supreme Court and Puerto Rico: The Doctrine of Separate and Unequal*, University of Puerto Rico Press (Editorial de la Universidad de Puerto Rico), Río Piedras, Puerto Rico (1988).

7. See Cagni, supra, at 7, 79-92.

8. Id. at 30.

9. Id.

10. Id. at 30-31.

11. These are more than adequately described in detail elsewhere. See Musicant, supra, at 191-234, 340-351, 432-466.

12. Id. at 190.

13. Id. at 221.

14. Id. at 225.

15. Id. at 227.

16. Id. at 233.

17. Spain too, of course, though it would soon become almost irrelevant.

18. Linn, supra; Blount, supra.

19. Id. at 310-313.

20. Id. at 311.

21. Musicant, supra, at 290.

22. Id. at 282-283.

23. Id. at 288.

24. Id. at 327.

25. Id. at 432-466.

26. Telegram dated June 28,1898, from General-in-Command Blanco, approved by the Government in Madrid on 1 July by telegram from Minister Auñon to General Blanco. *Colección de Documentos Referentes a la Escuadra de Operaciones de las Antillas*, 5th ed. Editorial Naval, Madrid (1989), at 194, 195.

27. Henry Clay Taylor, "The *Indiana* at Santiago," in "The Story of the Captains," *Century*, May, 1899, at 71-3.

28. Musicant, supra, at 352-370.

29. E. Ranson, "British Military and Naval Observers in the Spanish-American War," *Journal of American Studies*, 3 (1969), at 33 n.3. The report of the British military observer, Captain A.H. Lee, Royal Artillery, is found in *War Office Reports and Miscellaneous Papers*, W.O. 33/155 (Public Records Office), under the title *Reports of the Military Attachés with the Spanish and United States Forces in Cuba and Porto Rico*, London (1899). Part I is the *Report of the Military Attaché with the Spanish Forces in Cuba*, by Major G.F. Leverson, Royal Engineers, at 3-53 thereof. In his report, Major Leverson found the Cuban insurgents an inconsequential fighting force, suggesting that the Spanish army had failed to suppress the revolution because too many officers had a vested financial interest in keeping the war going. Ranson, supra, at 51. He found Spanish soldiers to be tough and brave, but poorly led, and the cavalry efficient but lacking spit and polish. He considered the artillery and engineers to be the elite corps. Id. The supply system was very bad, the rations late and short, the medical facilities inadequate, and the pay for all ranks several months in arrears. Id. Although the Spanish coastal defenses were inadequate, one battery at Matanzas dating back to 1721, the United States bombardment was ineffective, with an unacceptable number of defective fuses. One of the few casualties from American artillery was a mule, which the Spanish, exhibiting a touch of sarcastic humor, buried with full military honors. Id. at 52.

    The report of the British military observer with the United States Army in the Cuban campaign, Captain A.H. Lee, is found under Part II of the *Report on the Santiago Campaign*, at 54-102, while his report on the Puerto Rico campaign can be found in Part III of the *Report on Operations in Porto Rico*, at 103-121. Captain Lee's report on the Cuban campaign is highly critical of U.S. operations there. Starting with winter grade uniforms issued to the troops for use in tropical Cuba, the crass lack of familiarity with and incompetence in mounting an overseas amphibious operation, the poor or non-existent communications system, the failure to provide naval escorts to unarmed troop transports, the chaos in the loading of supplies and armaments aboard the vessels, the failure to black out the fleet at night, the inaccuracy of the naval bombardment preceding landings (at Daiquirí, the sole casualties were seven Cuban insurgents killed or wounded by "friendly fire," id. at 42), the lack of proper planning, compounded by an apparent absence of advance intelligence, and just plain general inefficiency and incompetence, all were claimed in his report. Id. at 36-50. His most acrimonious criticism was reserved for General Shafter, the obese American commander, whom he excoriated for his incompetence and lack of military ability, as well as for causing divisiveness in his command, particularly in regard to the naval component led by Admiral Sampson. Id. at 50. Despite the criticism, while in the field with the Americans, he acted like anything but a neutral, giving advice to the Americans from the moment he joined the troops in Tampa on everything from the use of hammocks to the need to pay with Mexican dollars. Id. at 35-36. Nor did he make any effort to conceal his partiality for the American cause. As he told Theodore Roosevelt in an exchange of letters shortly after the War, "I never pretended for a moment to be neutral, or to disguise my sympathies." Lee to Roosevelt, March 1, 1902. Id. at 46. Roosevelt in turn said that he was "as staunch a friend as America has" in a letter introducing him to the new Secretary of War, Elihu Root. Id.

Part III contains Lee's report on General Miles' Puerto Rico campaign and is much less critical of the U.S forces, which had gained considerable experience in Cuba, the Spanish resistance being less of a problem. Id. at 52-55. Lee concluded that "in Puerto Rico, the American methods of war were modern, at Santiago they were mediaeval." Id. at 55.

The report of the British naval observer, Captain Alfred W. Paget is found in *Spanish-American War of 1898, United Transport Service, Report*. Paget's brother was married to the daughter of Williams Collis Whiney, the former Secretary of the Navy under President Cleveland. Id. at 36 n.1. Paget more or less confirmed Lee's observations regarding the army, but considered the naval operations to be generally better prepared and commanded than those of the army. He was highly critical of the captain of the American vessel *Seguranca* for refusing assistance to Spanish sailors in the water at Santiago. Id. 52.

30. Musicant, supra, at 390-431. The fight for El Caney was equally fierce. Id. at 402-9. In 2001, the United States Congress posthumously awarded Theodore Roosevelt the Congressional Medal of Honor, citing him "for conspicuous gallantry and intrepidity at the risk of his life...while leading a daring charge up San Juan Hill... accompanied by only four or five men ... was the first to reach enemy trenches." See http: www.cmohs.org/recipients/transe_citation.htm.

31. Id. at 467-515.

32. Id.

33. Id. at 517-518.

34. Id. at 520.

35. Id. at 523.

36. Id.

37. Torruella, supra, at 23.

38. *Correspondence respecting the War between Spain and the United States (1898-1899)* (Confidential Print, 7267, Foreign Office, March 1900) (hereafter *CPFO*), No. 141, Declaration of neutrality signed by the Queen, April 24, 1898. Shortly thereafter, most nations followed suit: France, April 27 (No. 144, *CPFO*); Italy, April 26 (No. 271, *CPFO*); Sweden and Norway, April 27 (No. 287, *CFPO*); Portugal, April 29 (No. 299, CFPO); Denmark, April 29 (No. 311, *CFFO*); Japan, May 2 (No. 315, *CFFO*);Mexico, April 26 (No, 418, *CFFO*);Uruguay, April 27(No. 502, *CFFO*);Brazil, May 2(No. 505,*CFFO*);Greece, May 1(No. 507, CFFO); Rumania, May 17(No. 551, *CFFO*); Colombia, May 18(No. 592, *CFFO*); Sarawak, May 16 (No. 629, *CFFO*). *See also Disposiciones de España y de los Estados Unidos referentes a la guerra y declaraciones de neutralidad*, Ministerio de Estado, Madrid (1898) (hereafter DEEU), Belgium (April 26) at 67; the Netherlands (April 26) at 91; Russia (April 20) at 96; Argentina (June 11) at 100; Haiti (April 25) at 112; Venezuela (April 29) at 117; China (undated) at 118; and Liberia (June 20) at 126.

Some interesting situations arose regarding neutrality. Austro-Hungary indicated that it would not make a declaration of neutrality "as such notification would be contrary to the custom usually observed [in that country]." *CPFO*, No. 310(April 29, 1898). Germany followed suit in the *Nord Deutche* of May 5, 1898, indicating that there would be no German declaration of neutrality because there was "no obligation to do so" and such was their custom, and because"[a] formal Declaration of Neutrality is not allowed for under German Imperial law." *Id.*, No. 390. Neither Turkey or Serbia-Montenegro adopted formal neutrality declarations. *DEEU*, at 99.

Hawaii, still an independent republic at the time, took an ambivalent position, obviously favoring the United States, which it was actively seeking to join, while not openly declaring war against Spain. There were various U.S. warships in Pearl Harbor after hostilities commenced, the British consul reporting on May 10, "Hawaii [has] not yet declared neutrality...U.S. ships still here in harbour." *CPFO* at No. 475 (May 10, 1898). The ships continued to make use of those facilities and to take on coal and supplies. Id., at No. 479 (May 17, 1898). Two days later, on May 19, the *U.S.S. Bennington* was still in port and the United States consul in Honolulu bought all the coal that was available in the islands. Id. at No. 630 (May 19, 1898). On June 9, the Spanish vice-consul filed a formal protest with the Hawaiian government against the "constant violations of neutrality." Id. at No. 681 (June 9, 1898). In July, in the middle of the Spanish-American War, three U.S. troop ships with 2,500 troops stopped at Pearl Harbor, where they took on 200 tons of coal. Id. at No. 753 (July 11, 1898). They left for Manila on July 4, but not before the troops were feted by the American community in Honolulu. Id. Meanwhile, the U.S. consul purchased land and commenced to build a coal shed, Id., the precursor to the U.S. Naval Station at Pearl Harbor.

39. *See generally*, Rosario De la Torre del Río, *supra*; Charles S. Campbell, *Anglo-American Understanding, 1889-1903*, Johns Hopkins Press, Baltimore (1957); Charles S. Campbell, Jr., "*The Anglo-American Relations, 1897-1901*," in *Threshhold to American Internationalism. Essays on the Foreign Policies of William McKinley*, Paolo Coletta (ed.), Exposition Press, New York (1970); A.E. Campbell, *Great Britain and the United States, 1895-1903*, Longmans, London (1960); R.G. Neal, *Great Britain and United States Expansion: 1898-1900*, Michigan State University Press, Lansing (1966); R.A. Reuter, *Anglo-American Relations During the Spanish-American War*, New York (1934).

40. *CPFO*, Report No. 7 (March 28, 1898).

41. Id. at No. 63 (April 21, 1898).

42. de la Torre del Rio, supra, at 143.

43. Of the two, Carrol's activities were the most flagrant violation of his presence on purportedly neutral British soil. Id. at 138-41. The British Governor of Gibraltar, Sir Robert Biddulh, reported the activities of Carrol and Hall to the Foreign Office and recommended that their permits to remain in Gibraltar not be renewed when they expired on July 12. *CPFO*, at No. 739 (July 7, 1898). No action was taken on this recommendation, Biddulh instead being asked for proof that these activities were taking place. Biddulh supplied it in the form of copies of telegrams sent by Carroll through the Eastern Telegraph Company to the U.S. State Department, the last of which coincided with the departure of the Spanish fleet from Cadiz for the Suez Canal. Chamberlain, the Colonial Secretary, taking his time about it, asked for an opinion from the Legal Office, who on July 22 advised against any action being taken, a view with which Chamberlain agreed. Lord Salisbury agreed, considering this a "political" rather than legal issue. See also, id. at No. 646 (June 16,1898).

44. de la Torre del Río, supra, at 144.

45. Id.

46. Id.

47. Id. at 145.

48. See ante.

49. *Convention to Guarantee Neutrality of the Suez Canal*, October 29, 1888.

50. CPFO, at No. 671 (June 24, 1898).

51. Id.

52. Id. at No. 675 (June 25, 1989).

53. Id. at No. 678 (June 26, 1898).

54. Id. at No. 683.

55. Id. at No. 684.

56. Id.

57. Id. at No. 693 (May 29, 1898).

58. Id. at No. 699. The Hong Kong attorney general issued an opinion to the effect that nothing could be done. Id.

59. Id. at No. 711 (July 2, 1898).

60. Id. at No. 717 (July 4, 1898).

61. Id. at 744.

62. Id. at No. 730.

63. Id. at Nos. 748 and 749 (July 9, 1898).

64. L. Oppenheim, *International Law*, 7th ed., Vol. II, London (1951), at 623-879.

65. For a more detailed account of the incident, *see* De la Torre del Rosario, supra, at 141-153.

66. De la Torre del Río, supra, at 125-6.

67. Id. at 128-31.

68. Id. at 128-9; PRO, *FO72*, 2091, *Colonial Office to Foreign Office*, April 23, 1898.

69. De la Torre del Río, supra, at 129; PRO, FO72, 2091, *Report of the Law Offices of the Crown*, April 23, 1898.

70. CPFO at No. 554 (April 28, 1898).

71. Id. at No. 333.

72. De la Torre del Río, supra, at 158.

73. CPFO, supra, at No. 652 (June 16, 1898).

74. "El Honor militar" and "El timo de la bandera," *La Época*, May 22, 1898, at 1; "Barcos sin honra," and "El pabellón falso," *El Imparcial*, May 22, 1898.

75. De la Torre del Río, supra, at 160-1.

76. Generally, id at 133-8.

77. CPFP, at No. 568 (June 2, 1898)

78. Id. at No. 597 (June 7, 1898)

79. De la Torre del Río, supra, at 135.

80. Captain J.M. Ellicott, "The Cold War Between Von Diederichs and Dewey In Manila Bay," *United States Naval Institute Proceedings*, 81 (1955), 1236-39; E.A.M. Laing, "Admiral Dewey and the Foreign Warships at Manila, 1898," *Mariner's Mirror*, 52 (1966):167-71.

81. Admiral Otto von Diederichs, "A Statement of events in Manila, May-October, 1898," *Journal of the Royal United Service Institution*, Vol. LIX, No. 438, November, 1914.

82. For a somewhat more benign version of how events developed in Manila Bay, *see* Gottschall, supra, at 51-70.

83. Thomas A. Bailey, "Dewey and the Germans at Manila Bay," *American Historical Review*, 45 (Oct. 1939): 59-81.

84. At various times, the British cruiser *Bonaventure* and the gunboats *Swift, Pique, Rattler, Plover,* and *Pygmy* would also visit Manila.

85. French Admiral De la Bedoliére's contingent included the cruisers *Bayard* (which arrived on June 26), *Bruix* (which arrived on July 1) and the *Pascal*.

86. Admiral Nomura's fleet consisted of the cruisers *Akitsushima* and *Matsushima,* which arrived on June 24 and 27, respectively, as well as the *Naniwa* and the *Itsushima.*

87. The frigate *Freudsberg*.

88. In addition to the *Linnet* and *Immortalité*, three additional gunboats would join the British fleet at Manila during the months of May and June. The gunboat *Rattler* arrived in May and left on June 22, being replaced on that day by *Bonaventure* and *Iphigenia*, and *Plover* arrived on June 25.

89. J.K. Eyre, "Russia and the American Acquisition of the Philippines," *Mississippi Valley Historical Review* 28 (1942): 561-62.

90. Bailey, supra, 60-1.

91. Ellicott, supra, at 1237.

92. Id.

93. Lester Burrell Shipee. "Germany and the Spanish-American War," *American Historical Review*, XXX/4 (July, 1925), 754-777, at 764.

94. Id.

95. Bailey, supra, at 61.

96. Id. My assessment does not totally agree with others, including Bailey's, Id., and Shippee's, supra, at 774.

97. Quoted in Hugo, supra, at 84.

98. Gottshall, supra, at 18-21.

99. Hugo, supra, at 84.

100. Ellicott, supra, at 1237.

101. Bailey, supra, at 62. It might be added that von Diederichs received his last orders in Japan. He received no further instructions during his entire presence in the Philippines. His only military orders were to maintain strict neutrality. Id. at 61 n. 7.

102. Ellicott, supra, at 1238.

103. *See* Edwin Wilman, "What Dewey Feared in Manila Bay," *The Forum*, May, 1918, at 513-535; Bailey, supra, at 65.

104. Bailey, supra, at 63.

105. Id., at 63, n. 16.

106. Von Diederichs, supra, at 427.

107. Ellicott, supra, at 1238.

108. Id.

109. Id.

110. Bailey, supra, 64, n. 21, 66.

111. Id. at 67.

112. Id. at 67.

113. Id. at 68.

114. Id.

115. Id.

116. Id. at 76-8. There are several interpretations of these actions by the German fleet. Id. See also, Ellicott, supra, at 1239.

117. Id. at 78.

118. Hugo, supra, at 84.

119. Id. at 84-5.

120. Id. at 86.

121. Id. at 86 n. 58.

122. Holger H. Herwig and David F. Trask, "Naval Operations Plans between Germany and the USA, 1898-1913. A Study of Strategic Planning in the Age of Imperialism," in *The War Plans of the Great Powers 1898-1914*, ed. by Paul Kennedy, London (1979), at 39-74.

123. Payson J. Treat, *Diplomatic Relations Between the United States and Japan, 1895-1905*, Stanford University Press, CITY (1988), at 55 n. 10. See also full roster of the *Maine*'s crew, at pp. 248-270 of *The Maine, Personal Narrative of Captain Sigbee*, The Century Co., New York (1899).

124. Treat, supra, at 55.

125. Id.

126. Id. at 55-8: J.A.S. Grenville, "Diplomacy and War Plans in the United States, 1890-1917," *Royal Historical Society*, Fifth Series, Vol. II, London (1961), at 13.

127. Charles E. Neu, *The Troubled Encounter: United States and Japan*, John Wiley & Sons, Inc., New York (1975).

128. Storry, supra, at 30.

129. John R.M. Taylor, *The Philippine Insurrection Against the United States*, 4 Vols., Eugenio Lopez Foundation, Pasay City, Philippines (1971), at Vol. I, 62.

130. Id. at 81.

131. Musicant, supra, at 197, 547.

132. Id. at 547-8.

133. These activities were previously known and commented upon. See Blount, supra, at 328; Taylor, supra, at 496; Treat, supra, at 66-8, 70, 137-138.

134. On June 17, 1898, Agoncillo issued detailed instructions to Ponce and Lichauco regarding their activities in Japan. PID, 420-10.

135. During and after the Philippine insurgency, which lasted from 1899 to 1902, many of the insurgent records, which were considerably detailed, were captured. These were translated into English and filed, first in the State Department, and finally in the Library of Congress as the *Philippine Insurgent Records*, 1896-1901, 94 Entry 196-196A.

136. Id. at No. 416-9.

137. PID, No. 420-7.

138. Id. at No. 479-7.

139. Id. at No. 466-10.

140. Id. at No. 466-1.

141. Id. at No. 471-6.

142. Id. at No. 446-3.

143. Id.

144. Id. at No. 420-9.

145. This would appear to be a perfect cover for an intelligence agent.

146. Id. at No. 420-9.

147. Id. at No. 458-3.

148. Id. at No. 420-9.

149. Id. at No. 466-11.

150. Aguinaldo's constitutional adviser. Linn, supra, at 21.

151. Id. at No. 420-4.

152. Id. at No. 446-9.

153. Id. at No. 390-2.

154. Id. at No. 420-1.

155. Id. at No. 476-9.

156. Id. at No. 420-8.

157. Id. at No. 416-12.

158. Musicant, supra, at 616.

159. Id. at No. 390-9.

160. Id. at No. 420-3.

161. Id. at No. 390-6.

162. Id. at No. 390-8.

163. Id. at No. 390-6.

164. Id., at No. 420-3.

165. Musicant, supra, at 626.

166. PID, at No. 420-3.

167. Id. at No. 390-6.

168. Id. at No. 390-4.

169. Id. at No. 530-2.

170. Id. at No. 453-4.

171. Id. at No. 446-7.

172. Id. at No. 446-3.

173. Linn, supra, at 42.

174. Id. at 322-28.

175. Id. at 26.

176. PID, at No. 446-2.

177. Id. at No. 446-6.

178. Id. at No. 390-5.

179. Id. at No. 65-1.

180. Id. at No. 390-3.

181. Id. at No. 104.

182. Id. at No. 66-11.

183. Id. at No. 621-2.

184. A number of Murata rifles were found in the possession of the insurgents. Taylor, supra, Vol. II, at 496.

185. Treat, supra, at 67.

186. Id. at 67 n.6.

187. Similar charges were also leveled against a clerk in the German Consulate in Manila. Id. at 138 n. 26.

188. CPFFO, at No. 144 (April 27,1898). As will be discussed presently, French neutrality was not as clear cut as this statement indicates. *See* John L. Offner, *An Unwanted War: The Diplomacy of the United States and Spain over Cuba, 1895-1898*, University of North Carolina Press, Chapel Hill / London (1992), at 211.

189. See generally, James Louis Whitehead, "French Reaction to American Imperialism. 1895-1908," Unpublished Ph.D. dissertation, University of Pennsylvania, Philadelphia (1943), at 99-148; John L. Offner, "The United States and France: Ending the Spanish-American War," *Diplomatic History*, 7 (1983): 1-21; Offner, *An Unwanted War, supra*, at 210-224; Louis M. Sears, "French Opinion of the Spanish-American War," *The Hispanic American Historical Review*, 7 (1927): 25-44, at 37-44; Serge Ricard, "The French Press and Brother Jonathan," in *European Perceptions*, supra, at 145-49.

190. Whitehead, supra, at 114.

191. *Le Correspondant* regretted the French Ambassador's involvement in the peace effort and feared that his actions might someday be to France's disadvantage with relation to her Caribbean holdings in Martinique and Guadeloupe. *Le Correspondent*, August, 1898, at 830.

192. Offner, *Ending the Spanish-American War*, supra, at 2.

193. Id.

194. Id. at 3.

195. Id.

196. Id.

197. Id. at 7.

198. Offner, *An Unwanted War*, supra, at 210.

199. Id. at 211.

200. Id. at 212.

201. Offner, *Ending the Spanish-American* War, supra, at 10-11.

202. Id. at 11.

203. Id. at 11 n. 33.

204. Id. at 12.

205. Id. at 14.

206. Id. at 14-5.

207. Id. at 15.

208. Id. at 18.

CHAPTER IV

The Peace Negotiations

The composition of the United States peace commission in Paris was itself revealing. It was decidedly stacked in favor of the so-called expansionists.[1] Although the delegation was headed by Secretary of State Day, who held moderate views about the disposition of the Philippines, the majority was composed of decided expansionists. These included, among others, Republican Whitelaw Reid, the publisher of the *New York Tribune* and former ambassador to France, Republican Cushman K. Davis, the expansionist chairman of the Foreign Relations Committee, and Republican Senator William P. Frye. Opposing views were represented by Democrat George Gray, the ranking minority member of the Foreign Relations Committee, and a known anti-imperialist.

Spanish Prime Minister Sagasta had difficulty gathering a Spanish delegation, as no one wanted to be part of so thankless a task. The Conservative Party outright refused to participate. Sagasta was finally able to convince Liberal Eugenio Montero Ríos to head the Spanish delegation, and Liberals Buenaventura Abarzuza and José Garnica y Díaz to join him, together with diplomat Wenceslao Ramírez de Villaurrutia y Villaurrutia and General Rafael Cerero y Saenz.

Public opinion in the United States was to exercise overwhelming influence on President McKinley's decisions concerning the peace settlement overriding the views of other countries, public opinion elsewhere, and even issues of international law raised by the Spanish and other continental powers.[2]

From the beginning Spain tried to retain the Philippines arguing that they had not been conquered militarily since the capitulation of Manila took place after the signing of the protocol in Washington. Thus, Spain

157

claimed that the Philippines were not subject to retention by the United States. This contention was rejected outright by the United States delegation, answering that it was irrelevant whether its authority over Manila was before or after the protocol or capitulation. The Americans posited that "in either case, the powers of the military occupant are the same."[3] The question of United States retention of the Philippines became from the outset the defining issue of the Paris negotiations.

Spain, aware that it lacked negotiating power, attempted in vain to seek European aid in support of its position. León y Castillo sought to enlist the help of the German Ambassador to France, Count Herbert Munster. Although the German Ambassador met with Reid on the matter of the Philippines, he told León y Castillo that Spain should not hope for any European assistance, either moral or material.[4] France's main interests at this point were to contain the United States within the current theaters of war and its concern for French bondholders, whom the French foreign ministry undertook to represent directly with Madrid.[5]

The Filipino insurgents attempted to be heard regarding their own fate and sent an emissary to Washington, Felipe Agoncillo, who arrived there on October 1, 1898. Soon thereafter he was received by President McKinley himself. The president merely listened and asked that Agoncillo prepare an informal memorandum and submit it to the Department of State. The latter received it, while avoiding any implication of recognition of the Aguinaldo regime. Thereafter Agoncillo proceeded to Paris. The American commissioners failed to give him so much as a personal interview. Returning to Washington, Agoncillo attempted to meet with Secretary of State Day but he refused to meet with him.[6]

Thus the Filipinos, as had happened with the Indians when the United States became independent and thereafter, became irrelevant to the process that decided their destiny, while it was negotiated away by others in the mirrored hallways of Paris. Of course, the Cubans, Puerto Ricans, and Chamorros[7] suffered a similar fate without so much as a thought being given to their desires by the representatives of either the United States or Spain.

Early on, Montero Ríos had tried to saddle the United States with the $400 million Cuban debt incurred by Spain as a result of the Cuban conflict, as the quid pro quo for Spain's relinquishment of sovereignty over Cuba. As was to be expected, both formally and informally, the Spanish proposal was rejected out of hand. It thus appeared that the conference was at an impasse almost before it got started.

The Spaniards then decided upon a change in tactics and moved the discussions to the issue of the Philippines. On this point, Spain's greatest ally was the political circumstances of the United States itself, for although the American delegation was stacked in favor of annexation, there was a great divide among Americans, both in and out of positions of power, about what to do with the Philippines.[8] Even Admiral Dewey was non-committal.[9]

The president, with whom the final decision lay, gave little or no thought to the views of Spain but relied almost exclusively on the state of U.S. domestic opinion. To check this, he personally toured the Mid-West from October 11 to 21, making speeches and otherwise testing the waters. In the end, he learned that the great majority of his supporters approved the annexation of the Philippines.[10] Had he been left to his own devices, McKinley would probably have taken a different path, for from the beginning of the war he was against any territorial expansion outside of the continental mainland, including even Hawaii and Puerto Rico. But in the final analysis he did not control these events; they controlled him.

When the Paris delegations reconvened on October 31, Secretary Day announced the intention of the United States to annex the entire Philippine Archipelago, noting that the United States was willing to compensate Spain "for necessary works and improvements of a pacific character."[11] The Spanish, although expecting this outcome, when finally faced with its reality, nevertheless responded in a state of shock and could only attempt to delay final capitulation in the hope that something would save the Philippines for them. This was not to materialize although there were signs of European uneasiness with the situation. On November 27, with the relative positions then totally obvious, the United States gave Spain an ultimatum requiring an answer by the following day, November 28, to what it termed its final proposals. This included an offer by the United States to purchase the Philippine Archipelago for $20 million.

Germany had been following the negotiations with predatory interest, eyeing not only the island of Mindanao but the Sulus (both parts of the Philippines), as well as the Carolines and the Samoas. As far back as May 17, during the height of the Manila interchange between Dewey and von Diederichs, the German Ambassador to Great Britain, Count Paul von Hatzfelt –while denying that Germany had any unfriendly intentions towards the United States– stated to Ambassador Hay that Germany sought coaling stations in the Pacific, and that something might be worked out regarding the Philippines.[12]

In July, the temporary chief of the German Foreign Office, Baron Oswald von Richthofen, had unofficially approached the U.S. Ambassador in Berlin, Andrew Dickinson White, with the suggestion that in return for Germany's "good will," the United States should allow Germany to acquire the Samoas, the Carolines, and a naval station in the Philippines.[13]

Receiving no favorable response, the Germans commenced secret negotiations with Spain for the purchase of various of its island groups in the Pacific. In August, the Spanish responded that it was considering disposing of all of its overseas possessions, whereupon von Richthofen ordered studies of the Philippines, the Sulus, the Carolines, the Ladrones, as well as the Spanish Atlantic Islands, including the Canary Islands and Fernando Po. After the August 12 protocol, von Richthofen concentrated on the islands of Kusaie, Yap and Ponape in the Carolines, and on September 10, a secret agreement was reached with Spain for their purchase, subject to the outcome of the Paris treaty negotiations regarding the Philippines. This agreement was not even made known to the Spanish delegation in Paris.[14]

German reaction to the raising of the acquisition of the Carolines by the United States as an issue in the Paris negotiations was immediate but indirect. The German Ambassador to France, Count Herbert Munster, indicated to Whitehall Reid on several occasions that Germany had no present interest in the Philippines. On November 25, he went so far as to inquire whether Reid's name could be used in German negotiations concerning the Carolines with Madrid or Washington, a proposal which was emphatically rejected by Reid who proceeded to report the matter to Day.[15]

Germany's raptorial hovering around the edges of the Paris negotiations was at least one of the reasons why the Americans issued their ultimatum to Spain to conclude the negotiations and to sign a definitive treaty ending the War.

It was thus that, on November 25, the Sagasta Government ordered the Spanish delegation to sign the treaty under protest. The possibility of internal disorder in Spain, as well as the hopelessness of the Spanish bargaining position, led to its inevitable conclusion: on November 28, the Spanish delegation formally accepted the demands of the United States in the course of a somber and dignified session.

Thereafter, the two commissions met on December 10 and formally signed the Treaty, which contained seventeen articles whose text reflected the one-sided nature of the negotiations. The more important provisions of the Treaty of Paris, as it became known, were: (1) the relinquishment of Spain's sovereignty over Cuba, (2) the cession of Puerto Rico and Guam to the United States, and (3) the transfer of the sovereignty of Philippine Islands to the United States for a payment of $20 million.[16] There was no mention of the Carolines.

As to the Carolines, Spain and Germany completed their negotiations on December 21, 1898, with Germany acquiring the Carolines, the Palaus and the Marianas (minus Guam), for 25 million pesetas. A formal treaty was signed on February 10, 1899, and thereafter ratified in June.[17]

The Treaty of Paris was ratified and proclaimed on April 11, 1899.[18] The United States thus officially became an imperialist nation with overseas colonies. Furthermore, for the first time in its history, the United States acquired territory without granting its inhabitants citizenship and without the commitment of eventual incorporation into the Union as a state.[19]

NOTES

1. See Pratt, *The Expansionist of 1898*, supra.

2. Trask, supra, at 437.

3. Id.

4. Offner, supra, *Diplomatic History*, at 18.

5. Id.

6. Trask, supra, at 443.

7. Natives of Guam.

8. Trask, supra, at 430-56; Musicant, supra, at 614-6.

9. Trask, supra, at 450.

10. Id. at 453.

11. Id. at 457.

12. Id. at 462.

13. Id.

14. Id. at 463.

15. Id.

16. Musicant, supra, at 626.

17. Trask, supra, at 466.

18. 30 Stat. 1754 (1899).

19. See generally, Torruella, supra.

CHAPTER V

The Immediate Aftermath of the War and the Resulting World Order

An appropriate starting point for a discussion of the impact of the Spanish-American War on the World Order is a consideration of its repercussions on the United States, the major player in that conflict. Not only does the United States emerge from this clash as an important contender in the world arena of that epoch, it can fairly be argued that the Spanish-American War serves as the point from which the United States began to move toward its present unique superpower status. After the Spanish-American War, the United States had to be taken into account in almost every major event that has taken place around the globe since then.

The Treaty of Paris did not end hostilities in all the theaters of that war. If anything, it exacerbated the situation of the Philippines, with military operations continuing for three more years through 1902. That period of strife, although between two new adversaries, cannot be separated historically from the alleged main event any more than can the Cuban rebellion that started in 1895 be separated from the brief period of direct United States military intervention in 1898 in Cuba.

The confirmation of the United States' "permanent" presence in the Far East by its acquisition of its Philippine outpost on the fringe of mainland China changed the geopolitical map of the entire Pacific region. Now the United States had a ring of territories around the whole Pacific expanse, dotted by strategically located potential coaling and naval bases. The Pacific Rim was now a "Pacific Ring" bounded by the United States mainland to the East, by Alaska and the Aleutians to the North, by the Philippines to the far West, and by American Samoa to the South. In crossing this circle, there were the Hawaiian Islands, Guam, and the Midway and Wake Islands[1] running down the middle of the "Ring" from East to West (see Map 6).

The acquisition of the Philippines not only gave the United States an imposing strategic advantage in protecting its military, political, and commercial interests in the Far East, but it deprived all other competing nations of those same advantages. This American preemption forced those nations to seek mainland entrepots in contention with each other and with the United States. This took place at a time when those countries would be faced with China's growing resistance to additional foreign incursions (witness the Boxer Rebellion in 1900), and without the advantages of the local hegemony and control that could be exercised by the United States in the Philippines (especially after 1903).

The American incursion into the Western Pacific, particularly the Philippines, although initially causing friction, principally with Germany, was predictably[2] the source of more serious and long lasting controversy with the natural Pacific competitor of the United States: Japan. Until the mid-20th century, however, Japan would be content with the distraction that the Philippines and other colonial entanglements of the United States afforded, which kept America from focusing on Japan's Asian agenda. Japan would then be relatively free to pursue its own interests– closer to home, in China, Korea and Manchuria – and to concentrate on its more immediate antagonist: Russia. It would soon dispatch that rival in the 1904-1905 Russo-Japanese War. The winds of revolution in Russia would further handicap that adversary for some time to come.

But this *Pax Pacifica* was destined to come to an abrupt end within less than half a century, after which the Pacific and the Far East would be troubled by almost continuous warfare for the rest of the 20th century in the form of the Second World War, the Chinese Civil War and consequent rise of the People's Republic, the Korean Conflict, and the wars in Indochina.[3]

The expanded American empire that resulted from the Treaty of Paris, with its multitude of far-flung administrative, logistical, and constitutional[4] problems, in effect brought about the containment of the United States that the French had sought to achieve before and during the Spanish-American War. The United States was too busy with its new overseas colonial acquisitions to look elsewhere or to engage in further non-contiguous expansion, although its quest for "informal empire"[5] can be said to continue to this day.

U.S. expansion did in fact continue in the Caribbean even after the Spanish-American War. Almost literally, but certainly militarily and politically, the Caribbean became an American "lake" as a result of the Spanish-American War and its aftermath (see Map 7). Cuba became a de facto U.S. protectorate, with the Platt Amendment to the Cuban Constitution allowing U.S. intervention at the drop of a hat, and with a permanent U.S. naval enclave at Guantánamo (see Map 8). Puerto Rico, guarding the Eastern approaches to the Caribbean and the Panama Canal, became a colony over which the U.S. Congress exercises almost absolute plenary power to this very day.[6] Together with the Virgin Islands (acquired from Denmark in 1917), and the Panama Canal Zone (since relinquished) linking the Pacific and Atlantic Oceans (thus permitting the U.S. Navy to serve American interests on both oceans), the United States practices almost total control in the Caribbean and its contiguous lands. Recognition by Great Britain of American hegemony in the Caribbean, and the dusting off and expansive interpretation of the Monroe Doctrine by the United States, effectively froze Pan-Americanism in place to the detriment of Germany and all the other European powers, and blocked any further colonial expansion in the Americas, other than by the United States.

Probably the single most important long range consequence of the Spanish-American War was the permanent *rapprochement* that developed thereafter between Great Britain and the United States, the beginning of which can clearly be traced to events surrounding that conflict. This closer relationship commenced to bear fruit for the British almost immediately after the Spanish-American War, during the Boer War of 1899, and has continued almost uninterruptedly in the course of almost every international confrontation since then (the 1956 Suez crisis being the rare exception). At the same time, the Spanish-American War served to alert American politicians and the public as to who could be relied upon in future conflicts, and what the true intentions of several of the European Powers were, particularly those of France and Germany.

Of the three moribund empires that existed in 1898, only the Spanish empire was directly impacted by the Spanish-American War. Spain's international status declined even further as a result of its losing all of its overseas colonies except some minor strips of desert and islands in

Africa.[7] It was not until after World War I that the Ottoman Empire was reduced to the national territory of Turkey, with the balance of its lands distributed between France and Great Britain, or being granted various degrees of independence under the close tutelage of those countries. Interestingly, as evidenced by its resilience over the course of its long history and recent events, China proved to be the most durable of the "dying" empires, surviving the Boxer Rebellion in 1900 and numerous revolts and civil wars thereafter, as well as the almost fatal depredations by the Japanese during the Second World War. The sleeping Chinese giant has since reawakened and changed from apparent helplessness, to communist threat, to its present quasi-capitalist rivalry with the United States, and it will, most likely, be the world's next superpower probably before the end of the 21st Century. On the other hand, the Russian Empire, whose endemic dysfunctions led to revolutions and chaos, through brutal dictatorships and massive human and material loss during the Second World War, has, despite recent developments, failed to live up to the expectations of de Tocqueville. In fact, contrary to its historical tendency, rather than continuing its perpetual expansionism, Russia has lost large areas of its national territory in both Europe and Central Asia as a result of its various former "republics" choosing to take separate paths.[8]

In the final analysis, the Philippines did not turn out to be as big a boon to the United States in regard to the China market as was originally forecast, although initially,[9] U.S. trade with Asia jumped from $91.6 million in 1897 to $145.8 million in 1900. In the long run, the United States would probably have done about as well in China without the Philippines. There should be little doubt, however, that these islands were an important base from which to project the U.S. presence and prestige in the Far East during crucial periods of its modern history.

Cuba, on the other hand, the original focus of the Spanish-American War, has gone through various phases and transformations since that conflict, in which its fate was temporarily taken out of its hands by the United States' last minute war with Spain.[10] The apparently never-ending "Cuban problem," now inherited by the United States, in its most recent historical phase brought the world to the brink of atomic conflagration during the so-called Missile Crisis of 1962. Cuba's future is still an enigma under the world's longest-lasting dictatorship, led by its

"Comandante" Fidel Castro. In the meantime, as if the earth had not turned on its axis during the last hundred years, the United States still clings to its Spanish-American War anachronism in Guantanamo, using its base there to imprison so-called "enemy combatants" under doubtful constitutional authority,[11] while it pursues its also apparently never-ending "War on Terrorism" across the globe.

As it has turned out, the colonies acquired from Spain in the Pacific by Germany ended up in Japanese hands after World War I. They would be part of the fractious equation with United States that led to World War II.

NOTES

1. On January 17, 1899, the United States laid claim to Wake Island when Commander Edward D. Taussig, aboard the *U.S.S. Bennington,* took possession of that island despite German claims that it was one of the Marshall Islands, basing his actions on a visit paid there in 1841 by Captain Charles Wilkes. Trask, supra, at 468.

2. *See*, Homer Lea, *The Valor of Ignorance*, New York (1909).

3. As well as sundry insurrections and wars for independence such as in Indonesia and Malayia.

4. Torruella, supra.

5. *Cf.* Thomas J. McCormick, *The China Market: America's Quest for Informal Empire, 1893-1901*, Chicago (1967).

6. Torruella, supra.

7. Of these, only the Canary Islands and Ceuta remain Spanish today.

8. These include Estonia, Latvia, Lithuania, Belarus; Ukraine, Moldavia, Georgia, Armenia, Azerbaijan, Turkmenistan, Uzbekistan, Kazakhstan, Tajikistan, and Kyrgyzstan.

9. *Historical Statistics of the United States*, Washington, D.C. (1975), 250-51.

10. See generally, Thomas, *Cuba, The Pursuit of Freedom*, supra.

11. *See*, Juan R. Torruella, "On the Slippery Slopes of Afghanistan: Military Commissions and the Exercise of Presidential Power," 4 U. of Pa. J. Const. I. 648 (May, 2002). Cf. *Rasul v. Bush*, 542 U.S. 466 (2004); *Hamdan v. Rumsfeld*, 126 S.ct. 2749 (2006).

Epilogue

It is tempting and, admittedly, somewhat perilous, to draw comparisons or parallels between historical events or periods. Fully conscious of the risks that such analogies entail, it is nevertheless imperative that the events that transpired in relation to the Spanish-American War be assessed alongside those presently evolving in Iraq. Such an analysis is justified by the numerous points of resemblance between these two historically distant events. Obviously, the fact that the present conflict in Iraq is still unfolding presents added problems to such scrutiny, not least of which is that it involves developing, current events rather than strictly historical ones. Furthermore, not all the pertinent facts about the Iraq War are available at this time. On the other hand, there is a substantial amount of undeniable knowledge about many central facts which are unlikely to be changed by the passage of time. These are sufficient, when assessed in the light of our earlier experiences in the Spanish-American War, to allow us to conduct a predictive examination of the current Iraqi situation.

There are several remarkable points of coincidence not only in the conflicts themselves, but also in the attitudes and actions of the non-belligerents in both encounters, as well as in the personalities involved, particularly on the American side.

In both wars, a majority of the European countries, led by France and Germany, have used substantially the same arguments, more than a century apart, to vehemently oppose the undertakings of the United States. There is abundant evidence in both cases to support the conclusion that these oppositions have not been wholly altruistic, for in both wars Germany and France had substantial commercial and economic

169

interests at stake that were put in jeopardy by the belligerent actions of the United States. Furthermore, in both wars, the principal European exception to opposing the United States' action has been Great Britain. Additionally, there is a direct link between British attitudes toward the U.S. in the two wars, for it is from British-American exchanges that began during the period of the Spanish-American War that the "special relationship" has arisen and ever since has dictated the unspoken Anglo-American partnership, whose latest manifestation is the almost unqualified support that Great Britain has given the United States in the Iraqi conflict.

On the other hand, the avowed American purposes for engaging in the two wars were and are based on premises that are strikingly similar: both wars were allegedly undertaken by the United States[1] on moral and humanistic grounds, to free oppressed populations, and to bring the benefits of democracy to peoples heretofore lacking such traditions. The immediate provocation for intervention by the United States in what became the Spanish-American War, the so-called sinking of the *Maine*, allegedly by the Spanish, and the invasion of Iraq by the United States, allegedly because of the presence of weapons of mass destruction and an al-Qaida terrorist connection, have all proved to be unfruitful or fictitious.[2] Initially, the American public overwhelmingly supported both wars, but in both cases this support eroded, in the case of the Spanish-American War after the Filipino insurgency erupted, and under like circumstances, in the case of the Iraqi conflict with the appearance of post-invasion violence.

Both wars were preceded by considerable media blitzes designed to stir up public support for the actions of the United States. Alleged Spanish atrocities in Cuba and the sinking of the *Maine* led this list in the Spanish-American War, and atrocities by Saddam Hussein's government,[3] alleged terrorist connections and weapons of mass destruction did so in the case of the Iraqi conflict.

In both wars, the United States was able to obtain decisive initial military victories by the use of overwhelming, technically superior forces,[4] in a matter of a few weeks or months, and with relatively few casualties during the "conventional" part of the wars.[5] However, conventional war in both instances was / is being followed by violent insurgencies. In the Spanish-American War, the insurgency lasted from 1899 to 1903, at a cost of 4,200 Americans dead, 20,000 insurrectionists dead, and over 200,000 civilian casualties. Thus, American casualties during the period of insurrection exceeded actual Spanish-American War casualties by the thousands. Since the Iraqi War officially ended, there has been an ongoing guerrilla war[6] that to the present (October of 2006) has claimed over 2,700 American lives and more than 20,000 casualties, already many more than during the period of conventional warfare. Furthermore, unaccounted numbers of civilians, probably in the tens of thousands, have been killed and wounded during the period of insurrection, and the destruction of property has risen into the hundreds of millions of dollars.

In the Philippines, where the civilian population initially supported Aguinaldo's forces, there followed a period of reconstruction and "Americanization." This was interrupted by the brutal Japanese occupation from 1941 to 1945, and finally by the granting of independence and the withdrawal of United States forces from all but some leased naval bases (which have since also been given up). After several decades in the Philippines, the United States left behind a mix of successes and failures, particularly regarding the establishment of an American-style democracy.

At this point in time, only three years after the invasion, the situation in Iraq is also entirely a matter of conjecture.[7] It is probably safe to say, however, that democratic institutions are practically nonexistent, and that as in the case of the Philippines in 1898, there is no tradition of either democratic institutions or practices.[8] Even so, there have been recent U.S.-conducted, -supervised and -protected elections, and a provisional constitution, known as the "Transitional Administrative Law,"[9] has been approved. This lapsed when the occupation authorities turned over political leadership to the Iraqi Interim Government. In the meantime, the Iraqi armed forces remain under U.S. control, Iraq's finances remain under U.S. oversight, there is no local authority even to amend edicts issued by U.S. authorities or to enact new laws, and all key ministries are directed by American-appointed commissioners. Thus far, Iraq is almost a carbon copy of the initial U.S. colonial administration in the Philippines and Puerto Rico after the Spanish-American War.

One thing seems fairly certain, considering the state of U.S. domestic opinion and the apparent decrease in American public support for the Iraqi conflict and occupation: it is unlikely that U.S. presence in Iraq will (or more realistically, can) last nearly as long as it did in the Philippines. Yet, if the Philippine experience is any indication of how long it takes for democratic institutions to take hold in a society that lacks these traditions,[10] it will be difficult for them to take root in Iraq unless there is some type of U. S. tutelage there, or in the vicinity, for some time to come. This, of course, in itself presents a dilemma, for on the one hand, without the support (presence?) of U.S. forces in or near Iraq, it is unlikely that there is much chance of democracy gaining a foothold there, while conversely, the presence of the United States as an invading force to "promote democracy" is almost an oxymoron.

There may be more portentous, and less benevolent, reasons why it is likely that a U.S. presence in Iraq will have to be maintained for some time to come, and this may not be a gratuitous concern for the implantation of democracy there.

In this respect, it may be relevant to consider what is perhaps the most striking area of likeness between the Spanish-American War and the Iraqi War. This can be found in a comparison of the principal American personages in the two wars, and in that regard, the starting point is a comparison of the visions and attitudes that they promoted regarding the appropriate global role of the United States. It is apparent that the "hawkish," "Manifest Destiny" agenda of Theodore Roosevelt, Brookes Adams, Senator Cabot Lodge, Admiral Alfred Mahan and various other 1890's expansionist cohorts (also known as the "Large Policy" exponents), who planned, promoted and carried out the U.S. actions that resulted in the Spanish-American War, is patently similar, and largely duplicated by the policies advanced and actions taken by today's Washington cabal (sometimes referred to as the "Neo-Conservatives"[11]) of Vice President Richard Cheney, Secretary of Defense Donald Rumsfeld, Under Secretaries Ralph Wolfowitz and Douglas Feith, General Jay Garner, and others of similar persuasion. It is not difficult to detect in the actions of these modern-day "manifest destinists" advocacy for an American political, military, and economic hegemony that echoes the mantras of their 1890's soul mates, though on a larger and more ambitious scale, and framed in terms of an American "crusade"[12] – an unfortunate choice of words given the implications that this term has in the Muslim world, but a fitting one, considering that they are the modern day standard bearers of the "manifest destiny" banner, with its known religious connotations.

The policies promoted by the Spanish-American War expansionists were fueled, no pun intended, by the need for coaling bases to supply America's navy, and the merchant fleet that distributed U.S. goods throughout the World. Thus were acquired the strategically placed components of the American "Pacific Ring" and "Caribbean Lake".

Today's promoters of U.S. expansionism are no less concerned with the strategies of fuel than were their 19th century predecessors. Of course, what inspires their actions in Iraq is not coaling stations but rather the "oil imperative," for apart from other U.S. oil interests in the area, and it has many, the aggregate untapped oil reserves of Iraq are probably the largest in the world.[13] Thus the need to press democracy on the Iraqis, which by all accounts will take years, and may very well not be wanted by many if not most Iraquis, is entwined, not to say entangled, with other less altruistic purposes.

Ulterior strategic motives, as we have seen, were also present behind the scenes in the Spanish-American War era. As in that epoch, the United States already has the rudimentary equivalent of a "Middle East Ring," although obviously tempered by the times and the exigencies of a less malleable world than existed in the 19th century. Nevertheless, the relationship between nations is still ultimately determined by well-known "fire power disparities" as current events clearly demonstrate.

As in the case of the Pacific Ring, the United States has an equivalent "Middle East Ring" in place, from which to make its presence felt in the area: the U.S. military presence in Kuwait; its base on Diego Garcia Island in the Indian Ocean, is within easy striking distance by overwhelming U.S. air power[14]; there are substantial bases or facilities in Bahrain (NSA Bahrian / Muharraq Airfield), Oman (Masirah Island) and the United Arab Emirates (Fujairah); aircraft carrier task forces roaming the Indian Ocean, with substantial amphibious capabilities, supplement the lack of additional secure land bases in the area; and last but not least, in Israel, the United States has a steadfast, militarily proficient ally. To this should be added the assertion of the Neo-Conservatives that they intend to use Iraq itself as their main military base in the Middle East,[15] again emulating their Spanish-American predecessors in their use of the

Philippines, Puerto Rico and Guantanamo as U.S. staging points from which to exercise pressure in their respective areas. Thus the "Middle East Ring" is already substantially in place.

Last, but perhaps not least, the Spanish-American War and the Iraq conflict have in common an additional ingredient: the United States was the aggressor in both cases. Other than the War with Mexico in 1846,[16] the United States has been attacked or provoked by actions against it or its citizens, or has acted in aid of its allies, in all of the other wars in which it has been a participant. That was the case in the War for Independence, the War of 1812, the two World Wars, the Korean War, the Vietnam War, and even in the first Iraq War and in its attack on Afghanistan. This moral high ground cannot be claimed in either the Spanish-American War or the present Iraq War notwithstanding our government's attempts to do so in both conflicts. Thus in both wars, the United States ultimately damaged its image as the standard bearer of fairness and respect for international law; in the case of the Iraq War and its aftermath, this damage may be irreparable and long-lasting.

It may be that in the world of international power politics it is more important to be feared than to be admired or liked. Unfortunately, history seems to bear this cynical conclusion out. Nevertheless, the posture of the United States as an aggressor, even against such an infamous tyrant as Saddam Hussein undoubtedly was, makes for an uneasy world. For who is to cast the first stone? And once that is done, where does it stop?

Perhaps the comparisons and parallels between these two conflicts are too superficial to permit useful lessons or conclusions to be drawn regarding the attitudes and actions of nations in their intercourse with each other. It is, of course, evident that over and above all other considerations, nations will take the path of self-interest. It seems that this is a Malthusian commandment which cannot be avoided if survival is the foremost of all national priorities.

It probably is.

NOTES

1. Although I realize that the Iraqi War is not just a U.S. enterprise, I do not believe that it can be seriously questioned that, but for U.S. leadership and principal participation, the action would not have been taken.

2. It has been established beyond any doubt that the cause of the *Maine*'s sinking was an internal explosion provoked by unstable powder. *See* Admiral Hyman G. Rickover, *How the Battleship "Maine" Was Destroyed*, U.S. Naval Institute, Md. (1976). There is now no question but that there were no weapons of mass destruction in Iraq at the time of the 2003 invasion. *See*, Joseph Ciricano, Jessica T. Mathews. and George Petrowitch, *WMD in Iraq: Evidence and Implications*, Carnegie Endowment for International Peace, Washington, D.C. (2004); Robert Greenwald, *Uncovered: The Whole Truth About the Iraq War*, at *www.truthuncovered.com*. There has also been no credible evidence to date of any link between the government of Iraq and al-Qaida. See also, William R. Polk, *Understanding Iraq*, Harper Collins Publishers, New York (2005), at 168-169.

3. There is no question that these took place. Of course, the same can be said regarding other governments of the world.

4. The superiority of the U.S. fleet in the Spanish-American War has been amply discussed. U.S. firepower against Iraq was overwhelming, with the Iraqi forces being outgunned, outnumbered and outclassed. As an example, approximately 13,000 "cluster munitions," which separate into 2 million cluster bombs, were used against Iraq. Id. at 169.

5. In the conventional part of the Iraq War, only 128 American and 31 British soldiers were killed, many by "friendly fire," as compared to about ten thousand Iraqi civilians and tens of thousands Iraqi military personnel. Id.

6. By July 2004, American intelligence sources were reporting that at least 50 organizations comprising more than 20,000 combatants and active supporters were involved in the Iraq insurgency. *Id.* at 177. Although there are undoubtedly some foreign (i.e., non-Iraqi) infiltrators involved in this guerrilla war, it is mostly an indigenous movement. There does not appear to be a central umbrella movement or direction, a distinguishing factor from the Filipino insurgency.

7. Perhaps Rousseau's statement to the effect that "democracy is not a fruit for all climes" is apropos.

8. See generally, *Understanding Iraq*, William R. Polk, Harper Collins Publishers, New York (2005).

9. Written by American lawyers and only seen by a few Iraqis before it was pro-mulgated. Id. at 181.

10. And in fact distrusts them as a result of their experiences with the British. Id. at 88-90.

11. Id. at 166.

12. Id.

13. Id. at 9, 182. In 1980 alone, the oil revenues for the government of Iraq exceeded $25 billion. Id. at 128. In 2000, after the United Nations gave up all controls over its oil, following sanctions against Iraq resulting from the first Iraq War, Iraq was earning more than $30 billion annually from its oil. Id. at 165.

14. There are also substantial air bases in Turkey, although the Turkish Government has recently exercised restraint on their use in the area.

15. Id. at 207.

16. Or the Indian wars.

CHRONOLOGY OF RELEVANT EVENTS

A chronological listing of some of the most pertinent events of the Spanish-American War is useful, not only in locating this conflict temporally in its proper historical context, but also in helping to understand the geopolitical considerations that influenced the attitudes and actions of non-belligerents, when these are discussed in more detail in the text. The criteria used for inclusion is dictated in part by the limitations of space, as well as by my opinion as to what events are most relevant.

1862-70	The unification of Germany is completed.
1867	United States purchases Alaska from Russia for $7 million.
1868	The First Cuban War for Independence commences.
1869	The Suez Canal completed by a Franco-Egyptian financed company.
1870-1871	The Franco-Prussian War takes place.
1875	Great Britain acquires controlling interest in the Suez Canal Company.
1878	After ten years of fighting, the First Cuban War for Independence ends.
1881	France establishes a protectorate over Tunisia. Algeria had been subjugated in 1860.
1882	Great Britain occupies Egypt.
	France occupies Tongking.
1885	Germany acquires the Caroline Islands.

1886   Great Britain occupies Burma.

1890   As a result of a British ultimatum, Portuguese expansion into Central
                  Africa is halted.

1890-1892   French-German disputes over Morocco.

1894-1895   The Sino-Japanese War ended with Japan acquiring sovereignty over
                  Formosa and the Liao-Tung Peninsula.

1895   Russia (with Germany and France's backing) forced Japan to give up
                  Liaotung.

                  France granted mineral rights in Yunan, Kwangsi and Kwantung.

                  Germany granted a foothold in Hankow.

                  Russia acquires controlling interest in the Chinese Eastern Railway
                  being built through northern China, which when completed will link
                  with the eastern terminus of the Trans-Siberian Railway.

                  The Second Cuban War for Independence commences.

1896   The British-Venezuelan dispute over the Guiana border erupts, with
                  the United States intervening, claiming the preeminence of the Mon-
                  roe Doctrine.

                  Germany acquires the Tsingtao (Kiachow Bay) concession.

                  The Italian army is defeated at Adua.

1898   Great Britain forces France to back down at Fashoda in the Sudan.

                  The German Reichstag passes the Naval Law (calling for a fixed strength
                  of 19 battleships, 12 large cruisers and 30 small cruisers).

                  Great Britain leases Hong Kong from China.

On February 15, the *U.S.S. Maine* explodes and sinks in Havana Harbor, killing 260 of its crew, and is the immediate cause of the Spanish-American War which commences on April 21 and lasts until August 12; the Treaty of Paris is signed on December 10, whereby the United States acquired Puerto Rico, Guam and the Philippine Islands; the Philippine Insurrection continues until 1902.

Germany acquires the Carolines, Palau and the Marianas (except Guam) from Spain.

Russia gets a concession over Liao-Tung peninsula, including Port Arthur.

1899   The United States annexes the Hawaiian Islands.

Samoa is partitioned between Germany and the United States.

1899-1903 The Boer War takes place.

Great Britain and the United States resolve Canadian border dispute.

1900   The German Reichstag passes the Supplementary Bill (approving the doubling of the number of battleships).

1900-1901 The Boxer War takes place.

1902   Anglo-Japanese Treaty is signed.

1903   The United States acquires the Panama Canal Zone "in perpetuity."

1904-1905 Russo-Japanese War; Russia's Far East Fleet is annihilated at the Battle of Tsushima.

1914   The Panama Canal commences operations.

1917   The United States purchases the Danish Virgin Islands.

MAP 1
The British Empire, the End of the 19th Century

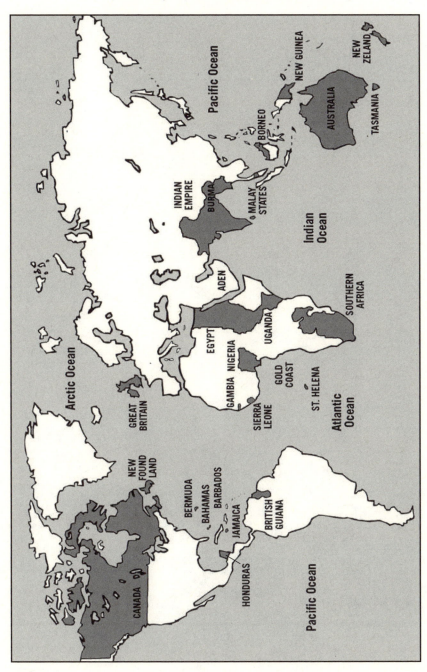

MAP 2
The Spanish Empire in 1770

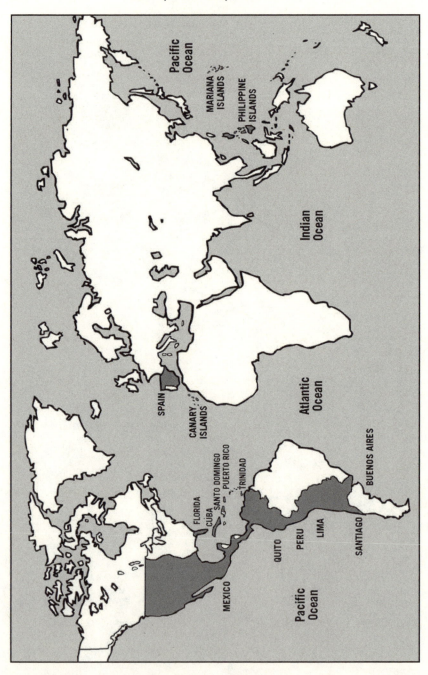

MAP 3

The Russian Empire at the End of the 19th Century

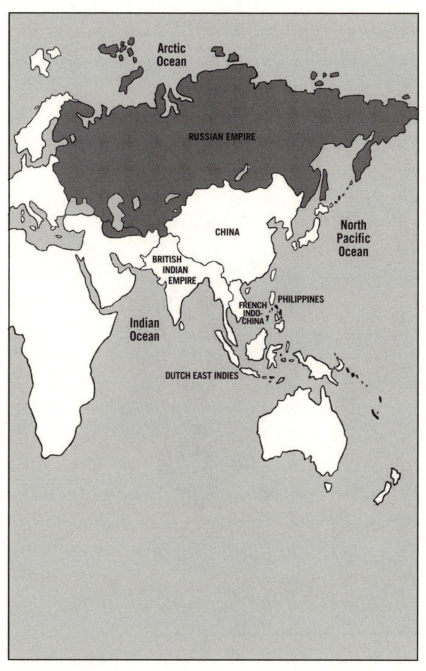

MAP 4
The Ottoman Empire in 1680

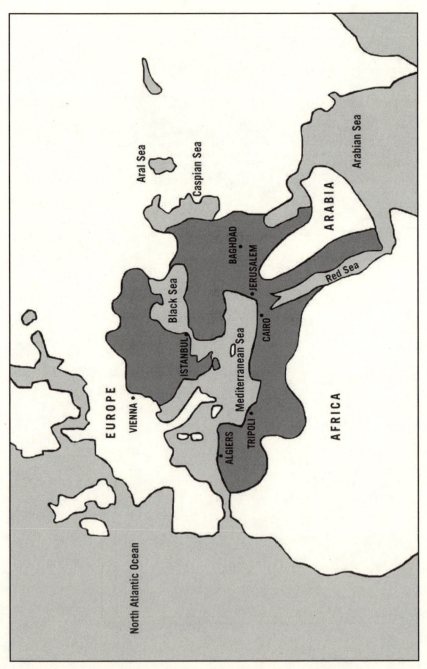

MAP 5

The Territorial Expansions of the United States, 1783-1853

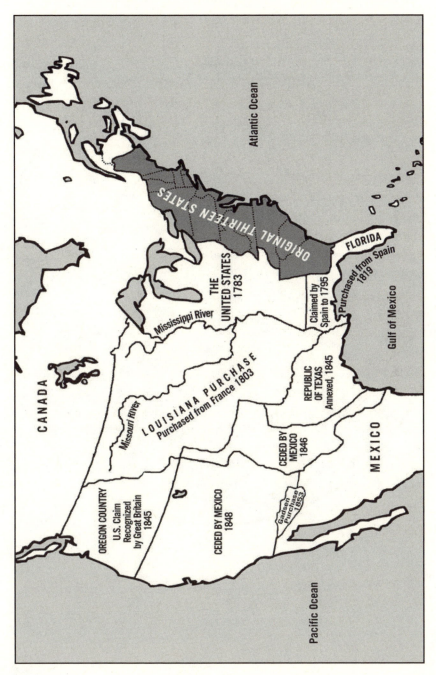

MAP 6
The "Pacific Ring": U.S. Territories in the Pacific Ocean by 1899

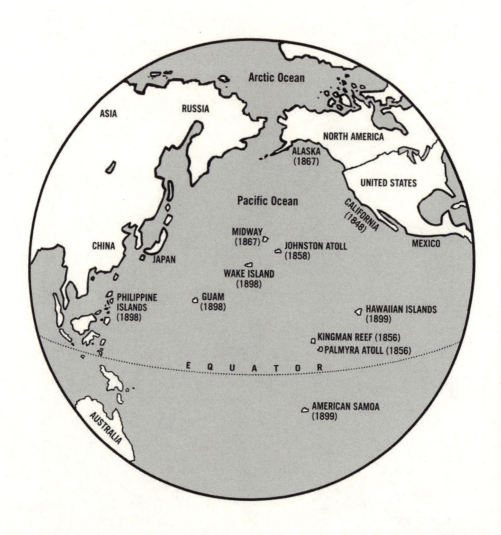

MAP 7

The "Caribbean Lake": U.S. Territories in the Caribbean Sea by 1917

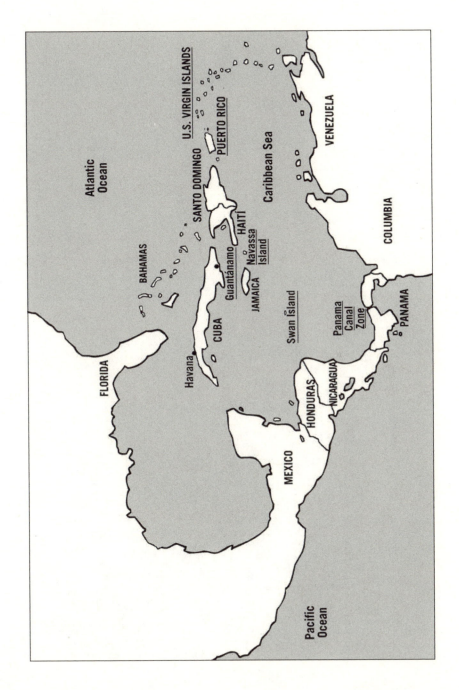

MAP 8
Cuba

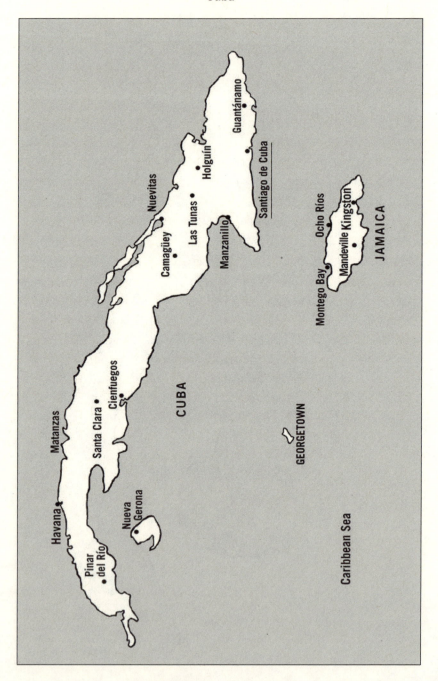

MAP 9
Puerto Rico

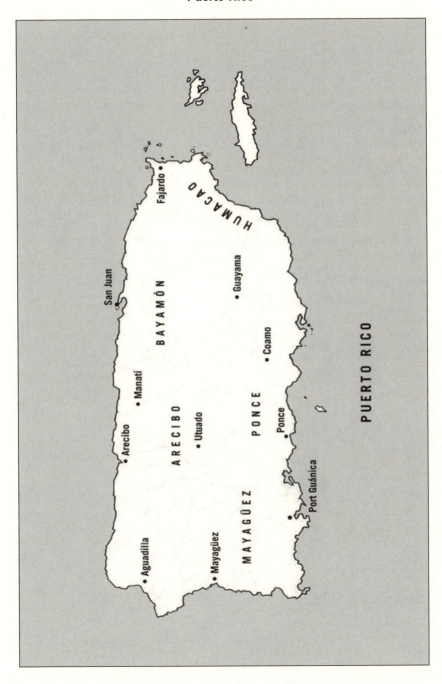

MAP 10
The South China Sea

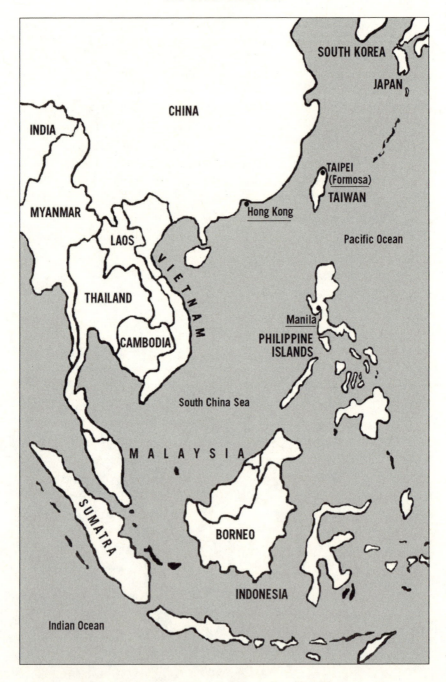

MAP 11
The Battle of Manila Bay (May 1, 1898)

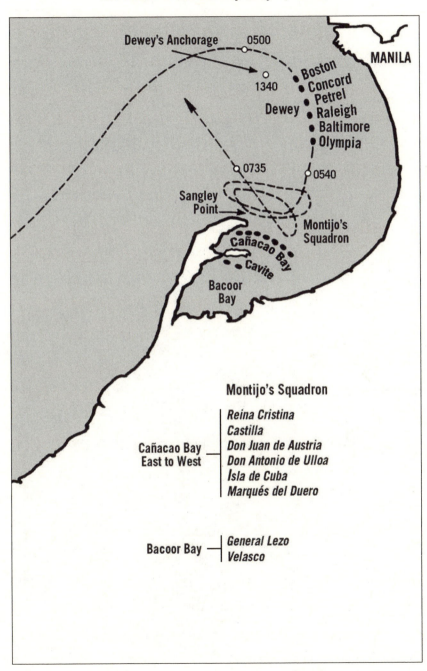

Dewey's Anchorage   0500

MANILA

Boston
Concord
Petrel
Dewey   Raleigh
Baltimore
Olympia

1340

0735   0540

Sangley
Point

Montijo's
Squadron

Cañacao Bay

Cavite

Bacoor
Bay

Montijo's Squadron

Cañacao Bay
East to West

Reina Cristina
Castilla
Don Juan de Austria
Don Antonio de Ulloa
Isla de Cuba
Marqués del Duero

Bacoor Bay

General Lezo
Velasco

MAP 12
The Battle of Santiago Bay, Cuba (July 3, 1898)

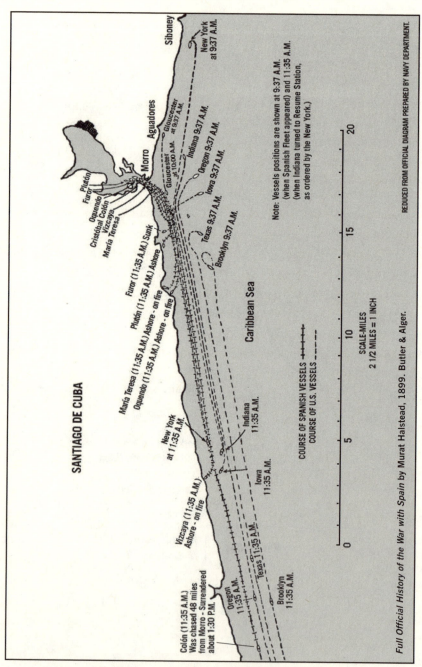

SANTIAGO DE CUBA

Siboney

New York
at 9:37 A.M.

Gloucester
at 9:37 A.M.

Indiana 9:37 A.M.

Oregon 9:37 A.M.

Iowa 9:37 A.M.

Gloucester
at 10:00 A.M.

Aguadores

Morro

Plutón
Furor
Oquendo
Cristóbal Colón
Vizcaya
María Teresa

Texas 9:37 A.M.

Brooklyn 9:37 A.M.

Furor (11:35 A.M.) Ashore

Plutón (11:35 A.M.) Sunk

María Teresa (11:35 A.M.) Ashore - on fire

Oquendo (11:35 A.M.) Ashore - on fire

Caribbean Sea

Note: Vessels positions are shown at 9:37 A.M.
(when Spanish Fleet appeared) and 11:35 A.M.
(when Indiana turned to Resume Station,
as ordered by the New York.)

New York
at 11:35 A.M.

Indiana
11:35 A.M.

Iowa
11:35 A.M.

Vizcaya (11:35 A.M.)
Ashore - on fire

Texas 11:35 A.M.

Brooklyn
11:35 A.M.

Oregon
11:35 A.M.

Colón (11:35 A.M.)
Was chased 48 miles
from Morro - Surrendered
about 1:30 P.M.

COURSE OF SPANISH VESSELS ┼┼┼┼┼
COURSE OF U.S. VESSELS ─ ─ ─ ─

SCALE-MILES
2 1/2 MILES = 1 INCH

0   5   10   15   20

REDUCED FROM OFFICIAL DIAGRAM PREPARED BY NAVY DEPARTMENT.

Full Official History of the War with Spain by Murat Halstead, 1899. Butler & Alger.

BIBLIOGRAPHY

I-Manuscript and archival sources

Philippine Insurgent Records, 1896-1901, Library of Congress, 94 Entry 196-196A. *Translations of Documents Captured from Filipino Insurgents, 1898-1900.*

II-Printed primary sources

Colección de documentos referentes a la Escuadra de Operaciones de las Antillas, compiled by Pascual Cervera Topete. Madrid: Editorial Naval, 1986.

Commercial Reports (Annual)-1900-XCIII, 47.
   Cuba, No. 2473- Report of Year 1899.
   Germany, No. 2400- Report on the Economic Position of the German Empire in 1900.

Correspondence respecting the War between Spain and the United States (1898-1900) (Confidential Print), 7267, Foreign Office, March, 1900.

Disposiciones de España y de los Estados Unidos referentes a la guerra y declaraciones de neutralidad. Madrid: Ministro de España, 1898.

German Diplomatic Documents, 1871-1914, edited and translated by ETS Dugdale. vol. 2. New York: Barnes and Noble, 1969.

Reports of the Military Attachés with the Spanish and United States Forces in Cuba and Porto Rico, War Office Reports and Miscellaneous Papers, W.O. 33/155 (Public Records Office), Parts I, II, and III.

Spanish-American War of 1898. United Transport, Services Report.

Spanish Diplomatic Correspondence and Documents, 1896-1900: Presented to the Cortes *by the Minister of State* (translations). Washington, DC: Government Printing Office, 1905.

The Philippine Insurrection Against the United States: A Compilation of Documents, edited by John R.M. Taylor. 5 Vol. Pasay City, Philippines: Eugenio López Foundation, 1971.

U.S. Bureau of the Census. *Historic Statistics of the United States*. Washington, DC: Government Printing Office, 1975.

III-Treaties and statutes

Convention of Constantinople: Convention to Guarantee the Neutrality of the Suez Canal (29 October, 1888)

Treaty of Paris of 1898, 30 Stat. 1754 (1898)

IV-Papal encyclicals

Cerum Novarum (1894)

Longinqua Oceani (6 January,1895)

Testem Benevolentiae Nostrae (22 January, 1899)

V-Printed secondary works
  A. Books

Álvarez Junco, José and Adrian Shubert, eds. *Spanish History Since 1808.* London: Oxford University Press, 2000.

Azárete, Pablo. *La Guerra Hispano-Americana de 1898.* La Coruña, 1993.

Ashton, T.S. *The Industrial Revolution, 1760-1830.* London: Oxford University Press, 1968.

Betts, Raymond F. *Tricouleur: The French Empire.* London: Gordon and Cremonesi, 1978.

Blount, James H. *The American Occupation of the Philippines, 1898-1912.* New York: G.P. Putnam's Sons, 1913.

Braudel, Fernand. *Civilization and Capitalism: 15th-18th Century.* 3 vols. London: Fontana Press, 1981-1984.

Buckle, George Earle, ed. *The Letters of Queen Victoria, Third Series: A Selection from Her Majesty's Correspondence between the Years 1886 and 1901.* 3 vols. London: 1930-32.

Bucholtz, Arden. *Molke and the German Wars.* Bersingstone: 2001.

Cagni, Horacio C. *La Guerra Hispanoamericana y el inicio de la globalización.* Buenos Aires: Centro Argentino de Estudios Estratégicos; Sevilla: IXBLIA, Universidad de Sevilla, 1999.

Campbell, A.E. *Great Britain and the United States, 1895-1903.* London: Longmans, 1960.

Campbell, Charles S. *Anglo-American Understanding, 1898-1903*. Baltimore: John Hopkins University Press, 1957.

Carr, William. *A History of Germany, 1815-1990*, 4th ed. London: Arnold, 1991.

Cervera Pery, José. *La guerra naval del 1898: a mal planteamiento peores consecuencias*. Madrid: Editorial San Martín, 1998.

Chesnaux, Jean, Marianne Bastid and Marie-Claire Bergére. *China from the Opium Wars to the 1911 Revolution*. Translated by Anne Destenay. Sussex: Harvester, 1976.

Churchill, Winston. *My Early Life: A Roving Commission*. London: Thornton Butterworth, 1938.

Cirincione, Joseph, Jessica Tuchman Mathews, George Perkovich and Alexis Orton. *WMD in Iraq: Evidence and Implications*. Carnegie Endowment Report, January 2004,<http://www.carnegieendowment.org/publications/index.cfm?fa=view&id=1435 >.

Coletta, Paolo, ed. *Threshold to American Internationalism: Essays on the Foreign Policies of William McKinley*. New York: Exposition Press, 1970.

Companys Monclus, Julián. *España en 1898: entre la diplomacia y la Guerra*. Madrid: Ministerio de Asuntos Exteriores, 1991.

Cortés Zavala, María Teresa, Cosuelo Naranjo Orovio and José Alfredo Uribe Salas, eds. *El Caribe y América Latina: el 98 en la coyuntura imperial*. 2 vols. Morelia: Universidad Michoacana San Nicolás de Hidalgo, 1998.

Crabtree, J.B. *The Passing of Spain and the Ascendancy of America*. Springfield, MA: The King-Richardson Publishing Co., 1898.

Craig , Gordon A. *Germany, 1866-1945*. Oxford: Clarendon Press, 1978.

Curtis, J. S. *Russia's Crimean War*. Durham: Duke University Press, 1979.

de La Torre del Río, Rosario. *Inglaterra y España en 1898*. Madrid: Editorial Eudema, 1988.

de Lema, Marqués. *Canovas o el hombre de estado*. Madrid: Espasa Calpe, 1931.

De Tocqueville, Alexis. *Democracy in America*. 2 vols. New York: Knopf, 1945.

Esdaile, Charles, J. *Spain in the Liberal Age: From Constitution to Civil War, 1808-1939*. Oxford: Blackwell Publishing, 2000.

Fieldhouse, D. *The Colonial Empires: A Comparative Survey from the Eighteenth Century*. London: Weidenfeld and Nicolson, 1966.

Flagg, Samuel. *The American Secretaries of State and their Diplomacy,* vol. 11. New York: Cooper Square Publishers, 1963.

Fogarty, G.P. *The Vatican and American Hierarchy from 1870-1965.* Stuttgart: Anton Hiesmann, 1982.

Freidel, F. *The Splendid Little War.* Boston: Little, Brown and Company, 1958.

Freeze, Gregory L. *Russia: A History.* Oxford: Oxford University Press, 1997.

Fromkin, David. *A Peace to End All Peace: The Fall of the Ottoman Empire and the Creation of the Modern Middle East.* New York: Henry Holt and Company, 1989.

Gernet, Jacques. *A History of Chinese Civilization.* 2 vols. London: The Folio Society, 2002.

Good, David F. *The Economic Rise of the Habsburg Empire, 1750-1914.* Berkeley: University of California Press, 1984.

Goran, Rystad. *Ambiguous Imperialism: American Foreign Policy and Domestic Politics at the Turn of the Century.* Lund, Sweden: Berlingska Boktryckeriet, 1975.

Grenville, J.A.S. *Lord Salisbury and Foreign Policy: The Close of the Nineteenth Century, 1895-1902.* London: University of London Press, 1964.

Harrison, John A. *China since 1800.* New York: Harcourt, Brace & World, 1967.

Hattaway, Herman and Archer Jones. *How the North Won: A Military History of the Civil War.* Urbana-Champaign: University of Illinois Press, 1983.

Hilton, Sylvia L. and Steve J.S. Ickringill, eds. *European Perceptions of the Spanish-American War of 1898.* Bern: Peter Lang AG, 1999.

Hobsbawn, Eric J. *Industria e imperio: una historia económica de Gran Bretaña desde 1750.* Barcelona: Ariel, 1977.

Hopkirk, Peter. *The Great Game: The Struggle for Empire in Central Asia.* New York: Kodansha, 1992.

Howard, Michael. *The Franco-Prussian War.* London: Rupert Hart-Davis, 1961.

Johnson, Paul. *A History of the American People.* London: Weidenfeld & Nicolson, 1997.

_____. *The Birth of the Modern World Society, 1815-1830.* New York: Harper Collins, 1991.

Jover Zamora, J.M. *1898: teoría y práctica de la redistribución colonial.* Madrid: Fundación Universitaria Española, 1979.

Kann, R.A. *A History of the Habsburg Empire, 1526-1918.* Berkeley: University of California Press, 1974.

Keiger, John F.V. *France and the Origins of the First World War.* London: Macmillan, 1983.

Kennedy, Paul. *Realities Behind Diplomacy: Background Influence on British External Policy, 1865-1960.* Glasgow: Fontana Press, 1981.

_____. *The Rise and Fall of the Great Powers.* New York: Random House, 1987.

Kent, Marian. *Oil and Empire: British Policy and Mesopotamian Oil, 1900-1920.* London: Macmillan, 1976

Krumeich, Gerd. *Armaments and Politics in France on the Eve of the First World War: The Introduction of Three-Year Conscription, 1913-1914.* Leamington Spa: Berg Publishers, 1984.

Langer, William. *The Diplomacy of Imperialism, 1890-1902.* New York: Knopf, 1951.

Lea, Homer. *The Valor of Ignorance.* New York: Harper & Brothers, 1909.

Lenin, Vladimir Ilich. *Imperialism I: Raskol Sosialissma Polnoye Sobranize Sachinelii,* vol. 30. Moskow: 1962.

Lewis, Bernard. *Istanbul and the Civilization of the Ottoman Empire.* Norman: University of Oklahoma Press, 1963.

_____. *The Emergence of Modern Turkey.* New York: Oxford University Press, 2001.

_____. *The Shaping of the Modern Middle East.* New York: Oxford University Press, 1994.

Liberati, Luigi Bruti. *La Santa sede e le origini dell'impero americano: la guerra del 1898.* Milano: Unicopli, 1985.

Linn, Brian McAllister. *The Philippine War, 1899-1902.* Lawrence: University Press of Kansas, 2000.

Longhorn, Richard. *The Collapse of the Concert of Europe: International Politics, 1890-1914.* London: Macmillan, 1981.

Mahan, Alfred Thayer. *The Influence of Sea Power Upon History, 1783-1812.* New York: 1890.

Mathias, P. *The First Industrial Nation: An Economic History of Britain, 1700-1914.* London: Methuen & Co. Ltd, 1969.

May, Ernest R. *Imperial Democracy: The Emergence of America as a Great Power.* New York: Harcourt, 1961.

McClain, James L. *Japan: A Modern History.* New York: W.W. Norton, 2002.

McCormick, Thomas J. *The China Market: America's Quest for Informal Empire, 1893-1901.* Chicago: Quadrangle Books, 1967.

McCullough, David. *The Paths between the Seas.* New York: Simon & Schuster, 1977.

México y el mundo: historia de sus relaciones exteriores. 9 vols. México: Senado de la República y El Colegio de México, 1990.

Morison, Samuel Eliot. *The Oxford History of the American People.* New York: Oxford University Press, 1965.

Mowat, R.B. *The Life of Lord Pauncefote: First Ambassador to the United States.* London: Constable & Co., 1929.

Musicant, Ivan. *Empire by Default: The Spanish-American War and the Dawn of the American Century.* New York: Henry Holt & Co., 1998.

Neale, R.G. *Great Britain and United States Expansion: 1898-1900.* East Lansing: Michigan State University Press, 1966.

Neu, Charles E. *The Troubled Encounter: The United States and Japan.* New York: John Wiley and Sons, 1975.

Noer, Thomas. *Briton, Boer and Yankee: The United States and South Africa, 1870-1914.* Kent: Kent University Press, 1978.

Nofi, Albert A. *The Spanish-American War, 1898.* Conshohocken, PA: Combined Books, 1996.

Offner, John L. *An Unwanted War: The Diplomacy of the United States and Spain over Cuba, 1895-1898.* Chapel Hill: University of North Carolina Press, 1992.

Oppenheim, L. *International Law.* 7th Ed, vol. 2. London: 1951.

Pabón y Suárez de Urbina, D. Jesús. *El 98: acontecimiento internacional.* Madrid: 1952.

Palacio Atard, Vicente. *La España del Siglo XIX, 1808-1898.* Madrid: Espasa Calpe, 1988.

Parish, P.J. *The American Civil War.* New York: Holmes & Meier Publisher, 1975.

Pérez, Joseph. *Historia de España.* Barcelona: Crítica, 2001.

Perkins, Bradford. *The Great Rapproachment: England and the United States, 1895-1914.* New York: Atheneum, 1968.

Polk, William R. *Understanding Iraq.* New York: Harper Collins, 2005.

Porter, Andrew. *European Imperialism, 1860-1914.* London: Macmillan, 1994.

Pratt, Julius W. *Expansionists of 1898: The Acquisition of Hawaii and the Spanish Islands.* Chicago: Quadrangle Books, 1964.

Remini, Robert V. *Andrew Jackson and the Course of American Empire, 1776-1821.* New York: Harper & Row, 1977.

Reuters, Bertha Ann. *Anglo-American Relations During the Spanish-American War.* New York: Macmillan, 1924.

Rickover, Hyman. *How the Battleship "Maine" Was Destroyed.* Annapolis, Md.: Naval Institute Press, 1976.

Rosario Natal, Carmelo. *Puerto Rico y la crisis de la Guerra Hispano-Americana, 1895-1898.* Hato Rey: Ramallo Brothers Printing Co., 1975.

Rodó, José Enrique. *Ariel.* Montevideo: 1900.

Ryden, George Herbert. *The Foreign Policy of the United States in Relation to Samoa.* New Haven: Yale University Press, 1933.

Shaw, A.G.L., ed. *Great Britain and the Colonies, 1815-1865.* London: Methuen & Co. Ltd., 1970.

Serrano, Carlos. *Final del imperio: España, 1895-1898.* Madrid: Siglo XXI, 1984.

Smith, Joseph. *The Spanish-American War: Conflict in the Caribbean and the Pacific, 1895-1902.* London: Longman, 1994.

Stoecker, Helmuth, ed. *Handbuch der Vertrage, 1871-1964.* Berlin: 1968.

Storry, R. *Japan and the Decline of the West in Asia, 1894-1943.* London: Macmillan, 1979.

Thomas, Hugh. *Cuba: The Pursuit of Freedom.* New York: Harper & Row, 1971.

Trask, David. *The War with Spain in 1898.* New York: Macmillan, 1981.

Treat, Payson J. *Diplomatic Relations between the United States and Japan, 1895-1905.* California: Stanford University Press, 1938.

Torruella, Juan R. *The Supreme Court and Puerto Rico: The Doctrine of Separate and Unequal.* Río Piedras: Editorial de la UPR, 1988.

Tuñón de Lara, Manuel, ed. *Revolución burguesa, oligarquía y constitucionalismo, (1834-1923)*, vol. 8 of *Historia de España.* Barcelona: Labor, 1988.

Uribe Salas, José Alfredo, María Teresa Cortés and Consuelo Naranjo Orovio, eds. *México frente al desenlace del 98. La Guerra Hispanoamericana.* Morelia, Michoacán: Universidad Michoacana de San Nicolás de Hidalgo, Instituto de Investigaciones Históricas, Instituto Michoacano de Cultura, Gobierno del Estado de Michoacán; Río Piedras: Universidad de Puerto Rico, 1999.

Vladimirov, L.S. *La diplomacia de los Estados Unidos durante la Guerra Hispano-Norteamericana de 1898.* Moscú: 1958.

Weigley, Russell F. *The American Way of War: A History of the United States Military Strategy and Policy.* Bloomingdale: Indiana University Press, 1977.

Widenor, William C. *Henry Cabot Lodge and the Search for an American Foreign Policy.* Berkeley: California University Press, 1980.

Wilhelm, Richard. *A Short History of Chinese Civilization.* London: George G. Harrap, 1929.

Wilkerson, Marcus Manley. *Public Opinion and the Spanish-American War: A Study in War Propaganda.* Baton Rouge: Louisiana University Press, 1932.

Wisan, Joseph Ezra. *The Cuban Crisis as Reflected in the New York Press (1895-1898).* New York: Octagon Books, 1965.

Young, L.K. *British Policy in China, 1895-1902.* Oxford: Clarendon, 1970.

Zea, Leopoldo and Adalberto Santana. *El 98 y su impacto en Latinoamérica.* Latinoamérica Fin de Milenio, no. 9. México City: Fondo de Cultura Económica, 2001.

2. Articles and Journals

Adams, Brooks. "The Spanish War and the Equilibrium of the World." *The Forum* 25 (1898): 641-651.

Álvarez Gutiérrez, Luis. "La diplomacia alemana ante el conflicto hispano-norteamericano de 1897-1898: primeras tomas de posición." *Hispania* 54, no. 186 (1994): 201-256.

_____. "Los imperios centrales ante el progresivo deterioro de las relaciones entre España y los Estados Unidos." *Hispania* 57, no. 196 (1997): 435-478.

Bailey, Thomas. "Dewey and the Germans at Manila Bay." *The American Historical Review* 45 (1939): 59-81.

_____. "Japan's Protest Against the Annexation of Hawaii." *The Journal of Modern History* 3, no. 1 (1931): 46-61.

_____. "The United States and Hawaii during the Spanish-American War." *The American Historical Review* 36 (1931): 550-560.

Beck, Earl R. "The Martínez Campos Government of 1879: Spain's Last Chance in Cuba." *Hispanic American Historical Review* 56, no. 2 (May, 1976): 268-289.

Blake, N.M. "The Olney-Pauncefote Treaty of 1897." *The American Historical Review* 50, no. 2 (1945): 228-243.

Bobadilla González, Leticia. "La opinión pública en México frente a la guerra hispano-cubano-norteamericana de 1898," in Uribe Salas, José Alfredo, et. al., eds. *México frente...*

Bootsma, Nico. "Reactions to the Spanish-American War in the Netherlands and in the Dutch East Indies," in Hilton, Sylvia L. and Steve J.S. Ickringill, eds. *European Perceptions...*

Braisted, William R. "The Open Door Policy and the Boxer Uprising," in Coletta, Paolo, ed. *Threshold to American...*

Campbell, Alec E. "Great Britain and the United States in the Far East, 1895-1903." *The Historical Journal* 1, no. 2 (September 1958): 154-175.

Campbell, Charles S. "Anglo-American Relations, 1897-1901," in Coletta, Paolo, ed. *Threshold to American...*

Casellas, Salvador. "Causas y antecedentes diplomáticos de la Guerra Hispanoamericana: 1895-98." *Revista de Ciencias Sociales* 9 (March, 1965): 55-76.

"Chronique Internationale." *Annales des Science Politiques* XVL.

Drechsler, Wolfgang, "Congress and the Spanish-Cuban/American War", in *The War of 1898 and US Interventions, 1898-1934: An Encyclopedia*, edited by Benjamin R. Beede, 119-121. New York: Garland Publishing, 1994.

Ellicot, John M. "The Cold War between Von Diederichs and Dewey in Manila Bay." *United States Naval Institute Proceedings*, 81 (1955): 1236-1239.

Espinosa Blas, María Margarita. "Cuba en la correspondencia consular mexicana, 1895-1900," in Uribe Salas, José Alfredo, et. al., eds. *México frente...*

Fernández-Armesto, Felipe. "The Improbable Empire." In *Spain: A History,* edited by Raymond Carr, New York: Oxford University Press, 2000.

Figueroa Esquer, Raúl. "El Correo Español: la prensa españolista mexicana y el 98." *Cuadernos Hispanoamericanos*, no. 577-578 (July-August, 1998): 87-98.

Field, Jr., James A. "American Imperialism: The Worst Chapter in Almost Any Book." *The American Historical Review*, 83, no. 3 (1978): 644-668.

Fiske, John. "Manifest Destiny." *Harper's New Monthly Magazine*, 70 (March, 1885): 578-590.

Ford, Peter. "Europe Cringes at Bush 'Crusade' Against Terrorists." *Christian Science Monitor*, September 19, 2001.

García Sanz, Fernando. "El contexto internacional de la guerra de Cuba: La percepción italiana del 98 español." *Estudios de Historia Social* 44-47 (1988): 395-310.

González Natale, Rodrigo, Carolina López and Patricia Orbe. "El 98 en Cuba: génesis de una nueva dependencia continental vista desde la Argentina," in Zea, Leopoldo and Adalberto Santana. *El 98 y su impacto...*

Greger, Rene. "The Austro-Hungarian Navy and the Spanish-American War of 1898." *Warship International*, 1 (1980): 61 ff.

Grenville, J.A.S. "Diplomacy and War Plans in the United States, 1890-1917." *Transactions of the Royal Historical Society*, 5th Series, 11 (1961): 1-21.

Goodrich, W.W. "Questions of international law involved in the Spanish War." *American Law Review*, 32 (1898): 481-500.

Herwig, Holger H. and David Trask. "Naval Operations Plans between Germany and the USA, 1898-1913: A Study in Strategic Planning in the Age of Imperialism." In *The War Plans of the Great Powers, 1880-1914*, edited by Paul Kennedy, 39-74. Boston: Allen & Unwin, 1979.

Journal du Droit Internationale Privé et de la Jurisprudences Comparés, XXV

Laing, E.A.M. "Admiral Dewey and the Foreign Warships at Manila, 1898." *Mariner's Mirror* 52 (1966): 167-71.

Lodge, Henry Cabot. "Our Blundering Foreign Policy." *The Forum* 19 (March, 1895): 8-17.

Louis, Paul. "À propos de la Guerre Hispano-Americaine." *La Revue Socialiste* (May, 1898).

Muñoz Mata, Laura. "México ante la cuestión cubana, 1895-1900," in Uribe Salas, José Alfredo, et. al., eds. *México frente...*

Offner, John L. "The United States and France: Ending the Spanish American War." *Diplomatic History* 7 (1983): 1-21.
_____. "Washington Mission: Bishop Ireland on the Eve of the Spanish-American War." *Catholic Historical Review* 73, no. 49 (October, 1987).

Pratt, Julius W. "John L. O'Sullivan and Manifest Destiny." *New York History* 14, no. 3 (july, 1933): 213-234.

Pérez, Blas Noel. "Visión rusa de la guerra hispano-cubano-norteamericana." *América Latina*, Havana (December, 1998).

Pérez Santarcieri, María Emilia. "El 98 español visto desde Uruguay." *Cuadernos hispanoamericanos* 577-578 (1998): 129-140.

Polisensky, Josef. "La Guerra Hispano-cubano-americana de 1898 y la opinión pública checa." *Histórica* 7 (1963): 99-113.

Popkova, Ludmilia N. "Russian Press Coverage of American Intervention in the Spanish War," in Hilton, Sylvia L. and Steve J.S. Ickringill, eds. *European Perceptions...*

Quijada, Mónica. "Latinos y anglosajones: el 98 en el fin de siglo sudamericano." *Hispania* 57, no. 196 (1997): 589-609.

Ranson, E. "British Military and Naval Observers in the Spanish-American War." *The American Historical Review* 30 (1925): 54-77.

Ricard, Serge. "The Anglo-German Intervention in Venezuela and Theodore Roosevelt's Ultimatum to the Kaiser: Taking a Fresh Look at an Old Enigma," in *Anglo-Saxonism in U.S. Foreign Policy: The Diplomacy of Imperialism, 1899-1919*, Serge Ricard and Hélene Christol, eds. Aix-en-Provence (1991): 65-77.

Rodríguez, Adriana, Natalia Fandussi and José Marciles. "El crucero 'Río de la Plata' como símbolo de 'Común-Unión', 1898-1902," in Zea, Leopoldo and Adalberto Santana. *El 98 y su impacto...*

Rodriguez, Agustín R. "Portugal and the Spanish Colonial Crisis of 1898," in Hilton, Sylvia L. and Steve J.S. Ickringill, eds. *European Perceptions...*

Rossini, Daniel. "The American Peril: Italian Catholics and the Spanish American War, 1898," in Hilton, Sylvia L. and Steve J.S. Ickringill, eds. *European Perceptions...*

Salom Costa, Julio. "La relación hispano-portuguesa al término de la época iberista". *Hispania* 25 (1965): 219-259.

Sears, Louis M. "French Opinion of the Spanish-American War." *Hispanic American Historical Review* 7, no. 1 (February, 1927): 25-44.

Shipetsky, Nicolas. "Austria and the Spanish-American War," in Hilton, Sylvia L. and Steve J.S. Ickringill, eds. *European Perceptions...*

Shippee, Lester B. "Germany and the Spanish-American War." *The American Historical Review* 30, no. 4 (July, 1925): 754-777.

Shippee, Lester B. and Royal B. Way. "William Rufus Day," in *The American Secretaries...*

Sloan, Jennie A. "Anglo-American Relations and the Venezuelan Boundary Dispute." *Hispanic American Historical Review* 18, no. 4 (November, 1938): 486-506.

Sneed, Geoffrey. "British Reactions to American Imperialism Reflected in Journals of Opinion, 1898-1900." *Political Science Quarterly* 73, no. 2 (1968): 254-272.

_____. "British Views of American Policy in the Philippines Reflected in Journals of Opinion, 1898-1907." *Journal of American Studies* 2, no. 1 (1968): 49-64.

Taylor, Henry Clay. "The *Indiana* at Santiago," in "The Story of the Captains," *Century*, May, 1899.

Torruella, Juan R. "On the Slippery Slopes of Afghanistan: Military Commissions and the Exercise of Presidential Power." *University of Pennsylvania Journal of Constitutional Law* 4 (2002): 648-734.

Von Diederichs (Admiral). "A statement of events in Manila, May-October, 1898." *Journal of the Royal United Service Institution* 59, (November, 1914): 421-446.

Wildman, Edwin. "What Dewey Feared in Manila Bay as Revealed by His Letters." *The Forum* 59 (1918): 513-35.

3. Newspapers

Deutsche Blatter
    May 29, 1898

Le Correspondent
    August 25, 1898

Daily Chronicle
    April9, 1898

La Época
    April 8, 1898
    May 22, 1898

El Imparcial
    May 22, 1898

Journal des Débates
    March 2, 1898
    April 3, 1898
    April 15, 1898

La Nación
    May 3, 1898

New York Journal
February 11, 1898

Nord Deutsche
May 5, 1898

L'Osservatore Romano
February 11-12, 1898
March 21-22, 1898
April 2-3, 1898

La Tribuna
December 29, 1897

VI-Unpublished Dissertations

Connor, William Patrick. "Insular Empire: Politics and Strategy of American Policy in the Pacific Ocean, 1879-1900" Ph.D. diss., Emory University, 1976.

Gottschall, Terrell Dean. "Germany and the Spanish-American War: A Case Study of Navalism and Imperialism, 1898." Ph. D. diss., Washington State University, 1981.

McMinn, John H. "The Attitude of the English Press Toward the United States During the Spanish-American War." Ph.D. diss., Ohio State University, 1939.

Whitehead, James Louis. "French Reaction to American Imperialism 1895-1908." Ph.D. diss., University of Pennsylvania, 1943.

INDEX